Foundation

MODERN WORLD HISTORY

for OCR specification 1937

David Taylor

Heinemann

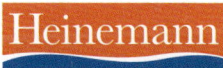

Heinemann Educational Publishers,
Halley Court, Jordan Hill, Oxford OX2 8EJ
Part of Harcourt Education

Heinemann is a registered trademark of Harcourt Education Limited

© David Taylor 2001

Copyright notice
All rights reserved. No part of this publication may be reproduced in any material form (including photocopying or storing it in any medium by electronic means and whether or not transiently or incidentally to some other use of this publication) without the prior written permission of the copyright owner, except in accordance with the provisions of the Copyright, Designs and Patents Act 1988 or under the terms of a licence issued by the Copyright Licensing Agency Ltd, 90 Tottenham Court Road, London W1P 0LP. Applications for the copyright owner's written permission to reproduce any part of this publication should be addressed to the publisher.

First published 2001

ISBN 0 435 30831 9

08 07 06 05 04
10 9 8 7 6 5 4

Photographic acknowledgements
The author and publisher would like to thank the following for permission to reproduce photographs:

A Krause/The Guardian: 255L; AKG: 58F, 80O, 108C, 113H, 116D, 121A, 124D, 129K, 227M; Bridgeman: 152L; British Library of Economics: 132A; Cartoons UKC/Solo Syndication: 63A; Cartoons UKC/Telegraph Group Ltd: 244T; Centre for the Study of Cartoon and Caricature: 229A, 236H, 245A; Christies Images: 106K; Corbis: 143B, 145D, 155C, 158F, 159H, 169J, 239J, 241M, 251G, 252H, 254K; David King: 92O, 177C, 179E, 180F, 185M, 191D, 192E, 195H, 198L, 200B, 201C, 205G, 208B, 211E, 212B, 240L; Hulton Getty: 51B, 51C, 83D, 98B, 99C, 105I, 117F, 172A, 173C, 181G, 183I, 189B, 190C, 193F, 232B, 247B, 248C, 249E; Hulton/Archive: 6A, 7B, 17J, 36B, 43G, 44H; Imperial War Museum: 28B, 29C, 34B, 38B, 40D; Low/Solo Syndication: 67B, 78K, 96A, 128J, 216A, 220E; Magnum: 250F, 258F; Mary Evans Picture Library: 10E, 19C, 22E, 26A, 42A, 45B, 46E; Museum of London: 24J; Peter Newark: 50A, 138B, 140D, 141E, 142A, 146E, 147F, 148H, 149I, 162D, 168I, 170L, 243P; Popperfoto: 88H, 95Q, 156D, 176B, 184L, 186N, 196I, 221G; Private Collection/Bridgeman Art Library: 39B; Punch: 8C, 13A, 43F, 62K; Scarfe/Sunday Times, 1980: 253I; Topham Picturepoint: 46F; Topham: 72D, 144C, 167H, 243Q

Cover photograph: © Hulton Getty

Designed and typeset by Visual Image, Taunton

Illustrated by Paul Bale and Jane Watkins

Printed and bound in Italy by Printer Trento s.r.l.

Index compiled by Indexing Specialists

The publishers have made every effort to trace copyright holders of material in this book. Any omissions will be rectified in subsequent printings if notice is given to the publisher.

Contents

Chapter 1: How was British society changed, 1906-18? — 5

Why did the Liberal governments introduce reforms to help the young, old and unemployed?	6
How effective were the Liberal reforms?	13
What were the arguments for and against women's suffrage?	18
How effective were the activities of the Suffragists and the Suffragettes?	21
How did women contribute to the war effort?	26
How were civilians affected by the war?	28
How effective was government propaganda during the war?	33
Why were some women given the vote in 1918?	35
What was the attitude of the British people at the end of the war towards Germany and the Paris Peace Conference?	37
Paper 2-type assessment: Britain and the First World War	39
Paper 2-type assessment: The Liberal Reforms	42
Paper 2-type assessment: The Suffragettes	45

Chapter 2: International relations 1919-c.1939 — 48

Were the peace treaties of 1919-23 fair?	50
Paper 1-type assessment: The Treaty of Versailles	63
To what extent was the League of Nations a success?	64
Paper 1-type assessment: The League of Nations	81
Why had international peace collapsed by 1939?	82
Paper 1-type assessment: The collapse of peace	96

Chapter 3: Germany 1918-45 — 97
Was the Weimar Republic doomed from the start? — 98
Why was Hitler able to dominate Germany by 1934? — 107
How effectively did the Nazis control Germany, 1933-45? — 114
What was it like to live in Nazi Germany? — 121
    Paper 1-type assessment: Germany 1918-45 — 132

Chapter 4: The USA 1919-41 — 134
How far did the US economy boom in the 1920s? — 136
How far did US society change in the 1920s? — 142
What were the causes and consequences of the Wall Street Crash? — 153
How successful was the New Deal? — 160
    Paper 1-type assessment: The New Deal — 172

Chapter 5: Russia 1905-41 — 174
Why did the Tsarist regime collapse in 1917? — 176
How did the Bolsheviks gain power, and how did they consolidate their rule? — 188
How did Stalin gain and hold on to power? — 199
What was the impact of Stalin's economic policies? — 206
    Paper 1-type assessment: Stalin's rule — 212

Chapter 6: International relations 1945-c.1989 — 214
Who was to blame for the Cold War? — 216
    Paper 1-type assessment: Causes of the Cold War — 229

How effectively did the USA contain the spread of communism? — 230
    Paper 1-type assessment: US policy in Cuba and Vietnam — 245

How secure was the USSR's control over Eastern Europe 1948-c.1989? — 246
    Paper 1-type assessment: Soviet control over Eastern Europe — 258

Glossary — 259

Index — 262

1 How was British society changed, 1906–18?

- Before 1900 the government did not think it was responsible for helping the old, the young, the sick, the unemployed and the low-paid.

- The Liberal government, elected in 1906, changed this and passed a number of laws to deal with the problem of poverty. For the first time the State (government) set out to provide a minimum standard of living for all its citizens. The foundations of the welfare state were being laid.

- In 1900 over half of all adults, including all women, were not allowed to vote in elections for parliament.

- Women, known as the Suffragettes, began to campaign for the right to vote. Between 1903 and 1914 the Suffragettes used violent tactics to try to achieve their goal, but parliament refused to give women the vote.

- At the start of the First World War in 1914, the Suffragettes called off their campaign and women played a big part in helping Britain to win the war. They were rewarded in 1918 when an act gave many women over the age of 30 the right to vote.

- Millions of men were recruited into the armed forces during the First World War. As these men left for the war, women filled their jobs at home. Women proved that they were more than capable of doing jobs once looked upon as men's work only.

- In order to win the war, the government became more and more involved in people's lives. The government took over industries, introduced conscription (compulsory military service) and food rationing. This was Britain's first experience of 'total war'. Once the war was won, Britain was never the same again.

This topic is examined in Paper 2 of the examination. Paper 2-type exercises are included at the end of the chapter. Mark schemes, sample answers and comments can be found in the accompanying Teacher's Resource Pack.

How was British society changed, 1906–18?

Why did the Liberal governments introduce reforms to help the young, old and unemployed?

In 1906 the Liberals came to power in Britain. Between 1906 and 1911 they passed a number of reforms that laid the basis for a '**welfare state**' in Britain. From now on the State (government) would look after the poorest members of society.

The Liberals said they would raise the money to do this by increasing **taxes**. The rich did not want to pay higher taxes, and said that helping the poor would only make them lazy. But the Liberals knew that most people had come to believe that it was the government's duty to look after the poor. Why were people now more sympathetic to the poor?

Working class housing in the East End of London, 1909.

SOURCE A

Reasons for the Liberal reforms

Changes in politics

At the start of the 1800s only upper class men were allowed to vote. Gradually more men were given the right to vote, including large numbers from the **working class**. By 1900 half the country's voters came from the working class. The trade unions then helped to set up the Labour Representation Committee (LRC), to help independent 'Labour' candidates stand in elections for parliament. Once elected these MPs would campaign for better pay and working conditions. In 1906, 53 LRC-backed candidates were elected to parliament. They became the Labour Party and were led by Keir Hardie. The new Liberal government of 1906 knew it had to pass acts to help working people, otherwise they would vote for the Labour Party in future elections.

QUESTION

1 Study Source A.
   a What can we learn from this source about London in 1909?
   b What was the attitude of the Liberals towards helping the poor?

SOURCE B

NOT A WISE SAW

A cartoon of 1903 commenting on the relationship between the Labour Party and the Liberal Party. It shows Keir Hardie, one of the Labour Party's early leaders.

Liberal governments' reforms

Social and economic changes

During the 1800s the **Industrial Revolution** brought the growth of factories and large towns. Living conditions in the new industrial towns were terrible.

The workers' houses were cramped, dirty and often without proper **sanitation**, like toilets or running water. Working conditions in the factories were dangerous and unhealthy. Not surprisingly diseases, such as cholera, spread easily. To begin with the government did nothing, but in time it was forced to pass some Factory Acts, Education Acts and Public Health Acts to try and improve things.

People gradually came to realise that only the government had the power to improve such awful conditions.

In 1906 the Liberals took this idea a step further by saying that government also had a duty to provide a basic minimum standard of living for everyone.

> **QUESTION**
>
> 1 Look at Source C.
>   a Explain the message of the cartoon.
>   b Do you think the cartoonist approved of the 'People's Budget'? Explain your answer.

The General Election result of 1906

Liberals	377 seats
Irish Nationals	83 seats
Labour	53 seats
Conservatives	157 seats
Liberal majority	84 seats

The main Liberal cabinet members

Prime Minister: Herbert Asquith
Chancellor of the Exchequer: David Lloyd George
President of the Board of Trade: Winston Churchill

A cartoon showing Lloyd George, and commenting on the 'People's Budget' of 1909.

8 How was British society changed, 1906–18?

Outstanding politicians

The Liberals had several outstanding politicians who were keen to pass social reforms. Two of the most important Liberals in this period were David Lloyd George and Winston Churchill.

Lloyd George was a talented and ambitious politician who came from a poor Welsh background. He was famous for his fiery speeches in which he supported the poor against the rich. As Chancellor of the Exchequer, Lloyd George drew up the 'People's Budget' in 1909, which raised taxes to pay for the government's reforms. Lloyd George went on to become Prime Minister from 1916-22.

Churchill helped to pass the National Insurance Act of 1911, which for the first time, provided workers with a certain amount of unemployment pay and sick pay (see pages 15 and 16). Churchill later became Prime Minister from 1940-5 and from 1951-5.

The problem of poverty in 1906

One of the biggest reasons for the Liberal reforms after 1906 was the growing awareness of the amount of poverty in Britain. Despite being one of the richest countries in the world, millions of British people lived in poverty. Many people said the poor were lazy and wasted their money on alcohol and tobacco.

Workhouses

Under the Poor Law of 1834 able-bodied poor people who wanted help had to enter the **workhouse**. Here conditions were deliberately made so hard that only the desperate would want to go there. There was not enough food, families were separated and people were made to feel ashamed at having to depend on the workhouse.

SOURCE D

When we entered the workhouse in 1895, my mother was taken to the women's ward. My brother and I were put in the children's ward. Once a week we were allowed to meet. How well I remember the first visiting day. I was shocked at seeing my mother in workhouse clothes. In just one week she had aged and grown thin.

Adapted from the autobiography of Charlie Chaplin, a famous comedian.

QUESTIONS

1. What changes were taking place in nineteenth-century Britain?
2. What was new about the attitudes of the Liberal governments after 1906 to social problems?
3. Why were David Lloyd George and Winston Churchill important?

The Poor Law fails to cope

The Poor Law of 1834 did not work all that well. When workers were made unemployed because fewer jobs were available, so many people wanted help that there were not enough places in the workhouses. In such times, people were given **outdoor relief** in the form of money and food (something the Poor Law was supposed to avoid). Another problem was that the Poor Law was not meant to solve the problem of poverty, but to cut the amount spent on the poor. Although many Poor Law authorities did their best, poverty remained a huge problem.

- **Helping the sick**
  As the sick could not work, they were given outdoor relief in their own homes. By 1900 a number of Poor Law hospitals had been built, which gave free treatment to the sick.

- **Helping the unemployed**
  By 1900 the attitude of the Poor Law authorities to the unemployed had softened a little. Poor Law authorities were now allowed to provide work for the unemployed.

- **Helping the elderly**
  Old age was one of the biggest causes of poverty. Many old people had to be taken into the workhouses because they were too frail (weak) to look after themselves.

> ### QUESTIONS
> 1. How did the Poor Law of 1834 deal with the able-bodied poor (page 9)?
> 2. Explain why the Poor Law failed to cope with the problems of poverty
> 3. Look at Source E. What can you tell about life in a workhouse from this source?

SOURCE E

Women eating a meal in the St Pancras workhouse in London in 1901.

Treatment of the elderly in the workhouses improved. Couples were not split up and they were allowed visitors and luxuries such as tea.

- **Helping the young**

  Pauper (poor) children usually had to go into the workhouse with their parents. Many Poor Law authorities, however, spared them the harsh surroundings of the workhouse and let them live with local families. Sometimes schooling was also provided.

Conclusion

By the end of the nineteenth century the treatment of the poor had improved. But the Poor Law only coped with the worst effects of poverty, and did not deal with its causes. Before this could be done people needed to have a better understanding of the problem of poverty.

> **QUESTION**
>
> 1 Look at Source F.
>   a Were these good or bad menus? Explain your answer.
>   b Do you think that the labourer's family were poor? Explain your answer.

SOURCE F

A week's menus for the labourer's family

Menu of meals provided during week ending June 21, 1901

	Breakfast.	Dinner.	Tea.	Supper.
Friday	Bread, butter, tea.	Bread, bacon.	Bread, butter, lettuce, tea.	
Saturday	Bread, butter, tea.	Meat, potatoes, Yorkshire pudding.	Bread, butter, tea, onions.	Fish, bread.
Sunday	Fish, bread, tea.	Beef, cabbage, potatoes, rhubarb pie (1).	Bread, butter, tea-cake, tea.	Bread, butter, tea-cake.
Monday	Bread, butter, tea-cake.	Cold meat, potatoes, pie.	Bread, butter, tea-cake, custard.	Bread, butter, pie.
Tuesday	Bread, bacon-fat, tea.	Cold meat, potatoes, pie.	Bread, meat, dripping.	Bread, cheese.
Wednesday	Bread, butter, tea, bacon.	Hashed cabbage, meat, bread.	Bread, butter, tea, lettuce.	
Thursday	Bread, butter, tea.	Liver, bread, bread pudding.	Bread, butter, tea.	Bread, butter.

(1) Rhubarb and cabbage given.

A week's menu for a labouring family in York in 1901.

Liberal governments' reforms

Studies of poverty

At the end of the nineteenth century two important studies about poverty were published.

- *Life and Labour of the People of London* by Charles Booth was published between 1886 and 1903. Booth visited the houses of poor people in London asking questions about their living conditions.

He said that people were poor if they had less than £1 a week for a family of five to live on.

Booth estimated that 30 per cent of the people in London lived in poverty.

He also said that poverty was caused by sickness, old age, unemployment, low wages and large families, rather than laziness.

- *Poverty: A Study of Town Life* by Seebohm Rowntree was published in 1901.

Rowntree carried out a study in York and he, too, found that about 30 per cent of the population was living in poverty with an income of £1 a week or less.

Both studies showed that the Poor Law could not cope with the problem of poverty. As a result of these studies, people became more sympathetic to the poor.

The Royal Commission on the Poor Law, 1905

In 1899, 40 per cent of the men who volunteered to fight in the **Boer War** were found to be physically unfit because of the effects of poverty.

There was no longer any excuse for a lack of action. So, in 1905 the government set up a Royal Commission to review the Poor Law.

Although its members disagreed over what improvements were needed, the appointment of the Royal Commission showed that there was a real concern about poverty in Britain.

It was against this background that the Liberals passed their great reforms.

SOURCE G

There are millions in this country living without enough food, clothes and shelter. Shame on rich Britain that she should put up with so much poverty. There is plenty of wealth in this country but it needs to be more fairly shared out.

Lloyd George writing in 1906.

QUESTIONS

1. **a** What did Booth and Rowntree find out about poverty?
   b Why was their work important?
2. Read Source G. Why did Lloyd George think the problem of poverty in Britain was shameful?

How effective were the Liberal reforms?

Reforms that helped children

1 The **School Meals Act** of 1906 gave local authorities the power to provide free school meals for poor children.

2 **Free school medical inspections** for children were introduced in 1907. All children were to be inspected once a year by a doctor.

3 The **Children's Charter** of 1908 introduced a number of measures affecting children:

- Child Care Committees helped families where children were suffering the effects of poverty or neglect.

- Special courts were set up to deal with young offenders. **Borstals** were set up so that young people were not kept in the same jails as adults.

- The sale of tobacco, alcohol and fireworks to people under 16 was made illegal.

- Working hours for children were limited and they were banned from doing unsuitable types of work.

Old age pensions

The Old Age Pensions Act was passed in 1908.

- The poorest people over the age of 70 who had an income of less than £21 per year would get a pension of 5 shillings [25p] a week.

- Smaller pensions were also paid on a sliding scale down to 1 shilling [5p] per week to those who were slightly better off and earning no more than £31 a year.

> **QUESTIONS**
>
> 1 What did the Liberals do to help children?
>
> 2 Look at Source A. Why did the cartoonist refer to Old Age Pensions as a 'gift'?

SOURCE A

THE NEW YEAR'S GIFT.

'The New Year's Gift' – a cartoon about the introduction of old age pensions, first paid in 1909.

- The pensions were paid for out of taxation and people did not have to pay anything towards them. This was a completely new idea, but the government felt it could afford it.

- Opponents of the government said that paying pensions to old people would discourage them from saving for their own retirement and rob them of their independence.

- By 1913 about one million old people were receiving a state pension, a lot more than the government had estimated.

> **QUESTION**
>
> 1 Read Sources B, C and D.
>   a Which two sources agree with pensions? Explain your answer.
>   b Which source disagrees with pensions and why?

Reactions to the introduction of old age pensions

Read Sources B, C and D and find out how people at the time reacted to the introduction of old age pensions.

SOURCE B

The Poor Law authorities gave old people who could not work a small weekly sum, but it was not enough to live on. Unless they had well-off children to help them, there came a time when the home had to be broken up. Old age pensions relieved old people of their worries. They were suddenly rich!

When they went to the Post Office to draw their pensions, tears of thanks ran down the faces of some. As they picked up their money, they would say, 'God bless that Lord George', because they could not believe that such a generous person could be a plain 'Mr'.

Adapted from *Lark Rise to Candleford* by Flora Thompson, an account of rural life in the late nineteenth century.

SOURCE C

We've often thought it would be best for us to die. We were just a burden to our children who kept us. They were good and wouldn't let us go into the workhouse if they could help it. But now we want to live forever, because we give them our ten shillings a week, and it pays them to have us.

The husband of an elderly couple talking to a journalist about the introduction of old age pensions.

SOURCE D

How can any sensible man think about pensions without dismay? The strength of this country has been its wealth and the independent character of its people. Old age pensions will destroy this.

They will take wealth from people by unfair taxation. Pensions will weaken the character of people by teaching them to rely on the state [government], rather than their own efforts.

Adapted from a letter to *The Times* (1908) about old age pensions.

Labour Exchanges

- Too many men had casual jobs from which they were often laid off. They then had the problem of finding another job. William Beveridge felt that people should be helped to find permanent employment, and this led the Liberals to pass the Labour Exchanges Act in 1909.

- Offices called Labour Exchanges were set up all over Britain. Employers looking for workers advertised their vacancies at the local Labour Exchange.

- Unemployed people were then put in touch with the employers. This meant that the unemployed no longer had to travel around looking for work.

- By 1914 there were 400 Labour Exchanges, filling a million jobs a year. Today we call them 'Job Centres'.

The Trade Boards Act, 1909

Many people worked in small-scale 'sweated' **industries** such as dressmaking and nail making.

These industries were not covered by any of the Factory Acts. Hours were long and wages low. The Trades Board Act set minimum wages for these industries.

The National Insurance Act, 1911

Before 1911 there was no National Insurance scheme in Britain. Most workers could not afford private insurance cover and therefore would have no money coming in if they fell ill or became unemployed. In such circumstances they would be plunged into poverty.

In 1911 the Liberals passed the National Insurance Act to deal with this problem. The Act was divided into two parts.

SOURCE E

The first person to draw an old age pension, 1909.

QUESTION

1 What did the Liberals do to help
   a the unemployed and
   b the low paid?

How effective were the Liberal reforms?

Part 1: Health insurance

- The scheme was compulsory for all workers who earned £160 a year or less.

- Out of their wages workers had to pay 4d a week into an insurance fund. The employers added 4d and the government 2d, making 9d for each worker. This allowed Lloyd George to tell opponents of the Act that the workers were getting '9d for 4d'.

- The employers collected the money from the workers and stamped their National Insurance card to show that payment had been received.

- In return if workers could not work because of illness they could claim sick pay of 10 shillings [50p] a week for a period of 26 weeks. They would also receive free medical care.

Many doctors were against the Act to begin with, but they changed their minds when they realised they would have more work than ever before.

Part 2: Unemployment insurance

- This part of the Act was designed to protect workers in industries that were affected by seasonal unemployment such as building, shipbuilding and engineering.

- About 2.5 million workers were covered.

- Both the workers and the employers paid 2.5d into the fund.

- When unemployed, workers could claim 7 shillings [35p] for up to 15 weeks. This was not enough to live on, but helped them cope until they found another job.

- This second part of the National Insurance Act was the work of Winston Churchill.

The significance of the Liberal reforms

Look at Sources G to J and decide how significant (important) the Liberal reforms were.

SOURCE F

Taffy was a Welshman.
Taffy was a thief.

A chant against Lloyd George by workers who did not want to pay National Insurance contributions.

QUESTION

1. Read Source F. Do you think it was fair to call Lloyd George a thief? Explain your answer.

SOURCE G

The 1911 National Insurance Act was not part of a programme towards a socialist state. By insisting on the insurance principle, the Liberals were making the point that individuals were paying for the benefits they received. The Liberals did not lay the foundations of the welfare state; they created a social service state in which everyone was expected to contribute towards the benefits they received.

Adapted from a British history book published in 1989.

SOURCE H

Between 1906 and 1914 the foundations of today's Welfare State were laid. The Liberals were prepared to go further than the Victorians by allowing the State [government] to take an active part in people's lives. By 1914 the Liberals had enlarged the field of direct state action and pointed the way to the future. Their proposals were not very extreme; for all the fuss, there was virtually no redistribution of income [when money is taken from one section of society and given to others].

Adapted from a British history book published in 1971.

SOURCE I

By this Act Lloyd George introduced the device of paying for social reform mainly out of the pockets of the poor. Instead of taxation falling mainly on the richer classes, the healthy and employed workers were made to contribute towards the needs of the sick and the workless.

Adapted from *A History of The Common People*, published in 1938.

SOURCE J

CRESCENDO;
OR, THE TUNE THE OLD COW'S LIKELY TO DIE OF.
THE COW. "STOP! STOP! THIS ISN'T MILKING; IT'S MURDER!"

'Income Tax Payer', a British cartoon of 1914, showing Lloyd George, who was Chancellor of the Exchequer at that time.

QUESTIONS

1. Look at Source J. How accurate is the impression this cartoon gives of the impact of the Liberal reforms?

2. Why does Source J give a different impression of the impact of the reforms from the other three sources?

3. How far do Sources G, H and I agree about the significance of the Liberal reforms? Explain your answer.

4. Which of these four sources do you think gives the fairest judgement on the Liberal reforms? Explain your answer.

How effective were the Liberal reforms?

What were the arguments for and against women's suffrage?

Attitudes to women in the nineteenth century

In the 1800s women were considered to be inferior to men. Women were financially dependent on men and had fewer legal rights. For example, they were not allowed to vote in parliamentary elections. Married women were not expected to work, unless they came from very poor families. By 1900, however, attitudes were starting to change.

- Women were able to enter professions such as teaching.

- Inventions such as the telephone and typewriter opened up new job opportunities for women. They could now become shop assistants and office workers.

- Young, single middle-class women benefited the most from these changes. They were now able to lead more independent lives. Out of these social changes the campaign for women's **suffrage** (the right to vote) began to develop.

> **QUESTIONS**
>
> 1 In what ways were women's lives changing by 1900?
>
> 2 Read pages 19–20 and Source A. Why did some people think it would still be a bad idea for women to have the vote?
>
> 3 Read Source B. Do you think Prime Minister Asquith wanted women to have the vote? Explain your answer.

SOURCE A

The inclusion of women in politics would harm the number, character and strength of our future race. It would limit women's ability and inclination for motherhood, and would lead to their unwillingness to manage the home, and home is the first and lasting strength of social life in all countries.

From a speech given in February 1912 by Charles Hobhouse, a member of the Liberal government.

SOURCE B

There are few issues in politics where such exaggerated language is used on both sides. I sometimes think, as one listens to the arguments of the supporters of women's suffrage, that there is nothing to be said for it. I also think, when I listen to the opponents of women's suffrage, that there is nothing to be said against it.

Prime Minister Asquith, speaking in the House of Commons in 1913.

Arguments against women's suffrage

1 Many men thought that women did not understand politics.

2 Many women, including Queen Victoria, were against the idea of women having the vote.

3 Not all men had the vote at this time, so why should women have it?

4 Few people thought it would be possible to give the vote to **all** women. But giving the vote to some women, such as the richest or most educated, would favour one political party (probably the Conservatives) over the other (the Liberals).

'Convicts and Lunatics Have No Vote', a British cartoon from 1910.

QUESTIONS

Look at Source C.
1 What is the message of this cartoon?

2 Was the cartoon drawn by someone in favour or someone against women's rights? Explain your answer.

5 Many people thought that the violent tactics of the **Suffragettes** (see page 21) proved that women did not deserve the vote.

6 Many people argued that women should not have the vote because they would not be strong enough to help protect the country in time of war.

Arguments for women's suffrage

1 Women in New Zealand, Australia and some parts of the USA were already allowed to vote.

2 Since 1888 some women in Britain had been able to vote in local elections. Why not parliamentary elections too?

3 Women were now more educated than before.

4 Through the 1800s more and more men had been given the vote. Surely it was now time to include women?

SOURCE D

Suppose the majority of men wanted a war against Russia, and the women were against it, or vice versa. In either case, as the men would supply more blood and money to fight such a war and would be better placed to judge the effects of the war on the country, then with them must rest the final decision.

Adapted from an article in *The Girl's Own Paper*, May 1896.

QUESTIONS

1 What arguments were there in favour of women having the vote?

2 Some of the arguments against women's suffrage seem strange to us now. Why, then, were these arguments used at that time?

How effective were the activities of the Suffragists and the Suffragettes?

The Suffragists

In 1897 Millicent Fawcett formed the National Union of Women's Suffrage Societies (NUWSS). Its members were known as **Suffragists**.

The NUWSS was orderly and law abiding, and believed in using calm persuasion to win the vote for women.

The Suffragists won a good deal of support for their cause and, given time, they probably would have succeeded. But some women did not want to wait.

The Suffragettes

In 1903 a group of Suffragists, tired with the slow approach of the NUWSS, broke away and formed the Women's Social and Political Union (WSPU).

Emmeline Pankhurst and her daughter, Christabel, were the leaders of this group.

Members of the WSPU were prepared to use direct action and, if necessary, violence to win the vote. They soon became known as the Suffragettes.

What action did the Suffragettes take?

At first the **Suffragettes** held demonstrations and carried out minor acts of public disorder, such as chaining themselves to the railings outside Buckingham Palace or heckling (rudely interrupting) politicians.

Parliament, however, refused to give women the vote. In their anger, the Suffragettes turned to violent, illegal tactics such as smashing windows, burning houses and assaulting politicians.

SOURCE A

Our heckling made women's suffrage a matter of news. The newspapers were full of us. We had defied the police, we were awake at last. We were prepared to do something that women had never done before – to fight for themselves, for their own human rights.

Adapted from Emmeline Pankhurst's autobiography.

SOURCE B

Do not open suspicious parcels arriving by post or leave them lying unopened in the house. They should be dealt with carefully and promptly. These Suffragettes are quite capable of trying to burn us out.

Adapted from a letter from Winston Churchill to his wife, 1913.

SOURCE C

From every part of the crowded and brilliantly lit streets came the crash of splintered glass. Scared shop assistants came out on to the pavements; traffic stopped; policemen sprang this way and that. Five minutes later the streets were full of excited groups, each surrounding a woman wrecker being led into custody at the nearest police station. Meanwhile the shopping quarter of London had plunged itself into a sudden darkness as shutters were hurriedly fitted. Guards of doormen and shop assistants were quickly mounted, and any unaccompanied lady in sight, especially if she carried a handbag, became an object of suspicion.

The *Daily Mail*, 2 March 1912, reporting on the Suffragettes' window-smashing demonstration.

QUESTIONS

1 Read page 21. What were the differences between the Suffragists and the Suffragettes?
2 Describe the violent tactics used by the Suffragettes.

SOURCE D

In 1913 the Suffragettes found their first martyr when Miss Emily Davison flung herself to death under the hoofs of the King's horse at the Derby.

A historian's account written in 1960.

SOURCE E

Emily Davison is knocked to the ground by the King's horse at the 1913 Derby.

22 How was British society changed, 1906–18?

Increased violence

By 1913 Parliament had still not given women the vote and the Suffragettes became even more violent. There was more window smashing, cutting telegraph wires and burning empty buildings.

Suffragettes tried to burn down the house of Charles Hobhouse, a well-known Liberal opponent of women's suffrage. Luckily, they only managed to set his back door on fire.

The 1913 Derby

On 4 June 1913 Emily Davison, a Suffragette, walked out in front of the horses during the Derby horse race at Epsom. She ran into the King's horse, 'Anmer' and was badly injured. She died in hospital four days later.

Davison was probably trying to draw attention to the Suffragette cause. Many people believed she committed suicide to be a **martyr** for the women's cause. Certainly this was how the Suffragettes treated her death. There is, though, real doubt about this view of events.

QUESTIONS

1. Look at Sources D to I. Did Emily Davison deliberately kill herself?
2. Was her death important? Explain your answer.

SOURCE F

The desperate act of the woman who rushed from the rails onto the course as the horses swept round Tattenham Corner, apparently from some mad notion that she could spoil the race, will impress the general public.

She did not interfere with the race, but she nearly killed a jockey as well as herself, and she brought down a valuable horse. A deed of this kind, we need hardly say, is not likely to increase the popularity of the cause with the public.

From *The Times*, 5 June 1913.

SOURCE G

In 1988 historians examined the contents of Emily Davison's handbag, and found she had bought a return ticket that day. Her diary [also] included a number of appointments in the days after the Derby.

From a recent history book.

SOURCE H

The cause needs a martyr.

Said by Emily Davison.

SOURCE I

The coroner said he did not think that Miss Davison aimed at the King's horse, but that her intention was to upset the race. The jury would probably dismiss the idea that she intended to take her own life.

A report on the inquest into the death of Emily Davison, published in *The Suffragette* newspaper, 13 June 1913.

The reactions of the authorities

1 Frustration

At first many men did not take the Suffragettes seriously. But they soon realised that the Suffragettes were not going to give up.

The authorities did not know what do with well-educated, middle-class ladies who were behaving in such a violent and 'unladylike' manner. This frustration resulted in many Suffragettes being roughly treated by men who did not like their activities.

2 The Cat and Mouse Act, 1913

The authorities sent more and more Suffragettes to jail. The Suffragettes responded by going on hunger strikes.

QUESTIONS

1 Look at Source J. Explain what is happening in this picture.

2 What techniques did the artist who painted the poster use to turn people's opinions against the government? Use details from the poster to explain your answer.

An election poster, using the issue of force-feeding to attack the government.

24   How was British society changed, 1906–18?

Frightened of a Suffragette dying of starvation in prison, the authorities force-fed the hunger strikers. This was a brutal and cruel process, which caused people to protest against the treatment of Suffragettes.

As a result, Parliament was forced to pass the '**Cat and Mouse**' Act in 1913. This said that prisons could release hunger strikers if their health was bad.

But once the hunger strikers had recovered they would be re-arrested and sent back to prison. The Act, however, did not stop Suffragettes such as Emmeline Pankhurst from going on hunger strikes.

Conclusion: Did the Suffragettes help the women's cause?

By the start of the First World War in August 1914 Parliament still had not granted women the vote.

Although the Suffragettes had caught the public's attention, their violent tactics lost them much support.

The Suffragettes decided to call off their campaign in 1914 and help the war effort. In the end it was not violent protests that won women the vote, but the contribution they made to winning the war.

QUESTIONS

1 'By 1914 the Suffragettes had not succeeded in winning votes for women. This means their campaign was a failure.' Explain whether or not you agree with the statement.

2 Do you think the Suffragists would have done better without the Suffragettes? Explain your answer.

SOURCE K

Emmeline Pankhurst being arrested at a Suffragette demonstration in 1914.

How did women contribute to the war effort?

Women in employment during the First World War

Women demand the 'Right to Serve'
As men rushed to join the armed forces at the start of the war, the women's movement immediately said their supporters were ready to fill the men's jobs at home. However, this happened only gradually. It took the government until March 1915 to set up a register of women willing to do war work.

In July 1915 the Suffragettes organised a huge demonstration in London, demanding the 'Right to Serve'. After this the number of women doing vital war work increased rapidly.

Conscription
The demand for female labour increased even more after the government introduced **conscription** (compulsory military service) in 1916. During the war a total of five million men served in the armed forces.

Women filled their jobs at home. They worked in factories, steel mills, in ship-building, as bus drivers, and on farms as part of the Women's Land Army.

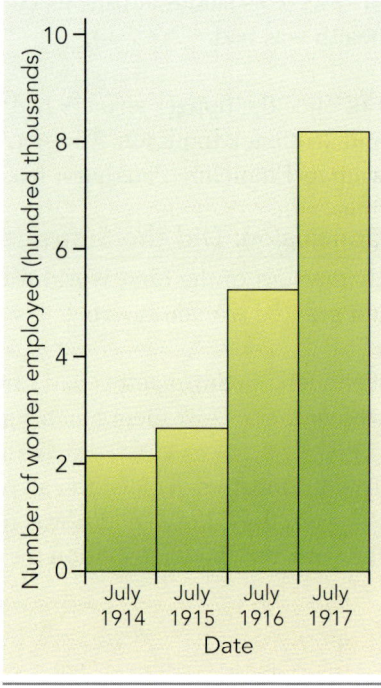

The employment of women in the munitions industry.

SOURCE A

Women working in an engineering factory in 1917.

QUESTIONS

1. Why were women needed to help the war effort?
2. What kind of work did women do in the war?
3. How did the experience of war work change women's lives?

26 How was British society changed, 1906–18?

They also worked in huge numbers in **munitions** factories, making bullets and shells for the soldiers at the front.

Some women went to the war zones and did valuable work in the Voluntary Aid Detachment, the Women's Auxiliary Army Corps and the Women's Royal Naval Service.

Women gain a greater sense of value

Middle-class women who were working during the war were receiving wages of their own for the first time, rather than having to rely on their husbands for money.

Industrial work was not new to working-class women, but the war gave them a greater sense of their value to society. The war changed attitudes to women's work for good.

Type of work	Number of women employed 1914	Number of women employed 1918
Industrial work	2,200,000	3,000,000
Transport	15,000	117,000
Commerce (office work)	505,000	934,000
Government (inc. teachers)	262,000	460,000

The increase in women's employment, 1914-18.

SOURCE B

I was working filling the bullets. You sat there with boxes of empty bullets, and you filled them with powder from a big thing like a dispenser. Then we put them into trays, and a couple of men came to take them away. There were people working with liddite and cordite. Their faces went all yellow from the stuff.

One day some flames started to come along the line towards us, and the two men in the shop got hold of us and threw us outside onto the grass. They knew something was going to happen. The alarm was going and Queenie, our supervisor, had to go back for her watch. She was blown to pieces.

A woman interviewed in 1984, describing her experiences as a munitions worker in the First World War.

SOURCE C

The wartime business girl is to be seen any night in London dining alone or with a friend. Before she would never have dined in town unless in the company of a man friend. But now with more money and without men she is beginning to dine out.

The *Daily Mail*, April 1916.

SOURCE D

They appear more alert and more critical of their working conditions. They have a keener appetite for pleasure and a willingness to protest against wrongs.

A comment about women workers from a factory inspector, 1916.

How were civilians affected by the war?

Recruiting

At the start of the war Lord Kitchener, the Minister for War, was in put in charge of raising a volunteer army. Men rushed to join the armed forces.

There was a strong feeling of **patriotism** and a belief that fighting in the war would be a great adventure. People thought the war would be over in a few months. By November 1914, over two million men had been recruited into the armed forces.

> **QUESTION**
>
> 1 Study Sources A, B, C. Explain the ways in which the government ensured enough men joined the armed forces.

SOURCE A

'Name please.'
'Austin J Heraty, 15 Bailey Street, Newcastle.'
'Age?'
'18, sir.'
The sergeant looked at me and said, 'Did you say 18, Mr Heraty? I am very sorry, but I'll tell you what you can do. You can walk around the town, but if you come back you must be 19.'
Only then did the penny drop. I walked around the town and in 60 seconds was back in the room. Soon I had signed up.

A soldier describes how he signed up for the war in 1914.

SOURCE B

BRITONS "WANTS" **YOU** JOIN YOUR COUNTRY'S ARMY! GOD SAVE THE KING

A recruitment poster for the First World War.

How was British society changed, 1906–18?

The enthusiasm soon wore off as people realised how horrible war really was. By 1915 casualties were rising and the government put up posters, urging men to join up.

Look at Sources B and C and see how the government tried to persuade men that it was their duty to fight.

New government powers and their impact on civilian life

In 1914 Parliament passed the Defence of the Realm Acts (DORA), which gave the government powers to interfere in people's lives more than ever before. Under DORA:

- British Summer Time was introduced to give more daylight to work in.

- Pubs had the right to water down beer to stop drunkenness.

- The government was given control of the media. Newspapers were not allowed to tell the truth about the high number of deaths in the war. Instead they told stories of heroic deeds and victories.

- The government was given the power to make workers stay in vital jobs, such as mining and the railways.

Conscription

The trench warfare of the First World War brought terrible casualties. Thousands of men could be killed in a single day. The longer this went on, the more men were needed.

In 1915 the government began to think about **conscription** – making military service compulsory. They knew this would be unpopular so they took things a step at a time.

- A National Register of all men between the ages 15 and 65 was drawn up, giving details of occupations.

A recruitment poster. The reference to Scarborough relates to German naval attacks on several East Coast towns in December 1914 in which over 100 people were killed.

QUESTIONS

1 What was DORA?

2 What was conscription?

3 Why do you think the Government did not introduce conscription at the start of the war?

How were civilians affected by the war?

- The 'Derby Scheme' was also introduced. Under this men were invited to 'attest' - promise to join up if they were asked. The scheme did not work well. Less than half of those old enough to join up bothered to come forward. The government now realised that relying on volunteers would not produce enough men for the armed forces. As a result they were in a stronger position to introduce conscription.

- In 1916 two Military Service Acts brought in conscription. The first was for unmarried men and the second for all men aged between 18 and 41. Men in 'reserved occupations' doing important war work, such as mining, did not have to join up.

- About 16,000 men, known as **conscientious objectors**, refused to join up because they were against fighting wars. Some agreed to do other kinds of war work, such as driving ambulances. However, about 1500 refused to do anything at all. They were imprisoned and treated brutally, with around 70 dying as a result.

- Conscription meant that most families were affected by the war. Of the five million who served in the British armed forces, 750,000 were killed and two million injured. Families at home lived in fear of hearing that a husband, brother or son had been killed.

SOURCE D

5 Questions to those who employ male servants

1. HAVE you a Butler, Groom, Chauffeur, Gardener, or Gamekeeper serving you who at this moment should be serving your King and Country?

2. Have you a man serving at your table who should be serving a gun?

3. Have you a man digging your garden who should be digging trenches?

4. Have you a man driving your car who should be driving a transport wagon?

5. Have you a man preserving your game who should be helping to preserve your Country?

A great responsibility rests on you. Will you sacrifice your personal convenience for your Country's need?

Ask your men to enlist TO-DAY.

The address of the nearest Recruiting Office can be obtained at any Post Office.

God Save the King.

An advertisement, December 1914: 'Five questions to those who employ male servants'.

SOURCE E

A postcard, published in 1917, showing the treatment of conscientious objectors.

QUESTIONS

1 What can you learn from Source E about the treatment of conscientious objectors?
2 Why were they treated this way?

Rationing

In 1914 most of Britain's food was imported, but German submarines (U-boats) began sinking the ships that carried the food. More food had to be grown in Britain and less eaten.

DORA allowed the government to take over land to grow food. The Women's Land Army provided women to work on farms.

Even so, because of the success of U-boats, there were still food shortages. In 1917, sugar rationing was introduced. Each household was sent a rationing card allowing the holder half a pound of sugar per week.

As goods became scarcer, so prices rose. The government began to **subsidise** the price of bread and potatoes. In 1918 other goods were rationed, including meat, tea and butter. Shopkeepers would clip coupons from ration books as they were used.

These measures meant people did not suffer severe hardship or shortages. In fact, rising wages during the war meant the less well-off could afford a better diet.

From the *Report of the Working Classes Cost of Living Committee*, 1918.

SOURCE F

Our figures show that families of unskilled workmen were slightly better fed in 1918, despite the rise in food prices. In London the number of poorly fed schoolchildren is less than half that of 1913. A similar improvement has taken place in Birmingham, Bolton, Bristol, Bradford, Glasgow and Nottingham. Fewer free school meals are being provided than before the war.

SOURCE G

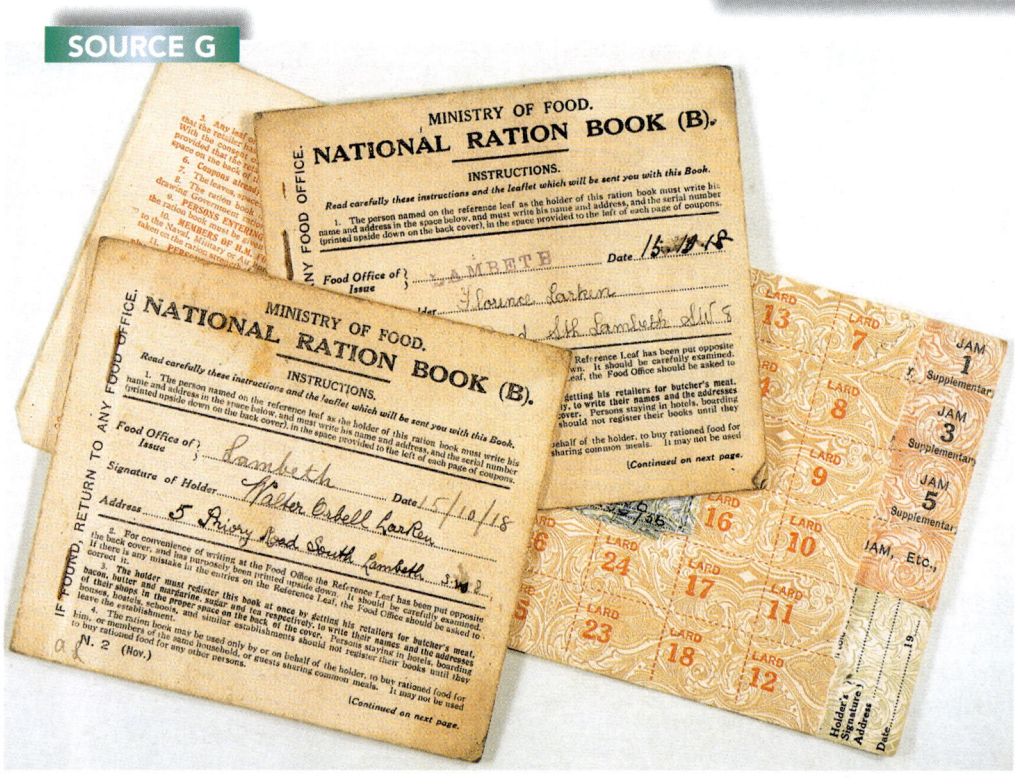

First World War ration books.

QUESTIONS

1 How did the government make sure that everyone had enough to to eat during the war?

2 Would you say that the civilian population of Britain suffered hardship during the First World War? Explain your answer.

How effective was government propaganda during the war?

Total support needed

During the First World War the government used **propaganda** to make sure people stayed favourable towards fighting the war.

In order to win a major war, a country needs the total support of its people. Without this support a country cannot rely on its workers to make an extra effort to produce weapons, ammunition and machinery.

It was vital that the people were made to believe that they were fighting a 'just' war and that the Germans were evil.

For this reason the government did nothing to stop stories that the Germans were carrying out terrible acts of violence, such as stabbing babies.

Attitudes towards the war

People soon realised that the war would not be 'all over by Christmas', and that it was going to drag on for much longer. It also became clear that war was terrible and not some glorious game. Despite this, most British people were still determined to win the war.

Exaggerated stories of brutality

Most people stayed fiercely patriotic and anti-German throughout the war, believing the stories of German brutality spread by the newspapers. Propaganda stories became exaggerated as they passed from one newspaper to the next.

In his book *Goodbye to all That*, Robert Graves showed how a simple report in a German newspaper grew into a false story about German brutality in Belgium, as it was spread from country to country (see page 40).

The Defence of the Realm Act (DORA) was used to make sure that the newspapers printed only stories that were approved by the government. But most newspapers were very happy to print what the government told them.

QUESTIONS

1. What is propaganda?
2. Why do governments use propaganda in war time?
3. Read Source A. Do you think this story was probably true? Explain your answer.

SOURCE A

I saw eight drunk German soldiers. They were singing, dancing and making a lot of noise. As they went along the street a small child, about two years old, came out of a house. The child was in the way of the soldiers. One of the soldiers drove his bayonet with both hands in the child's stomach, lifting the child into the air and carrying it away with his bayonet. He and his comrades were still singing. The child screamed when the soldier struck it with the bayonet, but not afterwards.

An account of German brutality in Belgium, included in a British report of 1915.

In addition, many private companies printed and displayed their propaganda posters.

This left the government free to concentrate on propaganda campaigns to get people to save food, buy savings bonds or encourage them to enter certain industries (see Source B).

The War Propaganda Bureau

Early in the war the government set up a secret War Propaganda Bureau. Its job was to look into the stories of German brutality and see if they were true. Not surprisingly, the Bureau reported that stories of German brutality (such as the one in Source A) were true.

The Department of Information

The Department of Information was set up in 1917. Its purpose was to:

- provide material to shape opinion
- oversee propaganda material used in the cinemas
- gather information from abroad
- control what news was printed in newspapers.

In 1918 the department was renamed the Ministry of Information under the leadership of Lord Beaverbrook, the owner of the *Daily Express* newspaper.

Conclusion

It is impossible to say how effective government propaganda was. The anti-German stories probably only strengthened **prejudices** already held by the British. But the stories may have persuaded neutral countries, such as the USA, to support the British side.

Most of the propaganda, however, was just information that the government wanted to get over in the most favourable way.

> **QUESTION**
>
> 1 Study Source B.
>
> a What is the message of this poster?
>
> b Explain how the poster tries to persuade the viewer to accept its message.

SOURCE B

'Put Strength in the Final Blow', a British propaganda poster.

34　How was British society changed, 1906–18?

Why were some women given the vote in 1918?

Women equal to men

Women made a big contribution to winning the war. They had shown that they were capable of doing all sorts of men's jobs.

Women now felt more independent and they were aware that they had more to offer society than men had previously allowed.

They had shared the burdens and dangers of winning the war, and began to feel the equals of men. If this was the case why should they not have the same rights as men?

Lloyd George supports votes for women

During the war political parties joined together in a **coalition** in order to fight the war. Old arguments that denied women the vote were put to one side, especially after Lloyd George became Prime Minister in 1916.

Lloyd George believed that women should be given the vote when the time came to deal with the issue again.

The right to vote is reviewed

Not all men had the right to vote at the time. But it became widely accepted that as men had faced the horrors and sacrifice of the war, then they should all have the right to vote afterwards.

If Parliament was to review the right to vote for men, then it would also be a chance to introduce votes for women.

The Representation of the People Act, 1918

In 1918 Parliament passed the Representation of the People Act, which said:

- All adult males over the age of 21 were given the vote.

- Women over the age of 30 who were householders (or the wives of householders) were given the vote.

Although the Act did not give all women the vote, this changed in 1928 when all women over the age of 21 were granted the right to vote.

QUESTIONS

1. Explain how the First World War helped women to win the right to vote.

2. What changes did the Representation of the People Act (1918) make to who would vote?

SOURCE A

It is some little comfort that the NUWSS, which was built up to promote votes for women, can now be used to help our country through a period of strain and sorrow.

Mrs Fawcett, leader of the Suffragists, writing in August 1914.

SOURCE B

Women voters going to the polls.

The first women MP

In 1919, Nancy, Lady Astor became the first woman Member of Parliament. Then in 1929, Margaret Bondfield, the Labour MP, became the first female Cabinet Minister.

SOURCE C

How could we have carried on the war without women? Short of bearing arms, there is hardly a service in which women have not been as active as men.

When the war is over questions will come up about women's labour and women's functions. I shall find it impossible not to grant women the power to make their voices directly heard.

Asquith, the former Prime Minister and opponent of women's rights, speaking in Parliament in favour of votes for women.

QUESTION

1 Read Source C. Why do you think Asquith changed his mind about votes for women?

What was the attitude of the British people at the end of the war towards Germany and the Paris Peace Conference?

The mood of the British people at the end of the war

Heavy casualties

When the war ended on 11 November 1918, the British people were in no mood to forgive and forget. The British armed forces had suffered high casualties in the war. Everyone knew someone who had lost a loved one.

Revenge

Germany was blamed for starting the war, and people wanted revenge. There was little pity in Britain for the Germans, even though they had lost more men than the British and Germany civilians had suffered more from food shortages.

There was a strong desire, stirred up by the newspapers, to make Germany pay. Headlines like 'Hang the Kaiser!' summed up the mood in Britain at the time.

The general election campaign 1918

During the General Election campaign in December 1918 politicians promised harsh treatment for Germany. Even Lloyd George, the Prime Minister, who understood the dangers of treating Germany too harshly, was swept along on the wave of anti-German feeling.

In Bristol Lloyd George told a meeting that 'Germany must pay to the uttermost farthing.'

Different attitudes about what should happen to Germany at the Paris Peace Conference

At the Peace Conference of 1919 Lloyd George had a difficult task in balancing his own personal views about how to treat Germany with the views of the British people.

> **QUESTIONS**
>
> 1. What was the attitude of the British people towards the Germans at the end of the war?
> 2. Read Source A. According to Winston Churchill, who stirred up people's feelings?

> **SOURCE A**
>
> The Prime Minister and his colleagues were astonished by people's feelings. People were stirred up into a fury by the newspapers. Crippled and mutilated soldiers filled the streets. Every cottage had its empty chair.
>
> Hatred of the beaten foe, thirst for his just punishment, rushed up from the heart of deeply injured millions.
>
> All over the country the most bitter were the women, of whom seven million were for the first time to vote.
>
> Winston Churchill, then Minister of Munitions, writing about the 1918 election campaign.

Lloyd George was under pressure to insist on a harsh peace, even though he knew this would anger the Germans and cause trouble in the future. Lloyd George realised that the demands of the British public could not be met.

SOURCE B

British Empire Union.
"ONCE A GERMAN—ALWAYS A GERMAN!"

REMEMBER!
This Man, who has shelled Churches, Hospitals, and Open Boats at Sea; This Robber, Ravisher and Murderer, AND This Man, who after the War, will want to sell you his German Goods, ARE ONE AND THE SAME PERSON! Men and Women of Britain! Have Nothing to do with Germans Until the Crimes Committed by Them against Humanity have been expiated! Help to Boycott Germans and German Goods by joining the British Empire Union, 346, Strand, London, W.C.2.

'Once a German, always a German', a British poster of 1919.

SOURCE C

I think that everyone here takes the view that a dissatisfied Germany would not be a good thing for Europe, but we are not the sole judges of the situation. Still I hope that our standing in international affairs may be enough to prevent an immoral peace.

A Liberal MP, writing to a friend about the peace conference, April 1919.

QUESTIONS

1. Study Source B. Explain why this poster was published in 1919.
2. Why was Lloyd George in a difficult position at the Paris Peace Conference?

Paper 2-type assessment: Britain and the First World War

The use of propaganda

Study the sources carefully. Then answer **all** the questions.

SOURCE A

Even for those who were not keen to join the army, there were enormous pressures to sign up. The government carried out a skilful propaganda campaign which portrayed the Germans as evil beasts. It was said that they had bayonetted babies and murdered nuns on their march through Belgium. Recruitment posters emphasised the need to help the country and to protect women and children from the horrors of war. Men who did not join up were made to feel like cowards.

An extract from a recent history book describing attitudes at the beginning of the war.

SOURCE B

RED CROSS OR IRON CROSS?

WOUNDED AND A PRISONER OUR SOLDIER CRIES FOR WATER.

THE GERMAN "SISTER" POURS IT ON THE GROUND BEFORE HIS EYES.

THERE IS NO WOMAN IN BRITAIN WHO WOULD DO IT.

THERE IS NO WOMAN IN BRITAIN WHO WILL FORGET IT.

A British poster issued early in the war.

SOURCE C

A Call from the Trenches.

(Extract from a letter from the Trenches.)

"I SAW a recruiting advertisement in a paper the other day. I wonder if the men are responding properly – they would if they could see what the Germans have done in Belgium. And, after all, it's not so bad out here – cold sometimes, and the waiting gets on our nerves a bit, but we are happy and as fit as fiddles. I wonder if _____ has joined, he certainly ought to."

Does '_____' refer to you?

If so

ENLIST TO-DAY.
God Save the King.

A recruiting advertisement in the *The Times*, 15 April 1915.

SOURCE D

TIME FOR ONE MORE

MITCHELL'S "GOLDEN DAWN" CIGARETTES.

A British poster advertising cigarettes in 1915.

SOURCE E

Extract 1
When the fall of Antwerp was announced the bells were rung in Cologne and all over Germany.

Written in the German newspaper, Kolnische Zeitung.

Extract 2
According to the *Kolnische Zeitung* the clergy at Antwerp were compelled to ring the church bells when the town was captured.

Written in the French newspaper, Le Matin.

Extract 3
According to what the British newspaper, *The Times*, has heard from Cologne, via Paris, the unfortunate Belgian priests who refused to ring the church bells when Antwerp was taken were sentenced to hard labour.

Written in the Italian newspaper, Corriere della Sera.

Extract 4
According to information which has reached *Corriere della Sera*, from Cologne, via London, it is confirmed that the barbaric conquerors of Antwerp punished the unfortunate Belgian priests for their heroic refusal to ring the church bells by hanging them as living clappers to the bells, with their heads down.

Written in Le Matin.

SOURCE F

We had been brought up to believe that Britain was the best country in the world. We were taught at school that we were better than other people – didn't we always win the last war? Now we wanted to show the Germans what we could do.

Private George Morgan, 16th battalion West Yorks Regiment, explains why he signed up in 1914.

How was British society changed, 1906–18?

SOURCE G

The airship was on fire and it was floating down. I could only think of people inside it being roasted to death. I was disgusted to see kind, good-hearted people dancing in the street as the men in that airship were dying. When I said it was a terrible thing, my friends said, 'but they're Germans, they're the enemy, they've been bombing us.' That's what the war did. It turned decent, gentle people into monsters.

An eye-witness description of the shooting down of a Zeppelin during the First World War.

SOURCE H

When the news came through that the Accrington Pals had been wiped out. I don't think there was a street in Accrington and district that did not have its blinds drawn.

The son of one of the Accrington Pals remembering the day the town heard about the losses in the Battle of the Somme. 720 of the Pals took part in the attack on the first day of the Somme (1 July 1916). Of these 584 were killed, reported missing or wounded.

QUESTIONS

1. Study **Source A**.
   How much could a historian studying the use of propaganda in the First World War learn from this source?
   Use the source and your own knowledge to explain your answer. (6 marks)

2. Study **Sources B** and **C**.
   Which of these two sources do you think would have had the greater impact on the British people?
   Use the sources and your own knowledge to explain your answer. (8 marks)

3. Study **Source D**.
   'This is an advertisement for cigarettes, not a piece of propaganda, so it is of no value to a historian studying the use of propaganda in the First World War'
   Use the source and your own knowledge to explain whether you agree with this interpretation. (6 marks)

4. Study **Source E**.
   Does this source prove that propaganda was just lies?
   Use the source and your own knowledge to explain your answer. (6 marks)

5. Study **Sources F** and **G**.
   Which of these two sources do you think would be most useful to a historian studying the effects of propaganda in the First World War?
   Use the sources and your own knowledge to explain your answer. (8 marks)

6. Study **Source H**.
   Do you think this source would have made the British people more or less likely to believe anti-German propaganda?
   Use the source and your own knowledge to explain your answer. (6 marks)

7. Study **all** the sources.
   'The use of propaganda in the First World War was subtle and extremely clever'.
   How far do the sources in this exercise agree with this interpretation?
   Use the sources and your knowledge to explain your answer. (10 marks)

Paper 2-type assessment: The Liberal Reforms

Old Age Pensions and National Insurance

Study the sources carefully. Then answer **all** the questions.

SOURCE A

A photograph showing living conditions for a London East End family in the early years of the twentieth century.

SOURCE B

David Lloyd George became Chancellor of the Exchequer in 1908. In his first budget speech he said that the government was going to introduce old age pensions. Old people would no longer be dependent on the Poor Law or the kindness of their friends and relatives. 'We are', he said 'lifting the shadow of the workhouse from the homes of the poor'.

An account of the work of Lloyd George, from a school textbook written in 1999.

SOURCE C

When the Old Age Pensions began, life was transformed for the aged. They were relieved of anxiety. They were suddenly rich. Independent for life! At first when they went to the Post Office to get their pension tears of gratitude would run down the cheeks of some – and there were flowers from gardens and apples from trees for the girl who merely handed them the money.

An extract from a novel by Flora Thompson. She had once been a Post Office worker handing out the benefits.

42 How was British society changed, 1906–18?

SOURCE D

Darby is 72, with a cataract in one eye and very little sight in the other. His wife Joan was 71 last October. They have lived on money given to them by their son and the meagre earnings from Joan's cleaning work. Interviewed by a reporter Darby chuckled and said 'It isn't wealth. No you couldn't call it wealth. But it's something for sure. The pension is not a charity. It's a right,' Darby said proudly.

An article in the *Daily Express* on 2 January 1909.

SOURCE E

Dear Sir,

The strength of this kingdom, in all its past struggles, has been its great wealth and the sturdy independent character of its people.

The measure will destroy both.

It will take the wealth from its possessors by unjust taxation and will sap the character of the people by teaching to rely, not on their own efforts, but on the State.

A letter written to *The Times* newspaper in 1908 complaining about the decision to introduce pensions.

SOURCE F

PUNCH, OR THE LONDON CHARIVARI.—August 5, 1908.

THE PHILANTHROPIC HIGHWAYMAN.

Mr. Lloyd-George. "I'LL MAKE 'EM PITY THE AGED POOR!"

A cartoon from *Punch* in 1909. It shows Lloyd George as a highwayman carrying out a robbery to pay for old age pensions.

SOURCE G

THE RIGHT TICKET FOR YOU!
YOU ARE TRAVELLING ON A SAFE LINE

1913 — GOVERNMENT LINE
MALE WORKER PAYS 4d
EMPLOYER PAYS 3d
STATE PAYS 2d

YOUR RETURN DURING ILLNESS
10/- Per Week FOR 26 WEEKS
5/- AFTERWARDS (TILL 70) WHILE INCAPABLE OF WORK
FREE DOCTOR & MEDICINE
30/- Maternity Grant
SANATORIUM BENEFIT

AND ARE ASSURED A SAFE RETURN

A government poster advertising the National Insurance Act. It was introduced in 1911 to provide payments for sickness and unemployment. This poster refers to the health insurance scheme.

Assessment: The Liberal Reforms   43

QUESTIONS

1. Study **Source A**.
   How useful do you think this source is for showing us what it was like to be poor in the early years of the twentieth century? Use the source and your own knowledge to explain your answer. (6 marks)

2. Study **Source B**.
   Do you think it is true that the Liberal government introduced old age pensions just to keep people out of the workhouse? Use the source and your own knowledge to explain whether you agree with this interpretation. (8 marks)

3. Study **Sources C** and **D**.
   Which of these sources do you think gives the better impression of the impact of old age pensions?
   Use the sources and your own knowledge to explain your answer. (6 marks)

4. Study **Sources E** and **F**.
   How similar are these two sources?
   Use the sources and your own knowledge to explain your answer. (8 marks)

5. Study **Sources G** and **H**.
   'These two sources are particularly important to a historian studying the impact of the Liberal reforms because they were issued by the government.' How far do you agree with this statement?
   Use the sources and your own knowledge to explain your answer. (10 marks)

6. Study **all** the sources.
   Do you think it is possible to decide how great an impact the Liberal reforms had from the sources in this exercise?
   Use the sources and your own knowledge to explain your answer. (12 marks)

SOURCE H

THE DAWN OF HOPE.

NATIONAL INSURANCE AGAINST SICKNESS AND DISABLEMENT

Mr. LLOYD GEORGE'S National Health Insurance Bill provides for the insurance of the Worker in case of Sickness.

Support the Liberal Government
in their policy of
SOCIAL REFORM.

A government poster advertising National Health Insurance. The doctor sitting by the bed is Lloyd George.

Paper 2-type assessment: The Suffragettes

How important were the Suffragettes in helping win the vote for women?

Study the sources carefully. Then answer **all** the questions.

SOURCE A

We believe that if we get the vote it will mean better conditions for our unfortunate sisters. We believe that only through new laws can any improvements be made and that new laws will not be passed until women have the same power as men to put pressure on governments.

We have tried every way. We have presented larger petitions than were ever presented before and succeeded in holding greater public meetings then men ever held. But we have been criticised and had contempt poured upon us.

Violence is the only way that we have to get the power which every citizen should have – the same kind of power that the worst of men have. The same kind of power that the wife-beater has, the same power that the drunkard has.

Emmeline Pankhurst speaking in her defence in court in 1912.

SOURCE C

'Hasn't Mrs Pankhurst the sense to see that the very worst kind of campaigning for the vote is to try to intimidate or blackmail a man into giving her what he would gladly give her otherwise'.

David Lloyd George, a member of the government, speaking in 1913 after his house had been bombed by Suffragettes.

SOURCE B

What a Woman may be, and yet not have the Vote

MAYOR | NURSE | MOTHER | DOCTOR or TEACHER | FACTORY HAND

What a Man may have been, & yet not lose the Vote

CONVICT | LUNATIC | Proprietor of white Slaves | Unfit for Service | DRUNKARD

A poster issued in 1912 by a group of woman artists supporting votes for women.

SOURCE D

By 1913 the activities of the militant Suffragettes had reached the stage at which nothing was safe from their attacks. Churches were burnt, public buildings and private residences destroyed, bombs were exploded, the police and individuals were assaulted and meetings broken up.
The feeling amongst MPs, caused by the extravagant and lawless action of the militants, hardened their opposition to the women's demands. So on 6 May the House of Commons voted against giving women the vote by a majority of 47.

Viscount Ullswater, a senior official in the House of Commons in 1913, writing in 1925 about the campaign for votes for women.

SOURCE F

THE CAT AND MOUSE ACT
PASSED BY THE LIBERAL GOVERNMENT

THE LIBERAL CAT ELECTORS VOTE AGAINST HIM! KEEP THE LIBERAL OUT!

BUY AND READ 'THE SUFFRAGETTE' PRICE 1P

A Suffragette postcard from 1913. It is attacking the Liberal Government for passing the 'Cat and Mouse Act'.

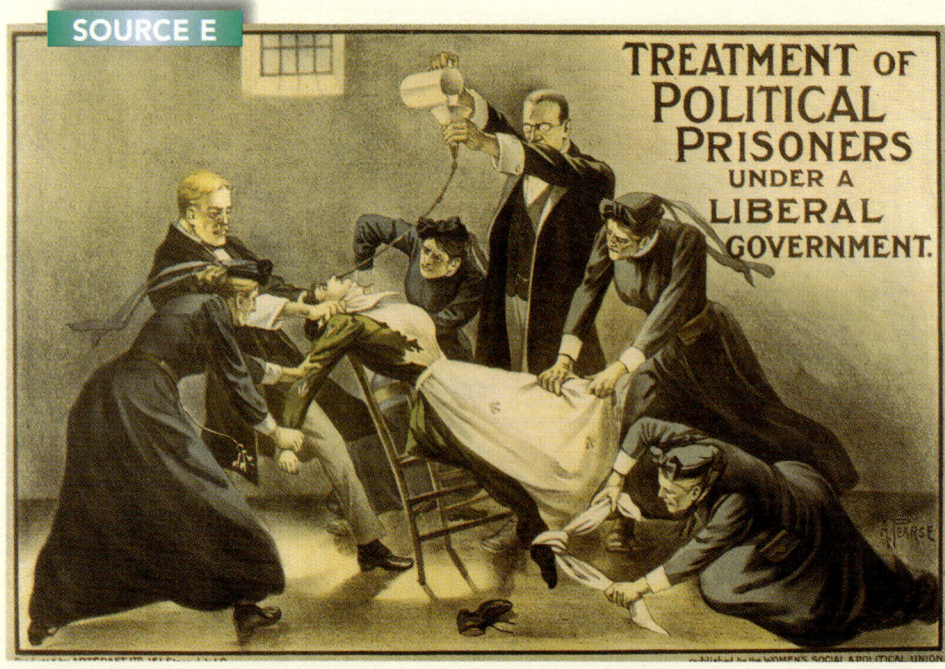

SOURCE E

TREATMENT OF POLITICAL PRISONERS UNDER A LIBERAL GOVERNMENT.

A Suffragette poster, probably published for the 1910 election. It shows the force-feeding of a Suffragette on hunger strike.

46   How was British society changed, 1906–18?

SOURCE G

It must be remembered that the behaviour of the Suffragettes served a very important purpose. Without it the government could have (and did before 1913) stated that there was no real 'evidence' that women even wanted the vote. The militants destroyed this theory. By destroying property, staging demonstrations and creating riots, the militants kept 'the cause' constantly in the public eye.

The effects of World War are important because they raised women in the eyes of Parliament and all men who remained in Britain – and they also raised many women's estimation of themselves. But the militancy of the Suffragettes is the main reason why women gained the vote in 1918.

An extract from an article written by a male member of the British Suffrage Society in 1996.

SOURCE H

It was in the year 1918 that disaster took place. A member of the House of Commons stood up and said, 'If you are extending the vote to our brave soldiers, how about our brave munition workers?' That argument was difficult to resist. Then…'How about our brave women munition workers?' And having agreed to the first argument it was impossible to resist the second.

An extract from the memoirs of Lord Birkenhead, a Conservative politician.

QUESTIONS

1 Study **Source A**.
   What could a historian studying the Suffragettes learn from this source?
   Use the source and your own knowledge to explain your answer. (6 marks)

2 Study **Source B**.
   'This source is obviously biased, so it is of no value to a historian studying attempts by women to win the vote'. Do you agree?
   Use the source and your own knowledge to explain your answer. (8 marks)

3 Study **Sources C** and **D**.
   Do you agree that these two sources show that the Suffragettes did not have the support of the men in the country?
   Use the sources and your own knowledge to explain your answer. (8 marks)

4 Study **Sources E** and **F**.
   Why do you think these two pictures were produced?
   Use the sources and your own knowledge to explain your answer. (8 marks)

5 Study **Sources G** and **H**.
   How similar are these two sources?
   Use the sources and your own knowledge to explain your answer. (8 marks)

6 Study **all** the sources.
   'The Suffragettes were vital in helping women win the vote'. How far do the sources in this exercise support this interpretation?
   Use the sources and your own knowledge to explain your answer. (12 marks)

Core Part I:

International relations 1919–c.1939

2 International relations 1919–c.1939

- In early 1919 politicians from the victorious countries met in Paris to draw up peace treaties to end the First World War. These treaties failed to bring a fair peace settlement and made it certain that Europe would face further problems in the future. The terms of the Treaty of Versailles were forced on Germany and left the Germans determined to reverse its terms.

- Yet the peacemakers of 1919 really believed that they had given the world the chance of a peaceful future. They set up the League of Nations, which aimed to prevent countries from ever going to war again. However the USA refused to join so the League was weak from the start.

- The League had some success in the 1920s, but the effects of the Great Depression made countries less willing to work together after 1929. The League's authority was further weakened by its failure to deal with Japanese aggression in China, and to stop Italy from invading Abyssinia in 1935-6.

- During the 1930s Hitler's wish to rebuild the military might of Germany and reverse the Treaty of Versailles was the biggest threat to peace. Ignoring the treaty, he built up Germany's armed forces and took control of Austria, Czechoslovakia and Poland. Britain and France followed a policy of appeasement, meaning they hoped they could settle Hitler's demands by negotiation. By September 1939 it was clear that appeasement had failed.

This topic is examined in Paper 1 of the examiniation. Paper 1-type exercises are included at the end of each section. Mark schemes, sample answers and comments can be found in the accompanying Teacher's Resource Pack.

Were the peace treaties of 1919–23 fair?

In January 1919 politicians met in Paris to make the peace settlement at the end of the First World War. Europe had been devastated by the war. Large areas of land had been destroyed and economies were ruined.

At least eight million soldiers and a further eight million civilians were killed in the fighting. The Austro-Hungarian empire had collapsed and communists had taken control of the Russian empire.

To agree a peace settlement that every country, winner and loser, would find fair was an impossible task. It is remarkable that the peacemakers achieved as much as they did. The peace treaties of 1919-20:

- redrew the map of Europe
- set up the League of Nations, an international body to keep the peace
- brought freedom to many people who had been under foreign rule before the war.

> **QUESTIONS**
>
> 1. How much damage had the war done in Europe?
> 2. Read pages 51 and 53. What were the differences in the aims of the 'Big Three'?

What were the motives and aims of the 'Big Three' at Versailles?

The 'Big Three' at the Paris Peace Conference were President Woodrow Wilson of the USA, Georges Clemenceau, the Prime Minister of France and David Lloyd George, the Prime Minister of Britain.

They represented the great powers that had won the war and had most of the say in making the decisions.

Traditional views of the 'Big Three'

Wilson is usually portrayed in books as an **idealist** whose plans were spoilt by the Europeans.

Clemenceau is traditionally looked upon as a cunning man who wanted revenge on Germany.

Lloyd George is seen as the man in the middle who was doing his best to make the treaty less harsh on Germany.

SOURCE A

Woodrow Wilson (President of the USA, 1913–21).

50   International relations 1919–c.1939

Although there is some truth in these views, things were much more complicated. Drawing up the treaty proved to be a very difficult task. There were frequent arguments among the 'Big Three', and on some issues they disagreed strongly.

It soon became clear they would have to compromise if a peace settlement were to be reached. All three got their way on some issues, but failed to do so on others.

Wilson's aims

Woodrow Wilson was a man of strong principles, who found it hard to accept the views of others. When the USA entered the First World War in 1917, Wilson said it was necessary for the Americans to fight the Germans in order 'to make the world safe for democracy'.

In January 1918 Wilson published his 'Fourteen Points' which he said should form the basis of the peace treaties at the end of the war (see page 53). The most important of these points outlined the policy of **self-determination** - the idea that people of different national groups had the right to rule themselves.

At the peace conference Wilson tried to have every decision discussed by all 32 countries. But this was too slow and most nations were only interested in their own problems. Wilson was forced to give way on many of the Fourteen Points.

Wilson's authority was further weakened because there was little enthusiasm for his ideas in the USA. The Americans did not want to get dragged into a war in Europe ever again.

In March 1920 the American government voted against signing the peace treaties and, as a result, the USA never joined the League of Nations.

SOURCE B

Georges Clemenceau (Prime Minister of France, 1917–20).

SOURCE C

David Lloyd George (Prime Minister of Britain, 1916–22).

Were the peace treaties 1919–23 fair?

Territorial terms of the Versailles settlement.

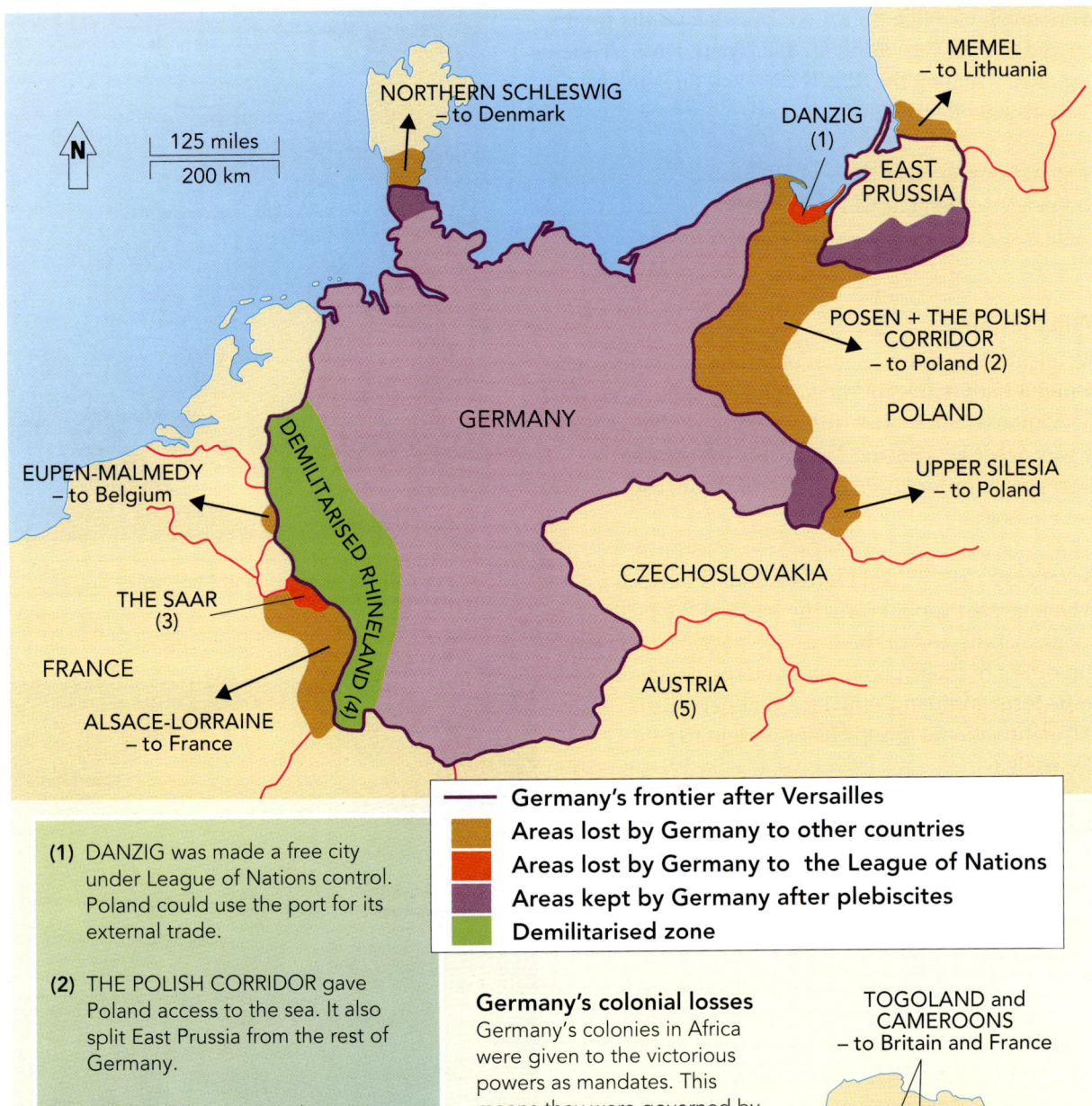

Map labels:
- NORTHERN SCHLESWIG – to Denmark
- MEMEL – to Lithuania
- DANZIG (1)
- EAST PRUSSIA
- POSEN + THE POLISH CORRIDOR – to Poland (2)
- POLAND
- UPPER SILESIA – to Poland
- EUPEN-MALMEDY – to Belgium
- GERMANY
- DEMILITARISED RHINELAND (4)
- CZECHOSLOVAKIA
- THE SAAR (3)
- FRANCE
- ALSACE-LORRAINE – to France
- AUSTRIA (5)

Legend:
- Germany's frontier after Versailles
- Areas lost by Germany to other countries
- Areas lost by Germany to the League of Nations
- Areas kept by Germany after plebiscites
- Demilitarised zone

(1) DANZIG was made a free city under League of Nations control. Poland could use the port for its external trade.

(2) THE POLISH CORRIDOR gave Poland access to the sea. It also split East Prussia from the rest of Germany.

(3) THE SAAR was put under League of Nations control for fifteen years. France was given the production of the Saar coalfields as part of reparations payments.

(4) THE RHINELAND was to be permanently demilitarised by Germany. It would be occupied by the Allies for fifteen years.

(5) ANSCHLUSS (union) between Germany and Austria was forbidden.

Germany's colonial losses

Germany's colonies in Africa were given to the victorious powers as mandates. This means they were governed by one of the victorious powers until they were ready for independence.

Germany's colonies in the Pacific were also allocated as mandates.

- New Guinea – to Australia
- Samoa – to New Zealand
- Pacific islands north of the Equator – the Marshalls, Marianas and Carolines – to Japan

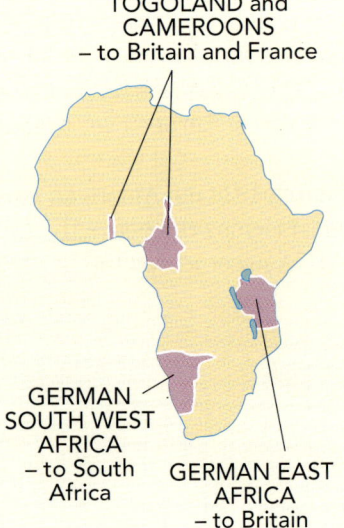

Africa map labels:
- TOGOLAND and CAMEROONS – to Britain and France
- GERMAN SOUTH WEST AFRICA – to South Africa
- GERMAN EAST AFRICA – to Britain

52 International relations 1919–c.1939

Clemenceau's aims

Clemenceau himself was willing to compromise to achieve a peace settlement that was acceptable to everyone, but the French people wanted revenge for the devastation left in northern France after the war. Much of the fighting in the war took place in north-east France. It was left a devastated area. The Germans had also deliberately blown up railways, factories and bridges when they retreated.

The French people wanted to make Germany pay for this damage to their country. They also wanted to make sure that Germany could never invade France again.

Neither Britain nor the USA wanted to punish Germany too severely. They would not accept Clemenceau's demand for the German border to be pushed eastwards to the River Rhine.

The question of how much money Germany should pay in **reparations** (compensation) was referred to a special commission. The French people were angry when they saw the Treaty of Versailles. They did not think it was harsh enough and voted Clemenceau out of power.

Lloyd George's aims

The British public blamed the Germans for the war and wanted to make them pay. Lloyd George won the 1918 election by promising to 'squeeze the German lemon until the pips squeak.' Privately, however, he knew that a harsh peace settlement would bring trouble in the future.

Lloyd George's main aim was to make sure that Britain remained the greatest naval power in the world. The Germans settled this issue themselves by sinking all their ships held captive by the British.

Lloyd George did not want Germany to be made to pay too much in compensation for war damage as it would slow down its recovery. He knew that Germany's recovery after the war was essential for Europe's trade and economy.

The Fourteen Points

1. No secret treaties.
2. Freedom of the seas.
3. The removal of economic barriers.
4. The reduction of armaments.
5. Settlement of all colonial claims.
6. Germans to leave Russian territory and a settlement of all questions affecting Russia.
7. Germans to leave Belgium.
8. French territory freed and Alsace-Lorraine returned to France.
9. Italian frontiers adjusted to take into account the nationality of the population.
10. The peoples of the Austro-Hungarian Empire to be given self-determination.
11. Germans to leave Romania, Serbia and Montenegro and international guarantees of their independence to be given.
12. The people of the Ottoman Empire to be given self-determination, and the Dardanelles to be permanently opened to international shipping.
13. An independent Polish state to be created with access to the sea.
14. A general association of nations to be formed to give guarantees of political independence to great and small states alike.

The terms of the Treaty of Versailles, June 1919.

This was the treaty signed by the Allies with Germany.

War Guilt
Germany had to accept the blame for the war.

Article 231 of the treaty:
'Germany accepts responsibility for causing all the loss and damage to which the Allied governments have been subjected as a consequence of the war imposed upon them by the aggression of Germany.'

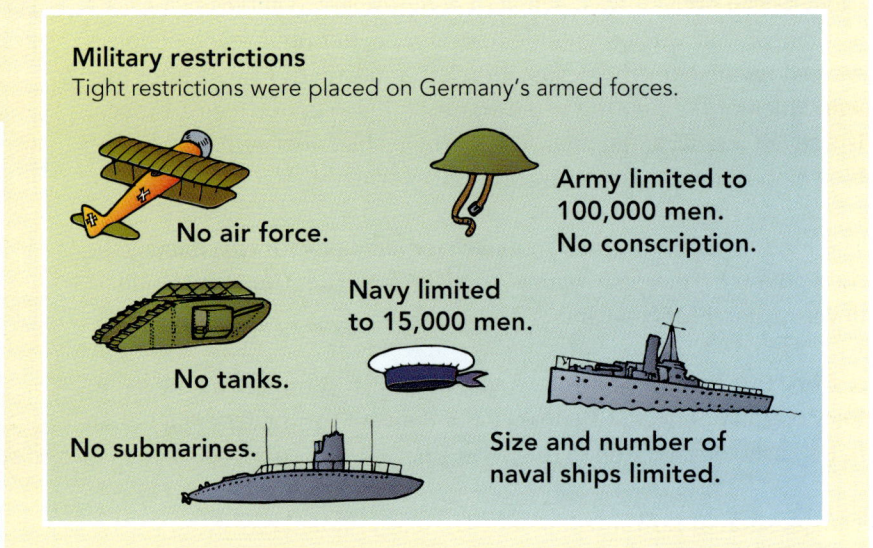

Military restrictions
Tight restrictions were placed on Germany's armed forces.

- No air force.
- No tanks.
- No submarines.
- Army limited to 100,000 men. No conscription.
- Navy limited to 15,000 men.
- Size and number of naval ships limited.

The League of Nations
The first item in all the peace treaties with the defeated nations was the 'Covenant' (the rules) setting up the League of Nations.

Reparations
As Germany accepted the blame for the war, the Allies could demand payment for all the damage caused. Germany was required to pay compensation – reparations – to the Allies.

A Reparations Commission was set up to fix the amount. It reported in 1921. Germany was presented with a demand for £6600 million.

Why did all of the victors not get everything they wanted?

The peace treaties were an uneasy compromise. None of the victors got the peace they wanted. This was because they all wanted a different kind of peace.

- The British and French would not accept all of the Fourteen Points.
- The British and the Americans would not back up France in making a peace that would keep Germany weak.
- The victors, however, were not free to make the peace they wanted. Four things limited their freedom.

1 Wartime commitments and secret treaties

During the war the Allies made promises of land to certain countries to get them to fight. When the war ended, these countries expected the promises to be kept.

Italy joined the war on the Allied side after signing the secret Treaty of London in 1915. The Italians were promised a share either of the Turkish Empire or of Germany's colonies, as well as land from the Austro-Hungarian Empire.

Woodrow Wilson was horrified to hear of the promises made to Italy. This was because they went against the principle of self-determination.

When the war ended Italy was not given all the land it had been promised in the peace settlement. South Tyrol, Trentino and Istria were taken from Austria and given to Italy. The port of Fiume, however, was given to Yugoslavia.

The Italians were angry that they had not been given all the land they had been promised. In September 1919 Italian nationalists seized Fiume by force and held it for a year. They were then driven out, but in 1924, Mussolini, the Italian dictator, recaptured Fiume.

2 The collapse of the Russian and Austro-Hungarian Empires

The Russian Empire In early 1917 Russia was losing the war and the Russian Tsar (Emperor) was forced to give up his throne. By the end of the year Russia was beaten.

In March 1918 Russia's new communist government signed the Treaty of Brest-Litovsk with the Germans. It was a harsh treaty. Russia lost large amounts of land, including the Ukraine, Finland and the Baltic States (Estonia, Latvia and Lithuania).

Although the treaty was cancelled when Germany was defeated, Russia did not get this land back (with the exception of the Ukraine). So, Finland and the Baltic States came into being as a result of Russia's collapse and Germany's defeat in the war, rather than the efforts of the peacemakers in Paris.

The Austro-Hungarian Empire The Austro-Hungarian Empire was a mix of many national groups. During the war the Empire started to fall apart and new countries set themselves up independently in its place. When the peacemakers met in Paris the new countries of Austria, Hungary, Czechoslovakia and Yugoslavia already existed. The peacemakers simply agreed their boundaries.

3 The terms of the armistice

When nations make peace at the end of a war, they first agree an **armistice**. This is when the two sides agree the terms (called the armistice) on which they will stop fighting. The terms of the armistice with Germany were very harsh. Germany agreed to accept reparations, give up Alsace-Lorraine and take its army away from the left bank of the Rhine. Each of these terms found its way into the Treaty of Versailles. So, the armistice terms, which were meant to end the fighting, actually became part of the treaty that punished Germany.

QUESTIONS

1. Look at the map on page 52. What territory did Germany lose under the Treaty of Versailles?

2. Look at the diagram on page 54. In what other ways did the Treaty of Versailles punish Germany?

SOURCE D

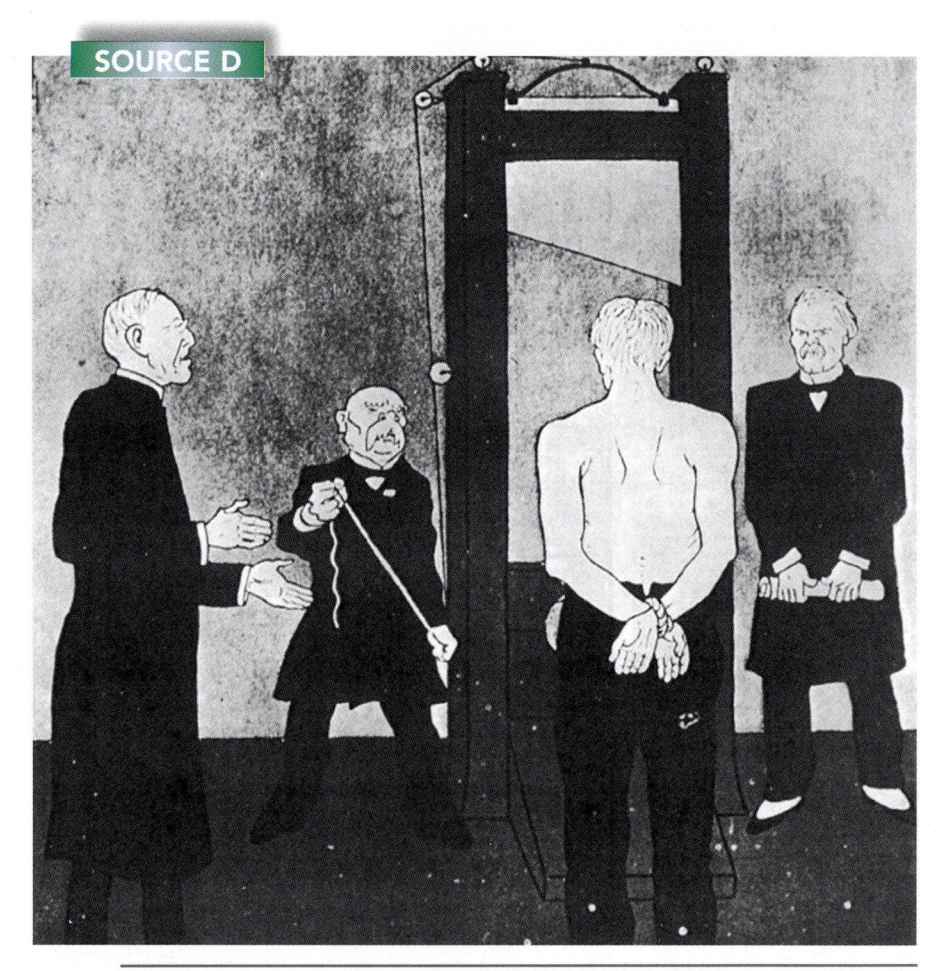

A cartoon about the Treaty of Versailles. It shows the figure of Germany about to be guillotined. The other figures (left to right) are Wilson, Clemenceau and Lloyd George.

4 Public opinion

Public opinion in each country wanted different things from the peace settlement. The Italian public wanted land to make them a great power. The French and British public wanted to make the Germans pay.

The American public wanted nothing to do with Europe at all. So, the 'Big Three' were not free to make the peace they wanted because of public opinion at home.

What was the immediate impact of the peace treaty on Germany up to 1923?

It took a little time for Germany's defeat in the First World War to hit the German people. Germany had not been invaded and right up to the end their leaders pretended they were winning. The Germans believed the peace would be based on Wilson's Fourteen Points. The Kaiser had fled to Holland and Germany had a new democratic government. The Germans hoped the Allies would show some mercy, but they were to be disappointed.

> **QUESTION**
>
> 1 Look at Source D.
>
> What is the message of this cartoon?
>
> Use your knowledge of the terms of the Treaty of Versailles to explain your answer.

Not one German politician was allowed to attend the Paris peace conference. The terms of the Treaty of Versailles were forced on the Germans, so they called it a **diktat** (a dictated peace).

The Germans were horrified by the harsh terms of the treaty but the Weimar Republic, the new German government, had no choice but to sign.

Many Germans said they had been 'stabbed in the back' by the government. They came to believe that Germany had not really lost the war, but had been betrayed by Jews and communists. The Germans thought it was a very unfair treaty, and wanted it abolished.

The weak Weimar Republic

1 The Kapp Putsch

The Weimar Republic was very unpopular for signing the Treaty of Versailles. This led to groups from both the left and right in politics to try to overthrow it. In 1920 a force of Freikorps (ex-soldiers with nationalist views), led by Dr Wolfgang Kapp, marched into Berlin.

They intended to overthrow the government. The army sat back and did nothing. In the end the uprising, known as the 'Kapp Putsch', failed because a general strike by the workers in support of the government brought Berlin to a standstill.

2 The 'War Guilt' clause and reparations

The Germans hated the 'War Guilt' clause in the treaty, which made them accept full blame for the war.

In 1921 Germany was ordered to pay £6600 million in reparations (compensation). The Germans resented this. John Maynard Keynes, a famous British economist, said that having to pay reparations would keep Germany weak. This would harm trade between nations and, therefore, hurt everyone.

Reparations were so unpopular in Germany that several German politicians were murdered for merely saying that Germany should try and pay them.

SOURCE E

einen Bessern findst du nicht

Paul von Hindenburg, President of Germany, 1925-34.

SOURCE F

French troops in the Ruhr in 1923.

3 Occupation of the Ruhr

Germany was deep in debt from the war. So the government printed more and more money to try and pay off the debt. This led to rising prices (**inflation**). At the end of 1922 the Germans said they did not have the money to pay any more reparations.

In January 1923 the French and Belgians sent troops to occupy the Ruhr, Germany's most important industrial area. They intended to take coal and iron ore as reparations.

The German government told the workers to go on strike. To pay the workers the government printed even more money, and soon there was **hyperinflation**. Prices shot through the roof.

In January 1923 a loaf of bread had cost 250 marks; by November the price had gone up to 201 billion marks. Germany was virtually bankrupt.

Gustav Stresemann helps Germany to recover

Gustav Stresemann was the chancellor of Germany from August–November 1923, and then foreign minister until 1929. He brought inflation under control by introducing a new currency called the Rentenmark.

In 1924 Stresemann agreed the Dawes Plan with the USA. This said how much should be paid each year in reparations, and provided Germany with American loans. In 1925 the French withdrew their troops from the Ruhr. Thanks to Stresemann Germany had started to recover from the war.

Peace treaties with other defeated nations, 1919–23

This was the treaty signed by the Allies with **Austria**. Austria accepted the break-up of the Austro-Hungarian Empire. Austria and Hungary were left as small independent states.

The Treaty of St Germain, September 1919.

(1) South Tyrol and Trentino to Italy.

(2) Istria and Trieste to Italy.

(3) Croatia, Bosnia and Herzegovina to Serbia, creating Yugoslavia.

(4) Transylvania to Romania.

(5) Galicia to Poland. The new state of Poland also received territory from Germany and Russia.

(6) The new state of Czechoslovakia was created.

Reparations
Austria agreed to pay reparations, but the collapse of the Bank of Vienna in 1922 meant nothing was paid.

Military restrictions
Austria was permitted an army of no more than 30,000 men.

The impact of defeat
- It was impossible to give every national group self-determination. Most of the new states contained dissatisfied minorities who continued to create problems.
- Splitting up the empire created economic problems. Roads and railways had not been built to suit the new states, and the new nations had their own taxes on trade, where previously trade had been free.
- Several small, weak states now existed where there had previously been one large state.

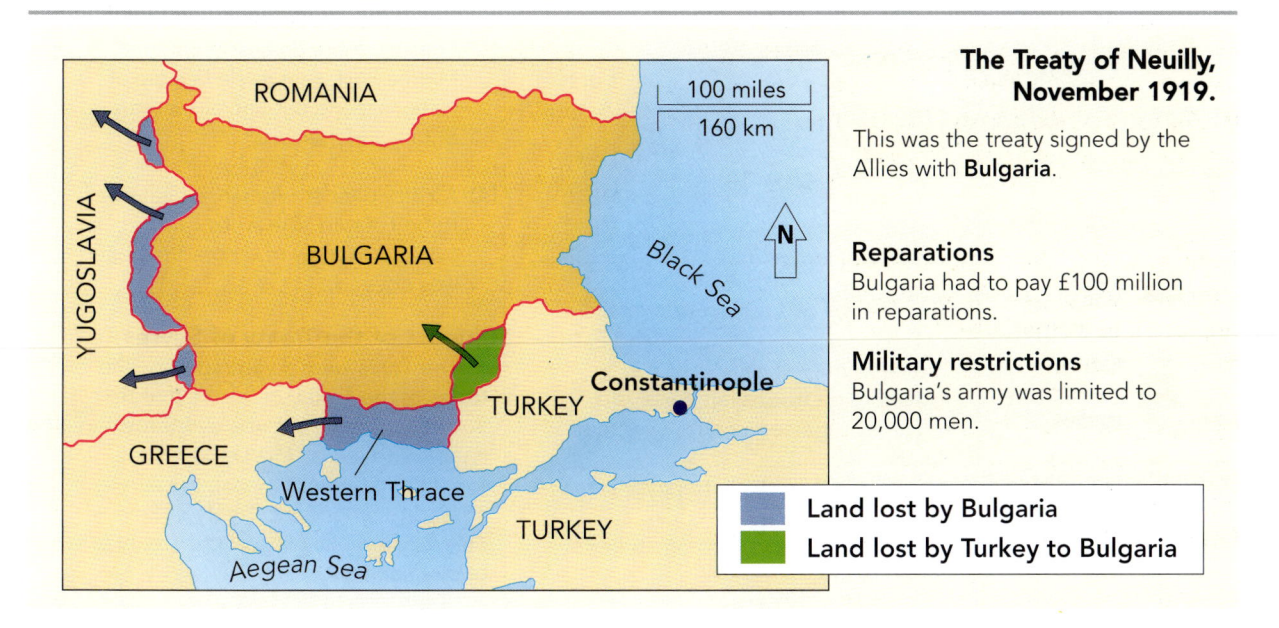

The Treaty of Neuilly, November 1919.

This was the treaty signed by the Allies with **Bulgaria**.

Reparations
Bulgaria had to pay £100 million in reparations.

Military restrictions
Bulgaria's army was limited to 20,000 men.

Land lost by Bulgaria
Land lost by Turkey to Bulgaria

Were the peace treaties 1919–23 fair?

The Treaty of Trianon, June 1920.

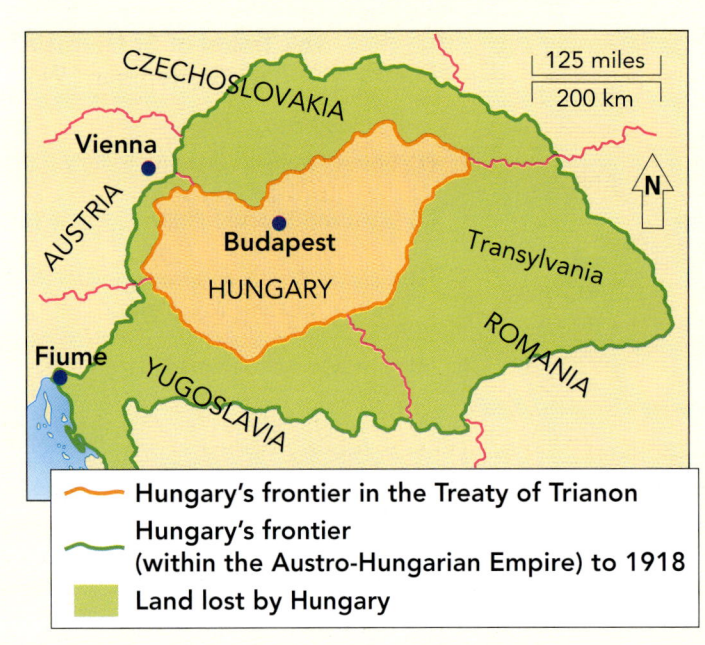

This was the treaty signed by the Allies with **Hungary**. With the Treaty of St Germain, it marked the break-up of the Austro-Hungarian Empire.

Reparations
Hungary agreed to pay reparations, but the collapse of Hungary's economy in the early 1920s meant nothing was ever paid.

Military restrictions
Hungary was permitted an army of no more than 35,000 men.

The impact of the defeat
- A communist state under Bela Kun was established in 1919. He was overthrown later in the year and a military dictatorship set up under Admiral Horthy.
- The Hungarians continued to resent a settlement that left up to 3 million Magyars (Hungarians) under foreign rule.

Map legend:
- Hungary's frontier in the Treaty of Trianon
- Hungary's frontier (within the Austro-Hungarian Empire) to 1918
- Land lost by Hungary

The Treaty of Sèvres, August 1920, amended by the Treaty of Lausanne, July 1923

These treaties were signed by the Allies with **Turkey**.

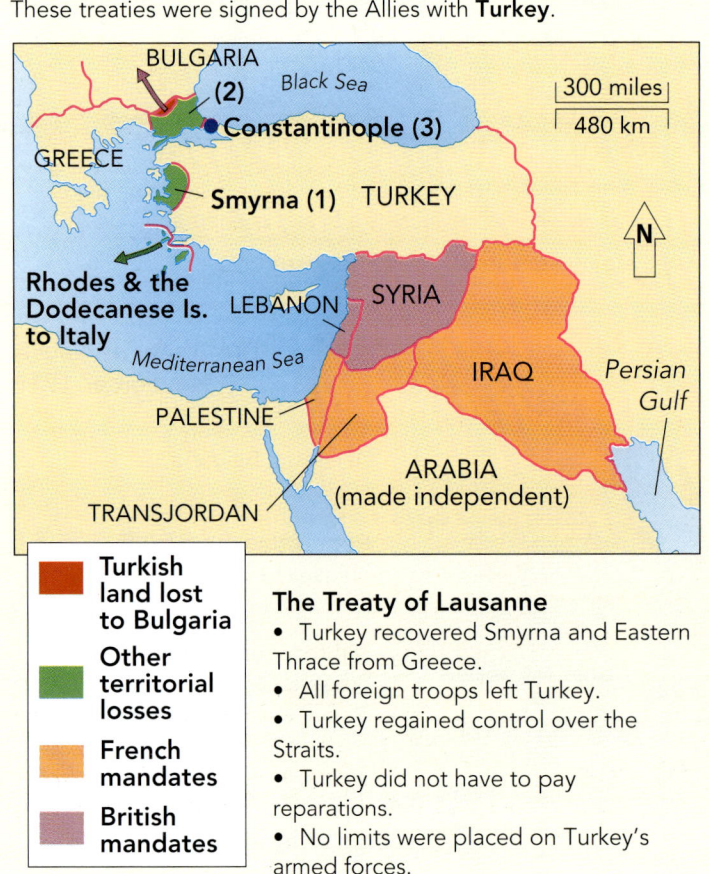

Map legend:
- Turkish land lost to Bulgaria
- Other territorial losses
- French mandates
- British mandates

The Treaty of Lausanne
- Turkey recovered Smyrna and Eastern Thrace from Greece.
- All foreign troops left Turkey.
- Turkey regained control over the Straits.
- Turkey did not have to pay reparations.
- No limits were placed on Turkey's armed forces.

The Treaty of Sèvres
(1) Smyrna and (2) Eastern Thrace were lost to Greece. In Europe Turkey was left with only the small area around Constantinople.

(3) The Straits of the Dardanelles and the Bosphorus were opened to ships of all nations.

The Ottoman Empire was split up. Arabia was made independent. Turkey's other possessions in the Middle East were made League of Nations mandates and allocated to Britain and France.

(4) An independent Armenian State was to be created. The Allies could keep troops in Turkey to ensure the treaty was obeyed.

Impact of the Treaty of Sèvres
- The Turks were so outraged by the terms of the Treaty of Sèvres that the Sultan's government was overthrown in an uprising led by Mustapha Kemal.
- Rather than fight Kemal, the Allies agreed to amend the Treaty of Sèvres. This led to the signing of the Treaty of Lausanne in July 1923.

Could the treaties be justified at the time?

The treaties which brought about the end of the First World War were very harsh on the beaten countries.

- Germany lost 13 per cent of its land. Nearly six million Germans now found themselves living outside Germany's borders. Germany had to pay huge reparations and the German armed forces were drastically reduced.

- The Austrian Empire was broken up. Austria also had to pay reparations and its armed forces were reduced. Bulgaria and Hungary suffered a similar punishment.

- The Turks were so angry at losing land in the Treaty of Sèvres that they overthrew the Sultan and his government who had signed the Treaty. The Allies then agreed to the Treaty of Lausanne in 1923, which was not so harsh.

At the time many historians said the treaties were too harsh and would lead to future war. Germany, especially, would want to get revenge. On the same day the Treaty of Versailles was signed, one German newspaper said, 'There will be vengeance for the shame of 1919.' Many other people shared this view (see Sources G-J).

SOURCE G

Lloyd George told one of his officials that the treaty was 'all a great shame. We shall have to do the same thing all over again in twenty-five years at three times the cost.'

Taken from a book on the Treaty of Versailles, written in 1969.

SOURCE H

This is not peace. It is an armistice for fifteen years.

Marshal Foch's view of the Treaty of Versailles. Foch was the Commander-in-Chief of the Allied armies in the final months of the war.

SOURCE I

The peace sowed a thousand seeds from which new wars might spring. It was though the devil had sat beside Clemenceau and whispered madness into the ear of Wilson, and grinned across the table at Lloyd George.

Taken from a book written by a British historian in 1929.

SOURCE J

PEACE AND FUTURE CANNON FODDER

The Tiger: "Curious! I seem to hear a child weeping!"

A cartoon by Will Dyson published in a British newspaper in 1919. Lloyd George, Orlando of Italy, Clemenceau and Wilson are leaving Versailles. Clemenceau (in front) looks at a weeping child labelled, 'The class of 1940.' Dyson thinks the Versailles Treaty will lead to another war in 1940. He was wrong by just four months.

Was the treaty a mistake?

Although the Treaty of Versailles was very harsh it was not a mistake – the peacemakers knew what they were doing.

- The peacemakers wanted to make sure that such a war could not happen again. They wanted to weaken Germany so it could never again invade France. This was done and the League of Nations was set up to keep the peace.

- The French people, in particular, wanted revenge on Germany. Much of the fighting had taken place in France with the loss of many lives. Many people in Britain wanted the Kaiser hanged.

- Europe was in chaos at the time. The Austro-Hungarian Empire was breaking up and large areas of Europe had been destroyed in the fighting. Also, many countries had been financially ruined by the war. There was a need to restore order quickly, and the peacemakers did this.

The strict terms of the treaty were not a surprise. When the Germans signed the armistice on 11 November 1918, they knew they would lose land, have their army cut in size and be made to pay reparations.

This was normal for a country that had been beaten in a war. In 1871 the Germans had made the French pay them 5 billion francs after beating them in the Franco-Prussian War. The Germans also took away more than a quarter of Russia's farmland and population under the Treaty of Brest-Litovsk in March 1918. This has led some historians to think the Germans would have made the Allies sign an even harsher treaty than the Treaty of Versailles if they had won the war.

SOURCE K

THE RECKONING.

Pan-German. "MONSTROUS, I CALL IT. WHY, IT'S FULLY A QUARTER OF WHAT WE SHOULD HAVE MADE *THEM* PAY, IF *WE'D* WON."

A British cartoon from 1919. The German is saying about the Treaty of Versailles: 'Monstrous I call it. These reparations are only a quarter of what we would have made them pay if we had won.'

Today, most historians think the peacemakers of 1918 did a reasonable job given the problems they faced. So, perhaps the peacemakers do not deserve the criticism they have received.

Paper 1-type assessment: The Treaty of Versailles

SOURCE A

"PERHAPS IT WOULD GEE-UP BETTER IF WE LET IT TOUCH EARTH"

Briand   Lloyd George

A cartoon from a British newspaper, 1921. Aristide Briand of France and David Lloyd George of Britain are looking at the effects of reparation payments on Germany.

QUESTIONS

Section A Questions

1 a Study Source A. Explain the message of this cartoon. Support your answer by referring to details of the cartoon and your own knowledge. (6)

b Explain why the Treaty of Versailles imposed such strict terms on Germany. (9)

Section B Questions

2 a How did the Treaty of Versailles try to make sure there would not be another war? (4)

b What did George Clemenceau of France hope to achieve in the Treaty? (6)

c 'The most important factor in deciding the terms of the Treaty of Versailles was Woodrow Wilson's desire for a fair and just peace'. Do you agree with this statement? Explain your answer. (10)

To what extent was the League of Nations a success?

The League of Nations was set up in 1920 to keep peace in the world. Although it was weakened by the USA's refusal to join, the League did have some success in the 1920s in settling arguments between countries. During the 1930s, however, aggressive nations who were ready to use war to achieve their aims, challenged the League's authority.

The League was unable to stand up to Japanese aggression in Manchuria. It also could not stop Italy from invading Abyssinia in 1935-6. After this the League lost all its authority and was unable to play an effective part in international affairs.

QUESTIONS

1. Look at the diagram on page 65.
   What was the work of the Assembly, the Council and the Secretariat?
2. In what ways was the League weak from the start?

How far did weaknesses in the League's organisation make failure inevitable?

From the start the League of Nations had a number of in-built weaknesses:

1. The countries defeated in the war were not asked to join.

2. The victorious countries disagreed about the League. Britain and France did not share Wilson's idealism and belief in co-operation between nations. They were half-hearted in their support for the League.

3. The American Congress (parliament) refused to accept the peace treaties, so the USA never joined the League. The absence of the world's most powerful country weakened the League's authority.

The structure and organisation of the League

The aims of the League were set out in the **Covenant**, which was written into each of the peace treaties.

SOURCE A

An American cartoon from 1919, showing the USA's unwillingness to join the League.

64 International relations, 1919–c.1939

The structure of the League of Nations

Secretariat
The permanent 'civil service' of the League. It carried out decisions taken by the Council.

Assembly
Met once a year. All member nations of the League had one vote here.

Council of the League
A committee that took major decisions. Most major nations were members.

International Labour Organisation
Each member nation sent two government ministers, one employer and one worker. They discussed working conditions and got countries to make improvements.

Permanent Court of Justice
Fifteen judges met at the Hague in the Netherlands. They settled international disputes, e.g. over frontiers or fishing rights.

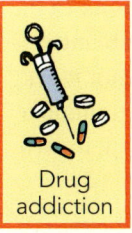

SPECIAL COMMISSIONS

Drug addiction | Health | Slavery | Help for undeveloped nations | Refugees | Minorities | Mandates | Women

The structure of the League of Nations.

The League's headquarters were in Geneva in Switzerland (a neutral country). The League was organised in a way that allowed countries to meet and discuss world problems.

1 The Assembly

All member countries could send three people to the Assembly, the League's parliament, which met once a year. In the Assembly all nations were equal and had one vote.

2 The Council

The Council was set up to deal quickly with quarrels between countries. It was made up of four permanent members (Britain, France, Japan and Italy) and four non-permanent members.

> To promote international co-operation and to achieve peace and security:
>
> - by not going to war;
>
> - by open, just and honourable relations between nations;
>
> - by the establishment of international law as the rule of conduct between governments;
>
> - by respecting all treaties.
>
> Adapted from the Covenant of the League of Nations.

To what extent was the League of Nations a success?

3 The Secretariat
The Secretariat carried out the League's administration. It prepared reports and organised the work of the Council and Assembly.

4 Special Commissions
The Special Commissions were set up to deal with particular issues. One of the most important was the one that dealt with disarmament. Other commissions dealt with such things as drugs, refugees, health and women's rights.

5 The Permanent Court of Justice
The Permanent Court of Justice was set up in The Hague in the Netherlands. It ruled on legal disputes between nations.

6 The International Labour Organisation (ILO)
The ILO encouraged countries to allow trade unions and improve workers' pay and conditions.

Membership of the League
The League had 42 members when it was first set up. The number of members increased over the years. At first the defeated nations were not allowed to join, but gradually they were let in. Germany joined in 1926, but left in 1933 after Hitler came to power. Russia was banned from joining until 1934, because other countries did not like its communist government. Two of the founder members, Japan and Italy, left the League in the 1930s.

Britain and France dominated the League, but they disagreed about the role it should play. Britain thought the League was no more than a 'talking shop'. The French, however, wanted the League to enforce the peace treaties. This difference in attitude weakened the League.

The League was never made up of all countries, or even of all the most important ones. No wonder it was sometimes called the League of *Some* Nations.

Settling disputes
What powers did the League have to settle disagreements between countries?

- The League did not have its own army. In theory it could ask member countries to provide an army, but this never happened in practice.

- The League had the power to ask member countries to apply **economic sanctions** (a ban on trade) against a country that was being aggressive to another. This, too, did not work very well. Countries were unwilling to impose sanctions because it would damage their own trade.

The League was able to make small nations obey it during the 1920s. But it was too weak to deal with large powers such as Japan and Italy in the 1930s.

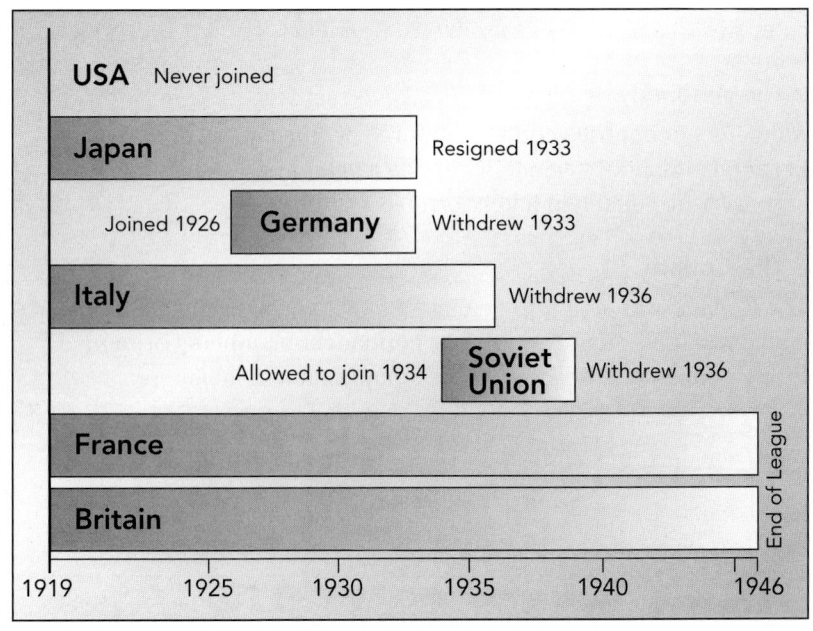

This graph shows when the major countries joined and left the League of Nations.

USA	Never joined
Japan	Resigned 1933
Germany	Joined 1926, Withdrew 1933
Italy	Withdrew 1936
Soviet Union	Allowed to join 1934, Withdrew 1936
France	End of League
Britain	End of League

1919 – 1946

SOURCE B

Mussolini — THE NEW MEMBER — Poincaré — Cecil

A British cartoon from the 1930s commenting on the League's ability to deal with the threat of war.

The Disarmament Commission

The work of the **Disarmament Commission** showed how powerless the League was in the face of opposition from individual countries.

The Covenant said that all members should reduce their arms, but it took until 1932 to set up a conference to work out how this should be done.

By this time any trust among the member countries had gone and the conference could not agree on anything. The French refused to disarm, and Hitler used this as an excuse to take Germany out of the League.

Conclusion

- The refusal of the USA to join made the League weak from the start.
- Not having an army of its own weakened the League.
- Some of the League's commissions did worthwhile **humanitarian** work and improved many people's lives across the world.
- The League was too idealistic in thinking that all countries would accept the League's authority.

QUESTIONS

1 Why was the League of Nations sometimes called the 'League of Some Nations'?

2 Look at Source B, drawn by David Low, a famous cartoonist, who worked for the *London Evening Standard*.

Did Low believe that the League would be able to prevent wars? Use details from the cartoon to explain your answer.

To what extent was the League of Nations a success? 67

How successful was the League in the 1920s?

Successes and failures in peacekeeping

The treaties of 1919-20 (see pages 54 and 59–60) did not solve all the disagreements over territory caused by the war:

- The Turks were so angered by the Treaty of Sevres (1920) they would not accept it. They went on fighting until the Allies agreed the Treaty of Lausanne in 1923.

- The Italians were unhappy at their gains and seized Fiume.

- The Poles were at war with Russia until 1921 and captured land in the Ukraine and Belorussia.

The League had mixed success in dealing with international disputes during the 1920s (see map).

Successes and failures for the League of Nations in the 1920s.

The Aaland Islands (1921)
Both Sweden and Finland claimed these islands and were ready to fight over them. They invited the League to settle the dispute. The League said the islands belonged to Finland, and Sweden accepted this.

Verdict on the League: A satisfactory result, but only because Sweden and Finland were willing to accept the League's authority.

Economic collapse in Austria and Hungary (1922-3)
In 1922-3 Austria and Hungary faced bankruptcy. Their economies did not recover after the war. Now with reparations to pay, it seemed they would collapse. The League arranged loans for the two countries. It then sent commissioners to check the money was spend properly. With this help, both Austria and Hungary began to recover.

Verdict on the League: The League took prompt and efficient action.

Corfu (1923)
In August 1923 five Italian surveyors were working for the League, mapping the Greek-Albanian border. They were shot and killed on the Greek side of the border. Mussolini, the Italian dictator, demanded compensation from the Greek government. His demand was ignored, so he bombarded and occupied the island of Corfu. This action was in defiance of the League, of which Italy was a major member. The League failed to condemn Italy's actions. Instead they put pressure on the Greek government to accept Mussolini's demands. Only when the Greeks apologised and paid up did Mussolini withdraw from Corfu.

Verdict on the League: A disaster! Faced by a great power willing to use force, the League had backed down.

Vilna (1920)
Vilna was made part of the new country of Lithuania after the war. Most of the people living in Vilna were Polish.

In 1920 Vilna was occupied by Polish troops. They refused to leave. It seemed a clear case for the League. Poland had been the aggressor against Lithuania.

The League seemed unwilling to get involved. It did not want to upset Poland, as it acted as barrier against communism Russia.

In 1923 the League confirmed Poland's occupation of Vilna.

Verdict on the League: Weak and useless.

The Greek-Bulgarian Dispute (1925)
Greece and Bulgaria quarrelled over their border. In October 1925 Greece invaded Bulgaria. The League condemned the Greeks. Pressure was put on the Greeks to withdraw, which they did.

Verdict on the League: The League's action was successful and brought a return to peace. But critics of the League said the League was only willing to take action when the great powers were not involved.

Upper Silesia (1921)
Both Poland and Germany claimed the industrial area of Upper Silesia. The people of Upper Silesia had the right to vote for which country they wished to join. In March 1921, in a plebiscite (vote) held by the League, the people of Upper Silesia voted to join Germany by 700,000 to 480,000. The League decided to partition (share) the area. Germany was given half the land and population. Poland was given most of the industry. The Germans were very angry they had not been given the industry. Both countries, however, accepted the decision.

Verdict on the League: A messy compromise. Whatever the decision someone would have been unhappy. The League did the best it could.

To what extent was the League of Nations a success?

International treaties

The League was at its best when it was dealing with small nations. The bigger powers, however, ignored the League. For example, the League could do nothing when the French invaded the Ruhr in 1923.

During the 1920s a number of treaties were signed without consulting the League. It seemed that the great powers thought some matters were too important for the League.

1 The Washington Naval Agreement 1922

- The USA, Britain, Japan, France and Italy agreed to limit the size of their navies.
- No major ships were to be built for ten years.
- The size of the American, British and Japanese navies would be in the ratio 5:5:3.

The League played no part in this agreement.

2 The Locarno Treaties 1925

These treaties were signed by Germany and the wartime Allies.

- Germany accepted its borders with France and Belgium (as laid down by the Treaty of Versailles).
- Germany accepted the **demilitarisation** of the Rhineland.

These treaties helped to bring Germany and France closer together, and led to Germany being allowed into the League in 1926.

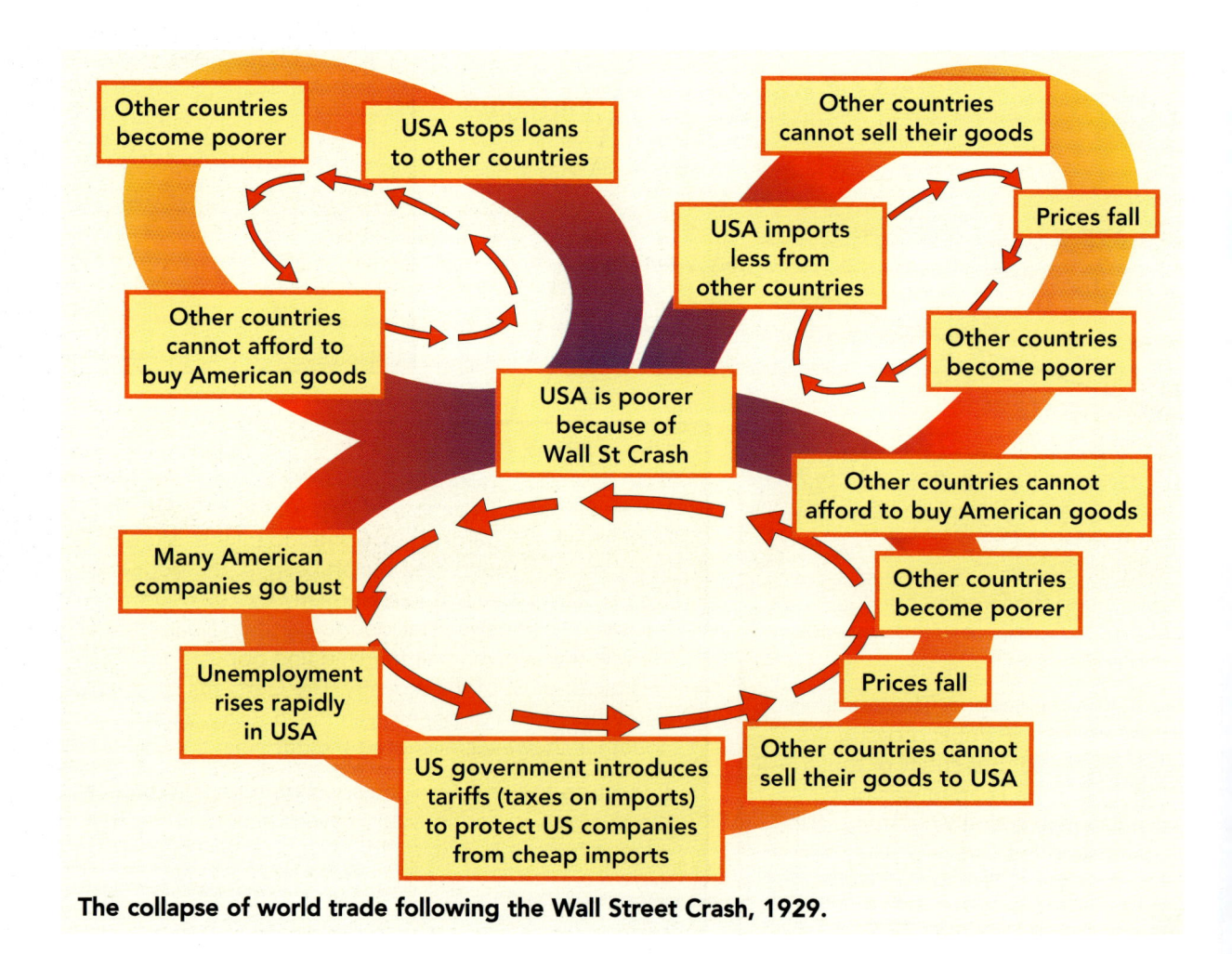

The collapse of world trade following the Wall Street Crash, 1929.

How far did the Depression make the work of the League more difficult?

The **Great Depression** was sparked off by the **Wall Street Crash** in October 1929. The American stock market collapsed and share prices slumped.

There was a wave of bankruptcies in the USA and this, in turn, affected almost every country in the world (see diagram on page 70). There was a worldwide slump in trade and unemployment rose dramatically.

The Great Depression did much to destroy the good will upon which the League had depended in the 1920s.

The 1930s brought tension and conflict as countries tried to cope with the Depression. This tension eventually led to the outbreak of the Second World War in 1939.

Out-of-work shipyard workers on a protest march from Jarrow to London in 1936.

SOURCE C

Members of the Italian Fascist Organisation receive their rifles in the presence of Mussolini.

SOURCE D

Unemployment

Millions of workers throughout the world lost their jobs because of the Wall Street Crash. In the USA, 30 per cent of the work force was unemployed. Politicians did not know how to cope with the situation.

Everywhere governments became uncertain. They were more concerned with settling their own problems than with tackling international disputes.

Extremism

In some countries extremist political parties came to power. In Germany, for example, people voted for the Nazis because they promised to end unemployment.

These extremist parties were often fiercely nationalist. This meant that they hated other countries and were only bothered about their own problems. They were also willing to use force to get what they wanted and did not care what the League of Nations said.

Militarism

Militarism is when a country tries to get what it wants by the use of military force. Political parties were run more like armies, with uniforms, parades and harsh discipline. These parties would not put up with any opposition to them. Men, women and children were expected to join party organisations.

During the 1930s there was growing militarism in Japan, Italy and Germany which did much to destroy the peace. Dictators, such as Mussolini and Hitler, adopted aggressive foreign policies. If they had success abroad it would distract people's attention from problems at home. These dictators rearmed their countries and it was only a matter of time before they used their military strength to threaten other countries.

Increasing militarism in Japan

In the early 1900s Japan took over territory in Asia. Japan's victory over Russia in the war of 1904-5 had given it control of part of Manchuria, a region in northern China. Then in 1910 Japan took over Korea. Despite this, the Japanese were dissatisfied.

- Japan's population and industry were growing quickly. This meant Japan needed to import more food and raw materials to survive.

- Japan had not been given any new territory in the peace settlement after the First World War.

- The Japanese government had signed the Washington Naval Agreement, which said the Japanese navy could only have three ships to every five built by Britain and the USA.

- The Japanese army and navy were angry with this, arguing that their politicians could not be trusted to protect Japanese interests. The army started to act without the government's approval.

The effects of the Depression

One of Japan's main industries was the making of silk cloth. During the Depression exports of silk to the USA fell. The production of silk was cut back and unemployment went up. The government could not cope with this slump.

The army said that Japan should capture more territory. This would provide Japan with raw materials and markets to sell its products.

The army grows more powerful

In September 1931 the Japanese army staged the Mukden incident, which led to the capture of Manchuria (see pages 75-7). The government disagreed with this, but failed to stand up to the army.

Gradually, the army became more and more powerful. Army generals became part of the government and Japan became more and more aggressive towards other countries.

QUESTIONS

1 Look at the diagram on page 70. Why did the Wall Street Crash in the USA also affect other countries?

2 a What is meant by militarism?

b Name three countries where militarism grew in the 1930s.

Militarism in Italy

The rise of Mussolini

- Italy was an unsettled country after the First World War. The Italians were unhappy that they had not been given more land in the peace treaties. Unemployment was high and there was a lot of poverty. In such an atmosphere the power of extremist parties grew rapidly.

- In 1922 Benito Mussolini's Fascist Party staged a march on Rome, after which he was invited by the king to become the prime minister. By 1926 Mussolini had become the dictator of Italy and had complete control of the country. He was known as 'Il Duce' (The Leader). Mussolini soon made a name for himself, banning other political parties and building up the armed forces. He also drained the Pontine Marshes and built new roads and railways.

- During the Depression, however, unemployment in Italy rose even more quickly. Mussolini became more aggressive to foreign countries in order to distract people from the problems at home.

- In 1935-6 he invaded Abyssinia. The League of Nations could not do anything effective to stop this aggression. Mussolini also sent troops to support the nationalists in the Spanish Civil War.

- In 1936 he signed the Rome – Berlin Axis with Hitler, which was the first move towards the alliance of Italy and Germany in the Second World War.

SOURCE E

Mussolini making a speech.

QUESTION

1 Why did Mussolini adopt an aggressive foreign policy?

Why did the League fail in Manchuria and Abyssinia?

1 Failure in Manchuria, 1931-3

Manchuria, a region in northern China, was rich in raw materials such as coal and iron ore.

The Japanese had an army in Manchuria to protect the land it had gained from Russia in 1905. They also owned the South Manchurian Railway.

The Mukden incident

- The Japanese army wanted to take control of the whole of Manchuria. Japan would then have a supply of coal and iron ore.

- In 1931, army officers staged the Mukden incident. On the night of 18 September, there was an explosion on the South Manchuria Railway near the city of Mukden. The Japanese said the Chinese had planted a bomb, and then fired at Japanese railway guards.

- The Chinese denied this. They said all their soldiers had been in their barracks at the time.

- Whatever the truth, it gave the Japanese army the excuse to begin the take-over of Manchuria.

- The Japanese government did not agree with the army's actions, but there was little the politicians could do.

- The Japanese army's invasion of Manchuria was very popular with the people.

- By 1932 the Japanese army had taken over most of Manchuria and renamed it Manchukuo.

SOURCE F

The Sleeping Giant Begins to Feel It

An American cartoon of 1937, commenting on the Japanese invasion of China.

The reaction of the League

The Chinese asked the League of Nations for help. On the surface it looked as though Japan was guilty of an act of aggression against China.

But the Japanese had some rights in Manchuria that had been agreed in a treaty with China. In addition, it was not clear what had happened at Mukden. The Japanese claimed they were only defending themselves.

The League told the Japanese to take its troops out of Manchuria. The instruction was ignored and Japanese troops advanced further into Manchuria. The League was powerless to stop them.

The Lytton Commission

In order to discover what had happened the League decided to set up a Commission of Inquiry under Lord Lytton. He was sent to Manchuria to gather information.

In October 1932 Lytton published a report in which he said that Japan was in the wrong.

The Japanese simply ignored the report and left the League.

In 1937 the Japanese invaded China itself and by 1938 many Chinese cities were under Japanese occupation.

SOURCE G

Japanese troops after a victory over Chinese troops in December 1931.

Verdict on the League

The League had been shown to be powerless to stop Japan. But, as these events took place in far away Asia, they were not too damaging to the League's authority.

People still thought that the League would cope with a similar crisis in Europe.

> **SOURCE H**
>
> On arrival at the site of the explosion, the patrol was fired upon. Lieutenant Kawamoto ordered his men to return the fire. The attacking group, thought to be five or six men, then stopped firing and retreated. The Japanese patrol followed them. After about 200 metres they were fired upon by a bigger group, thought to be three or four hundred soldiers.

The Japanese version of what happened at Mukden in 1931.

> **SOURCE I**
>
> Orders had been given that care was to be taken to avoid any clash with Japanese troops. On the night of 18 September all soldiers, numbering about 10,000, were in the North Barracks. The gate in the wall surrounding the camp, which gives access to the railway, had been closed. At 10 p.m. the sound of a large explosion could be heard, followed by rifle fire.

The Chinese version of what happened at Mukden in 1931.

> **SOURCE J**
>
> An explosion undoubtedly occurred on or near the railway between 10 and 10.30 p.m. The damage caused was not enough to justify military action. The military action of the Japanese cannot be seen as lawful self-defence.

Taken from Lord Lytton's report, published in October 1932.

QUESTION

1 Read Sources H, J and I. Did Lord Lytton believe the Chinese or the Japanese? How can you tell?

2 Failure in Abyssinia, 1935-6

Plans for an invasion

Abyssinia was a poor, developing country in north-east Africa, not yet under European control, but next to Italian colonies.

The Italians had been beaten by the Abyssinians at the Battle of Adowa in 1896.

Mussolini, the Italian dictator, said the time had come for revenge.

In December 1934 Italian and Abyssinian soldiers clashed at the oasis of Wal Wal and Mussolini started to plan an invasion.

The attitude of Britain and France

The League was in a difficult position. Both Italy and Abyssinia were members of the League and, in theory, had to do as the League told them.

In practice, the authority of the League would depend on the attitude of Britain and France.

As Britain and France had large empires, Mussolini thought that they would not mind him taking another colony in Africa.

He was therefore surprised when Sir Samuel Hoare, the British foreign secretary, gave a speech to the League warning Italy not to invade Abyssinia. Privately, however, Britain and France did not want to fall out with Mussolini, so that he would side with them against the growing power of Hitler.

Italy invades

On 3 October 1935, Italy started the invasion of Abyssinia. The Abyssinians stood little chance against the modern Italian army. The League immediately condemned Italy as an aggressor. Then it imposed economic sanctions against Italy. Member countries of the League were forbidden to trade with Italy.

However, the sanctions did not include the vital war commodities of coal, iron and oil. Mussolini later said that this would have stopped the invasion within a week.

The Hoare–Laval Plan

Unknown to the League, Britain and France were secretly planning to bring the invasion to an end. Sir Samuel Hoare of Britain and Pierre Laval, the French Prime Minister, met in December 1935. They came up with a plan to end the invasion. The plan was very favourable to the Italians, giving them half of Abyssinia (see map on page 79).

The details of the plan were leaked to the press and there was a public uproar. Hoare and Laval were forced to resign.

Although Britain and France had been talking tough about Mussolini in public, it seemed that they really wished to reward him for his aggression.

SOURCE K

A British cartoon of 1935, commenting on Mussolini's invasion of Abyssinia.

The fall of Abyssinia

The League was powerless when its two most important members, Britain and France, failed to take any effective action against the Italians.

By 5 May 1936 the Italians had captured Addis Ababa, the capital of Abyssinia. The Italian army had bombers, tanks and poisonous gas, but the Abyssinians had only spears. They did not stand a chance.

Haile Selassie

On 30 June 1936 Haile Selassie, the Abyssinian Emperor, gave an emotional speech to the League in Geneva. He complained bitterly about the League's failure to stop Mussolini.

After the League's failure to prevent Mussolini invading Abyssinia, no country took the League seriously again, and there was nothing it could do to stop the Second World War from breaking out in 1939.

The Hoare–Laval Plan.

- Italian territory in 1934
- Territory to be transferred to Italy
- Proposed area of Italian economic rights
- 'Corridor for camels' (to be given to Abyssinia)

SOURCE L

I, Haile Selassie, Emperor of Abyssinia, am here today to claim justice for my people. I also claim the help promised to me eight months ago, when fifty nations said that aggression had been committed against Abyssinia.

Part of Haile Selassie's speech to the League in Geneva on 30 June 1936.

SOURCE N

The real death of the League came in December 1935, not 1939 or 1945. One day it was a powerful body; the next it was a sham, everyone running from it as quickly as possible. What killed the League was the Hoare-Laval plan.

The view of A.J.P. Taylor, a British historian, on the effect of the Hoare-Laval plan.

SOURCE M

The bombing was magnificent fun. One group of Abyssinian horsemen looked like a budding rose unfolding as the bomb fell on them and blew them up.

A description by Mussolini's pilot son of a bombing raid by the Italian air force.

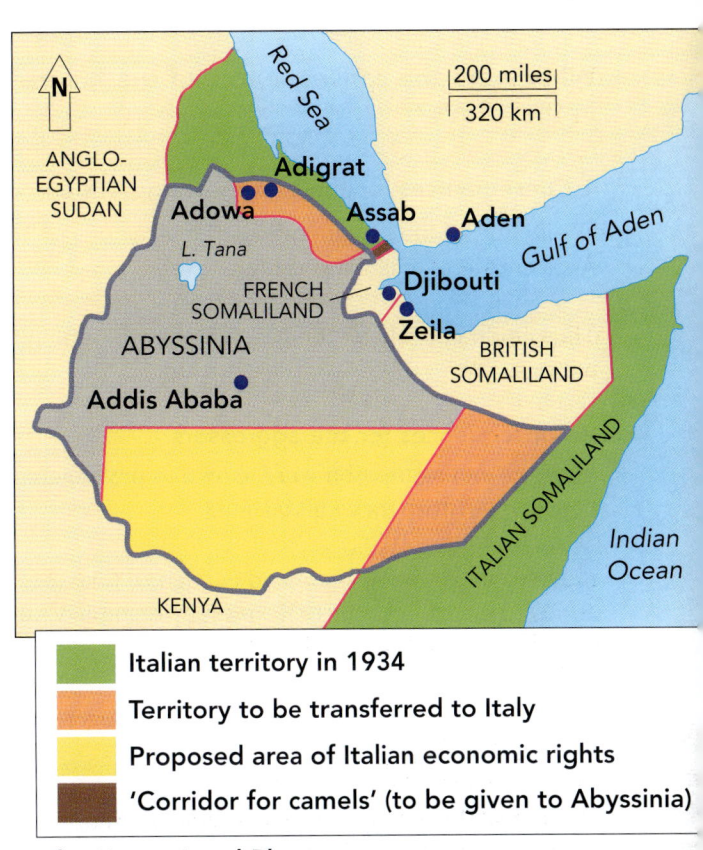

QUESTIONS

1. **a** Why did Mussolini invade Abyssinia?
   b What action did the League take?
2. Why was the League's action a failure?
3. What effect did the League's failure in Abyssinia have on world peace?

To what extent was the League of Nations a success?

What were the consequences of the failure of the League in the 1930s?

1 Consequences for the victims of aggression

The failure of the League to stop the invasions of Manchuria and Abyssinia left small nations defenceless.

They could not rely on the League to protect them from aggressive nations.

2 Consequences for the aggressors

Violence and aggression were shown to pay. Aggressive countries kept the territory they had invaded.

Italy and Japan were even bold enough to take more land. Japan attacked China again in 1937 and Italy occupied Albania in 1939.

3 Consequences for Britain and France

It was now clear that the League was no longer going to be able to keep peace.

Britain and France would have to find another way of dealing with aggressive dictators, such as Mussolini. They began to face up to the fact that they might have to fight another war.

SOURCE O

4 Consequences for the League of Nations

The events in Manchuria and Abyssinia showed that the members of the League would not stick together against aggression.

People's belief in the League of Nations as a peacekeeping body was destroyed.

Japanese soldiers celebrating the capture of a Chinese town in 1938. The League failed to stop this attack.

Paper 1-type assessment: The League of Nations

SOURCE A

A German cartoon of 1936 commenting on the Abyssinian crisis. The soldier is saying to the League: 'I am sorry to disturb your sleep, but I wanted to tell you that you don't need to bother yourself about this Abyssinian business any more. It's been settled elsewhere.'

QUESTIONS

Section A Questions

1 a Study Source A. Explain the message of this cartoon. Support your answer by referring to details of the cartoon and your own knowledge. (6)

b Explain why the Italian invasion of Abyssinia was important in the history of the League of Nations. (9)

Section B Questions

2 a What were the aims of the League of Nations? (4)

b Explain why not all the major powers joined the League of Nations when it was set up. (6)

c 'The most important factor in the failure of the League of Nations was the fact that the USA was not a member.' Do you agree with this statement? Explain your answer. (10)

Why had international peace collapsed by 1939?

The Second World War started just twenty years after the First World War had finished.

The Great Depression and the aggression of Germany, Italy and Japan during the 1930s destroyed hopes of peace.

Hitler's takeover of Germany in 1933 was a turning point. He defied the Treaty of Versailles and put Europe on the road to war.

What were the long-term consequences of the peace treaties of 1919-23?

1 German resentment

The peace treaties left many countries unhappy. In Germany the Treaty of Versailles was bitterly resented. In 1920 Hitler said the Nazis would destroy the treaty and gain **Lebensraum** (living space) for the Germans by capturing land in eastern Europe.

Hitler also said he would unite all Germans in a new German Reich (Empire).

Hitler knew other countries would oppose him, so he began rearming Germany (which was forbidden by the Treaty of Versailles).

Other, more moderate Germans, such as Gustav Stresemann, also wanted to abolish the Treaty of Versailles. Stresemann was the German foreign minister from 1923-9. Unlike Hitler, he wanted to achieve his aims by peaceful means rather than violence.

Nevertheless, the Germans did not accept the peace settlement and this left the future of Germany uncertain.

2 The League could not cope with aggressors

With countries unwilling to work together after the Great Depression, the way was open for Hitler to make Germany a great power again. He was helped by the weakness of the League of Nations. The League had no armed forces and war helpless in the face of determined aggressors.

SOURCE A

Three great tasks face Germany.

1. A solution to the reparations problem in favour of Germany.
2. The protection of 10-12 million Germans living abroad under foreign rule.
3. The recovery of Danzig, the Polish Corridor and the correction of the border in Upper Silesia.

From a letter written in 1925 by Stresemann, the German foreign minister.

SOURCE B

If only we could sit down at a table with the Germans and run through their complaints, it would greatly relieve all tension.

Neville Chamberlain, speaking in 1938.

SOURCE C

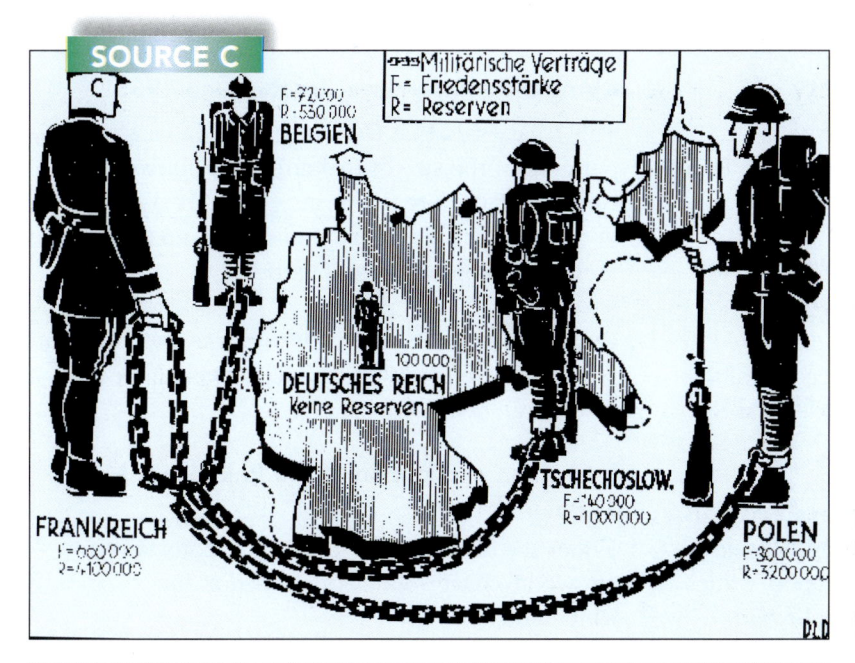

A Nazi cartoon opposing the Treaty of Versailles. Germany, with its army limited to 100,000 by the Treaty of Versailles, is surrounded by hostile countries.

SOURCE D

Neville Chamberlain.

3 Britain and France disagree

Britain and France did not agree about how to treat Germany. The British felt that Germany had been harshly treated at Versailles. They saw nothing wrong in helping the Germans. The French were frightened that Germany would grow strong again. In the end, both countries adopted a policy of **appeasement** towards Germany (see box).

Appeasement

Not wanting another war, Britain and France followed a policy of appeasement during the 1930s.

By the 1930s many British and French politicians felt that the unfair Treaty of Versailles had to be changed. It was right that Germany's complaints about the treaty should be settled. They thought the Treaty of Versailles was too harsh on Germany and hoped that giving in to some of Hitler's demands would make him happy. In this way war could be avoided.

If it was to work, appeasement needed Hitler to keep his side of the bargain. But he was not a man to be trusted. He was prepared to use violence to get what he wanted. However, Neville Chamberlain (British Prime Minister from 1937-40) kept faith with appeasement because he was desperate to avoid war.

QUESTIONS

1. How did the aims of Stresemann and Hitler differ?
2. Study Source C. How can you tell that the cartoonist was against the Treaty of Versailles?
3. What was appeasement?

Why had international peace collapsed by 1939?

How did Hitler destroy the Treaty of Versailles?

Between 1933 and 1936 Hitler destroyed the Treaty of Versailles.

1 Germany leaves the League of Nations and the Disarmament Conference, October 1933

The League's Disarmament Conference started in 1932. The Germans said they would get rid of the few weapons they had if other countries also disarmed.

France, however, refused to disarm and was also against Germany having a bigger army. This gave Hitler the excuse to leave the Conference, while pretending he wanted peace. (In fact, he had already started to rearm Germany.) Hitler also took Germany out of the League of Nations.

2 The people of the Saar vote to rejoin Germany, January 1935

The Saar was an important coal-mining region on the Franco-German border (see map on page 52). The Treaty of Versailles placed the Saar under the control of the League of Nations for fifteen years.

In January 1935 the people of the Saar voted by a large majority to rejoin Germany. This was a great propaganda success for Hitler and the Nazis.

3 German airforce and army, March 1935

In March 1935 Hitler announced that Germany had an air force (the **Luftwaffe**). He also said he was introducing conscription (compulsory military service). The army was to be enlarged to 500,000 men.

Although this was openly against the Treaty of Versailles, Britain, France and Italy took no action against Hitler.

From a letter written in 1934 by a British Labour Party politician. It helps to explain why Hitler could get away with rearming Germany.

4 Anglo-German Naval Treaty, June 1935

This treaty said that Germany could have a navy 35 per cent of the size of Britain's. This allowed Germany to ignore the terms of the Treaty of Versailles. Now Germany could build up its navy, including submarines and battleships.

By agreeing to this treaty, Britain was showing that it thought the Treaty of Versailles was unfair on Germany.

5 German occupation of the Rhineland, March 1936

Under the Treaty of Versailles, Germany was not allowed to have soldiers stationed in the Rhineland.

Hitler realised that this made Germany open to an invasion from the west. He wanted to have soldiers in the Rhineland to protect Germany's western border.

On 7 March 1936 Hitler took a big gamble and sent troops into the Rhineland. The British did not do anything. They said that Hitler was only putting soldiers into 'his own backyard'.

The French said they would not take action on their own. Once again Hitler had broken the Treaty of Versailles and got away with it.

SOURCE E

I think it would be a mistake to be on the side of France over the rearming of Germany. If we take France's side it would look as though we are in favour of the wicked Versailles Treaty. It would also appear that we are in favour of the evil policy of France of not making friends again with Germany. The danger from Germany is bad enough, but the dangers from France are equally as serious.

6 The Rome–Berlin Axis and Anti-Comintern Pact

The Rome–Berlin Axis (1936) was an agreement between Mussolini and Hitler to work more closely together.

Both leaders sent troops to help the nationalists in the Spanish Civil War (1936-9). This war gave Hitler the chance to try out his new planes and weapons.

The Anti-Comintern Pact (1936) was an agreement between Germany and Japan against the communist Soviet Union. Italy joined the pact in 1937.

How far was Hitler's foreign policy to blame for the outbreak of war in 1939?

Anschluss, March 1938: why did Hitler bother to invade Austria?

- The Treaty of Versailles forbade the union of Germany and Austria (**Anschluss**). Hitler, however, had been born in Austria, a German speaking country, and wanted to unite all German-speaking people into a Greater Germany. Joining Austria to Germany would help to achieve this.

- Hitler first tried to take over Austria in 1934, but was forced to back down because Mussolini opposed him.

- On 12 February 1938 Hitler invited Schuschnigg, the Austrian chancellor, to a meeting in Germany.

- Schuschnigg agreed to appoint Seyss-Inquart, an Austrian Nazi, to the post of Minister of the Interior, giving the Nazis a voice in the Austrian government.

SOURCE F

A British cartoon from 1936 about the remilitarisation of the Rhineland. The 'goose-step' was the style of marching used by the German army.

QUESTIONS

1. How did Hitler manage to get away with sending troops into the Rhineland in 1936?

2. Look at Source F.

   What did the cartoonist think of the remilitarisation of the Rhineland?

- By giving in to Hitler on this issue, Schuschnigg hoped to keep Austria independent.

- Schuschnigg then called a **plebiscite** (vote) to ask the Austrian people if they wanted to unite with Germany.

- Hitler was furious because he knew that if the Austrians voted to stay independent it would make it very difficult for him to take over Austria.

- On March 11 Hitler told Schuschnigg to cancel the plebiscite.

- Faced with this pressure, Schuschnigg resigned and was replaced by Seyss-Inquart, who promptly invited German troops to enter Austria.

Invasion

On 12 March German troops invaded Austria. The Austrians did not resist and there was no bloodshed. The *Anschluss* had taken place and Austria was united with Germany.

This time Mussolini did not object. Since 1936 Hitler and Mussolini had worked more closely together.

Britain and France also did nothing to stop Hitler taking over Austria.

A vote was held on 10 April in which over 99 per cent of the Austrians approved of *Anschluss*.

The Czechoslovakian crisis, 1938

Czechoslovakia was the next country on Hitler's list. Czechoslovakia had strong defences and a modern army.

Hitler knew the Czechs could make it difficult for Germany to fight a war in the west. Furthermore, there were 3.5 million Germans living in the Sudetenland, an area of north-west Czechoslovakia that bordered Germany. The Sudetenland was rich in iron and coal.

Hitler demanded that the Sudetenland should become part of Germany.

SOURCE G

GOOD HUNTING

Mussolini. "All right, Adolf—I never heard a shot"

A British cartoon from February 1938. Mussolini (left) is saying to Hitler, 'All right, Adolf, I never heard a shot.'

QUESTION

1 Why do you think Hitler was so keen to take over Austria?

A Czech–German war?

All of Czechoslovakia's border defences were in the Sudetenland. If the Czechs gave Hitler the Sudetenland it would leave them defenceless.

Also, if Hitler gained the Sudetenland he could easily capture the rest of Czechoslovakia. It looked as though war might break out between Germany and Czechoslovakia.

Britain and France did not want war to break out, so they tried to appease Hitler.

Neville Chamberlain

On 15 September 1938 Chamberlain, the British Prime Minister, met Hitler at Berchtesgaden in Germany. He told Hitler he had no objections to Hitler taking the Sudetenland, as long as it was done peacefully.

Chamberlain flew to meet Hitler for a second time at Bad Godesberg on 22 September. This time Hitler told Chamberlain he wanted the Sudetenland handed over by 1 October. If this demand was not met he said he would invade. Europe was on the brink of war.

The Munich Conference

Chamberlain was desperate to avoid war. When Mussolini called for a conference to discuss the Sudetenland, Chamberlain agreed to attend along with Hitler and Daladier, the French Prime Minister.

On 29 September the four leaders met in Munich. This is what they agreed:

- to give the Sudetenland to Germany

- to let Poland and Hungary take territory from Czechoslavia (see map)

- as long as Hitler promised not to demand any more territory in Europe.

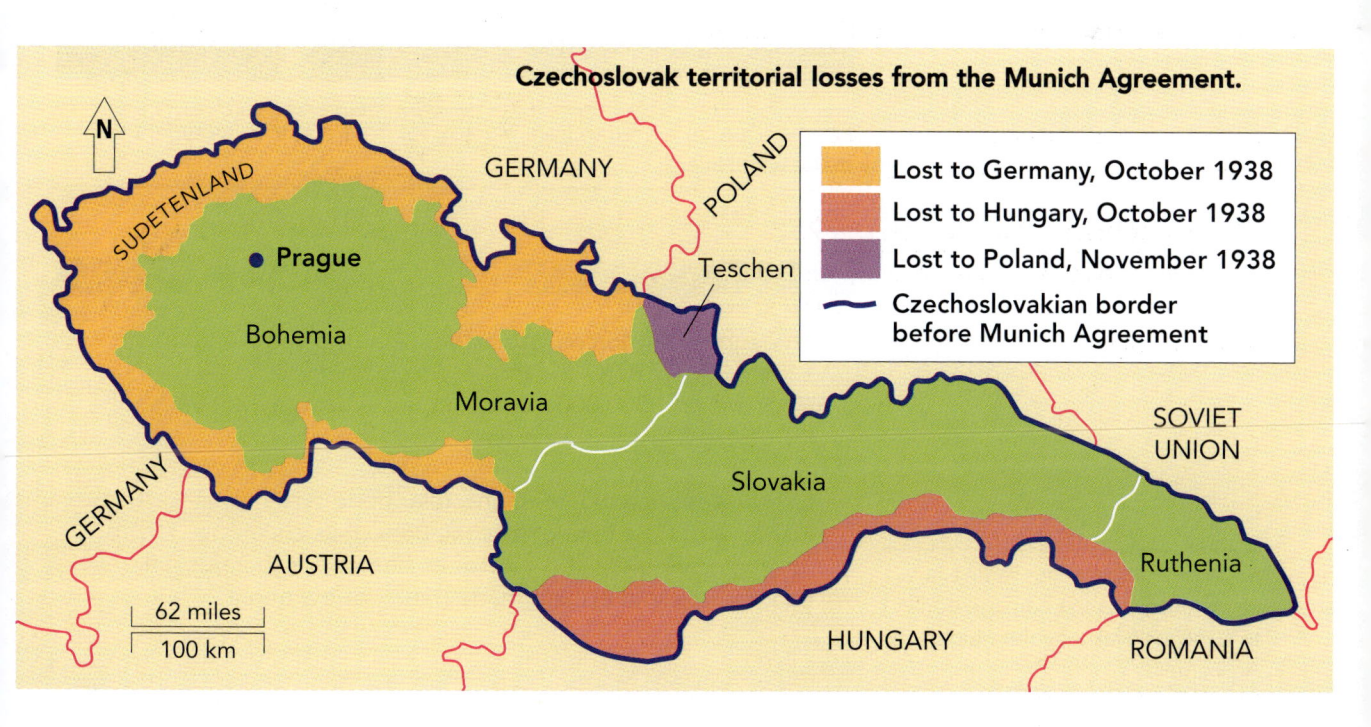

Czechoslovak territorial losses from the Munich Agreement.

- Lost to Germany, October 1938
- Lost to Hungary, October 1938
- Lost to Poland, November 1938
- Czechoslovakian border before Munich Agreement

Why had international peace collapsed by 1939?

'Peace for our time'

Stalin, the Soviet leader, was not invited to the Munich Conference. Everyone knew he would not have agreed to Hitler's demands.

The Czechs were also not consulted but, without the support of Britain and France, they had no choice but to agree.

While in Munich, Chamberlain managed to get Hitler to sign a declaration saying that Germany would never again go to war against Britain.

Chamberlain returned home and triumphantly told the British public, 'I believe it is peace for our time' (see Source H).

By 10 October 1938, the Germans had fully occupied the Sudetenland.

Czechoslovakia was left defenceless against its enemies.

An American historian, writing in 1959, describes the damage done to Czechoslovakia by the Munich Agreement.

SOURCE H

Chamberlain on his return from Munich. He is waving the agreement he made with Hitler.

SOURCE I

The agreement forced Czechoslovakia to give Germany 11,000 square miles of land, in which lived 2,800,000 Germans and 800,000 Czechs. In this area [the Sudetenland] lay all the Czech fortifications.

Czechoslovakia's rail, road and telephone system was disrupted. It lost 66% of its coal, 86% of its chemicals, 70% of its electrical power and 40% of its timber. A rich industrial country was split up and made bankrupt overnight.

Hitler destroys Czechoslovakia, March 1939

Hitler did not keep the promise he had made at Munich. Within six months his army was on the march again.

On 15 March 1939 German troops occupied Bohemia and Moravia, two areas of Czechoslovakia that had been protected by the Munich Agreement.

Next, Slovakia was brought under the control of Germany. Czechoslovakia had been destroyed.

On 23 March 1939 Hitler seized Memel from Lithuania. It was now clear to everyone that appeasement had failed.

Chamberlain told the Poles that Britain would help them if Hitler invaded their country.

The sources that follow show how different people reacted to the Munich Agreement.

SOURCE L

At the airport Daladier [of France] turned up his collar to protect his face from the rotten eggs he expected from the crowd. To his amazement, there were no eggs. Instead they cheered him, shouting 'Vive Daladier', 'Vive la France!' Daladier turned to a friend and whispered, 'The fools!'

From Daladier's own account of his return to France from Munich.

SOURCE J

Give thanks to your God. People of Britain, your children are safe. Your husbands and sons will not march to battle. Chamberlain's conquests are mighty and lasting. Millions of happy homes and hearts have had a burden lifted.

The *Daily Express* comments on the Munich Agreement, 30 September 1938.

SOURCE K

The events of the last few days are one of the greatest political defeats this country and France have ever suffered. There can be no doubt that it is a victory for Hitler. Without firing a shot he has achieved a dominant position in Europe.

Clement Attlee, the leader of the Labour Party, speaking about the Munich Agreement, October 1938.

QUESTIONS

1. Read Source I.

   How was Czechoslovakia damaged by the Munich Agreement?

2. Why do you think Daladier (Source L) expected eggs to be thrown at him?

3. When did it become clear that appeasement had failed?

Why had international peace collapsed by 1939?

SOURCE M

Early in the morning of 15 March 1939, a meeting took place in Berlin between Hitler, and a group of Czech politicians under the leadership of President Emil Hacha. Hitler was about to bring the independence of Czechoslovakia to an end.

- Hitler told the Czechs that his armies would invade Czechoslovakia at 6 a.m. Any attempt at resistance would be broken by brute force. Of course, he said, they had a choice. If the defenders laid down their weapons, they would be treated them generously. Hitler suggested the Czechs went into the next room to talk it over.

- Waiting for them in the next room were Goering [head of the *Luftwaffe*] and Ribbentrop [the German foreign minister]. They shouted that if the Czechs refused to let German troops into Czechoslovakia, within two hours, half of Prague [the Czech capital] would be bombed to ruins.

- Suddenly Goering shouted out, 'Hacha has fainted!' A thought crossed the minds of the Germans: the world would think Hacha had been murdered. Dr Theodor Morrell, Hitler's doctor, gave Hacha an injection to bring him round. Hacha then rang his ministers in Prague and told them to let the Germans invade.

- Two hours later German troops swarmed over the Czech border. Hacha was appointed governor of Bohemia and Moravia. But the world knew it was really the Germans who ruled the country now. Before going to bed that night Hitler issued a triumphant statement: 'Czechoslovakia has ceased to exist.'

Adapted from an account by an American historian, written in 1988.

Was the policy of appeasement justified?

Historians have many different opinions about the policy of appeasement. After the Second World War, many British historians said that Chamberlain was a weak man who was taken in by Hitler.

More recently, some historians have tried to restore Chamberlain's reputation. They have explained why he acted as he did and how he had little choice at the time.

Read the arguments for and against appeasement. Decide if you think appeasement was right or wrong.

The arguments for appeasement

1 Sympathy for Germany
The British thought that the Treaty of Versailles was too harsh on Germany. They felt that Germany had the right to be treated more fairly. So the British gave in to many of Hitler's demands, even though they went against the Treaty of Versailles.

The British signed the Anglo-German Naval Agreement in 1935, and did not object when Germany reoccupied the Rhineland in 1936. Britain also did nothing to stop Hitler joining Austria to Germany in 1938. Each of these events, they said, could be justified. The British hoped that after each claim was satisfied, Hitler would make no more demands.

2 The desire for peace
Memories of the horrors of the First World War were still strong in Britain and France. People did not want another war, and they hoped that the League of Nations would be able to settle quarrels between countries.

Also, during the 1930s, countries were short of money because of the Great Depression. They knew that they would not be able to afford to fight a war and were desperate to keep the peace.

3 The threat of communism

Britain and France could not hope to protect countries such as Czechoslovakia and Poland from German aggression. They were simply too far away.

The only country that could protect them was the communist Soviet Union.

Britain and France feared the spread of communism as much as they feared Hitler. Therefore, they decided it was best to try and keep the peace.

4 Time to rearm

The biggest reason for following appeasement was that Britain was not ready for a war. When the Sudeten crisis occurred in 1938, Britain needed more time to build up its armed forces.

By giving in to Hitler at Munich war was put off for a year, which gave Britain more time to get ready for war.

The arguments against appeasement

1 The appeasers misjudged Hitler

Opponents of appeasement said that politicians such as Neville Chamberlain trusted Hitler too much.

Opponents argued that politicians who believed in appeasement did not realise that Hitler was a **tyrant** who would do anything to get his way. The more they gave him, the more he wanted.

2 Appeasement was morally wrong

Many argued that following a policy of appeasement showed weakness and cowardice. They said it was wrong to sacrifice Czechoslovakia to Hitler.

Britain and France were so afraid of another war that they let Germany break international agreements without punishment. Some people, such as Winston Churchill, said that Britain should have stood up to Hitler and not given in.

SOURCE N

STEPPING STONES TO GLORY

A cartoon from a British newspaper, 1936.

QUESTIONS

1. What point is being made in Source N?
2. Do you think Chamberlain was right or wrong to follow a policy of appeasement? Explain your answer.

Why had international peace collapsed by 1939?

3 The appeasers missed chances to stop Hitler

Britain and France could easily have stopped Hitler from sending troops into the Rhineland in 1936, but they chose not to take any action. (Hitler had actually given his generals orders to retreat if they were challenged.)

In 1938 Britain and France gave up Czechoslovakia to Hitler when, in fact, the Czechs had a good enough army to resist the Germans.

How important was the Nazi-Soviet Pact?

Hitler turns to Poland

After the invasion of Czechoslovakia, Hitler turned his attention to Poland. Under the Treaty of Versailles Germany had lost land to Poland, including the 'Polish Corridor'.

It had also lost the city of Danzig to the League of Nations (see map on page 52). Hitler wanted this land back. He also wanted Polish land as *Lebensraum* (living space) for the German people.

SOURCE O

A Soviet cartoon of 1936, showing western countries protecting Hitler.

Up until 1939 the Poles had got on quite well with Hitler. They had, for example, helped him to destroy Czechoslovakia by grabbing Teschen in 1938.

The Poles therefore found it hard to accept that Hitler was now threatening them and demanding Polish territory.

Britain's promise

Britain promised to help the Poles if Hitler attacked them. In early August 1939 Britain, France and the Soviet Union tried to make an agreement over Poland, but the talks broke down.

But, in reality, there was little Britain could do to stop Germany invading Poland - it was too far away.

Why was the Nazi-Soviet Pact important?

1 What was the Nazi–Soviet Pact? Nazi Germany and the communist Soviet Union had always hated each other. So the world was amazed when, on 23 August 1939, news broke that the two countries had signed the Nazi–Soviet Pact. In this pact Germany and the Soviet Union had agreed not to fight each other and to split Poland between them.

The pact meant Britain and France were left to fight Germany alone. Britain signed an alliance with Poland on 25 August 1939. This time Britain and France would stand up to Hitler. They were more ready for war than they had been in 1938.

Hitler invaded Poland on 1 September 1939. Two days later, on 3 September 1939, Britain and France declared war on Germany.

SOURCE P

For us Poland is a matter of expanding our living space in the east. There is no question of sparing Poland. We are left with the decision to attack Poland at the earliest opportunity. There will be war.

Hitler speaking to his generals, 23 May 1939.

QUESTION

Why was the world amazed at the signing of the Nazi–Soviet Pact?

2 The Nazi–Soviet Pact made war unavoidable

Hitler launched a **Blitzkrieg** attack (lightning war) on the Poles. Within two weeks the Germans had taken over much of Poland.

In mid-September, Soviet troops invaded Poland from the east, and also occupied Estonia, Latvia and Lithuania.

The Nazi–Soviet Pact was the most important short-term cause of the Second World War. The pact meant Hitler could invade Poland without the Soviet Union interfering.

The fact that Britain had promised to help Poland, however, meant war was almost certain to break out.

Why did Britain and France declare war on Germany in September 1939?

Britain and France tried to get the Poles to talk to Hitler about the land he wanted from them. But the Poles did not want to talk to Hitler. They knew he could not be trusted.

In any case, under the Nazi-Soviet Pact, Germany and the Soviet Union had already decided to split Poland between them. Talking to Hitler was a waste of time.

QUESTIONS

1 When did the Second World War begin?
2 Read Source S on page 95. Why was Chamberlain so upset about the outbreak of war?

Advantages for Germany of the Nazi–Soviet Pact

1 Hitler knew he could now invade Poland without having to fight the Soviet Union.

2 Hitler would be able to get back land lost to Poland at Versailles, and begin to acquire *Lebensraum*.

3 There would be no alliance between the Soviet Union, Britain and France to prevent Hitler carrying out his plans.

Advantages for the Soviet Union of the Nazi–Soviet Pact

1 The Soviet Union would not be drawn into a war with Germany over Poland.

2 The Soviets did not trust Britain and France enough to ally with them to save Poland, and now would not have to.

3 Poland was hostile to the Soviet Union and the two countries had fought a war in the 1920s. Much of Poland's territory had been taken from Russia when Poland was created. Now the Soviet Union could get this land back. This area would be a useful 'buffer zone' against any future German attack.

4 Stalin still believed that war with Germany would come eventually, but the pact gave him time to build up the strength of Soviet armed forces.

A 'state of war'

Britain and France did not go to war immediately. They held back, hoping Hitler would change his plans.

On 3 September the British sent Hitler an **ultimatum** (Source R). When no reply was received by the deadline of 11 a.m., Britain declared war on Germany.

This time Hitler had gone too far. Britain and France finally realised that they had to resist him or accept German domination of Europe.

SOURCE R

Unless by 11 a.m. today [3 September] satisfactory assurances have been given by the German government and have reached the British government, a state of war will exist between the two countries.

The ultimatum from the British to the German government, 3 September 1939.

SOURCE S

This is a sad day for all of us. Everything that I have worked for, everything that I have believed in has crashed into ruins.

Chamberlain speaking in Parliament, 3 September 1939.

SOURCE Q

British people reading about the invasion of Poland, 3 September 1939.

Why had international peace collapsed by 1939?

Paper 1-type assessment: The collapse of peace

SOURCE A

"EUROPE CAN LOOK FORWARD TO A CHRISTMAS OF PEACE", SAYS HITLER

A British cartoon from October 1938.

QUESTIONS

Section A Questions

1 a Study Source A. Explain the message of this cartoon. Support your answer by referring to details of the cartoon and your own knowledge. (6)

b Explain why Hitler followed an aggressive foreign policy in the period 1938-9. (9)

Section B Questions

2 a What was agreed at the Munich Conference in September 1938? (4)

b Explain why Germany invaded Poland in 1939. (6)

c 'The most important cause of the Second World War was the weakness of Britain and France'. Do you agree with this statement? Explain your answer. (10)

International relations 1919–c.1939

3 Germany 1918–45

- Germany came out of the First World War much weaker than it had been in 1914. The army was beaten, the economy was in ruins and extremist groups were trying to seize power.

- The new democratic government, the Weimar Republic, soon ran into difficulties. It was unpopular because it signed the hated Treaty of Versailles. It soon faced uprisings in Berlin and Munich. The government failed to keep up with reparation payments in 1923, which led to the French occupying the rich industrial region of the Ruhr and rapidly rising prices (hyperinflation).

- Gustav Stresemann helped to restore the German economy and improve relations with foreign countries. Germany entered a period of prosperity between 1924 and 1929. Then the Wall Street Crash brought economic ruin once again to Germany. Support for extremist parties, such as the Nazis, increased.

- In 1933 the Nazi leader, Adolf Hitler, became Chancellor (Prime Minister) and set about restoring Germany's greatness. Hitler gave people jobs and took back land lost by Germany under the Treaty of Versailles.

- But this success came at a high price for the German people. Hitler was a cruel dictator who limited personal freedom and crushed opposition. He also enforced Nazi beliefs about the supremacy of the Aryan race. This had horrific consequences for the Slavs, gypsies and the Jews.

This topic is examined in Paper 1 of the examination. Paper 1-type exercises are included at the end of the chapter. Mark schemes, sample answers and comments can be found in the accompanying Teacher's Resource Pack.

Germany 1918–45

- In 1914 the Germans thought they would quickly win the war, but they were wrong. The war dragged on for four long years and ended in defeat for the Germans.

- In 1918 a new government called the Weimar Republic was set up in Germany. The Weimar Republic was unable to deal with the high unemployment that followed the Wall Street Crash in 1929.

- By 1933 Adolf Hitler and the Nazis had come to power in Germany. Hitler managed to put people back to work and took over large amounts of territory in Europe. But, overall, his policies caused enormous damage.

SOURCE A

We sat in our trenches and heard about the unrest back home in Germany. We felt that the French and British were no longer our enemies. We were more worried about the trouble brewing at home.

A German soldier describing his thoughts on the unrest in Germany in November 1918.

Was the Weimar Republic doomed from the start?

How did Germany emerge from defeat in the First World War?

The 'German Revolution'

By September 1918 Allied troops had broken through the German defences on the Western Front. Germany was on the brink of defeat. There was a shortage of food in Germany and many Germans were desperate for peace.

German sailors were also tired of the war. There were **mutinies** at the naval bases of Wilhelmshaven and Kiel. Workers and soldiers all over Germany set up councils similar to the soviets in Russia.

The leaders of Germany were frightened by this 'German Revolution' and realised they had to seek peace if order was to be restored.

SOURCE B

Kaiser Wilhelm II, who abdicated on 9 November 1918 and went to live in the Netherlands.

Kaiser Wilhelm II abdicates

Germany's leaders knew that the Allies would not make peace while the **Kaiser** remained in office. On 9 November 1918 they persuaded the Kaiser to **abdicate** (resign).

Friedrich Ebert of the Social Democratic Party (SPD) announced that Germany was now a republic. Ebert himself would be the president of the new republic and Philipp Scheidemann the Chancellor.

Problems for the new government

The 'November Criminals'

The new German government quickly signed the armistice (truce) with the Allies on 11 November 1918. Many Germans were shocked by this surrender, believing that the politicians had 'stabbed Germany in the back' and that the German army could have carried on fighting.

German nationalists called members of Ebert's government the **November Criminals** because they had signed the armistice. The new government had got off to an unpopular start.

The Spartacist uprising

The biggest problem for Ebert was deciding how Germany should be governed. The **Spartacists**, led by Karl Liebknecht and Rosa Luxemburg, wanted Germany to be a communist country.

In 1919 the Spartacists tried to seize power with an armed uprising in Berlin. Groups of ex-soldiers known as the **Freikorps** (Free Corps) were used to crush the revolt. Liebknecht and Luxemburg were arrested and executed on 15 January 1919.

QUESTIONS

1 What was the 'German Revolution' of 1918?

2 Why did some Germans call Ebert's government the 'November Criminals'?

3 Describe the Spartacist uprising of 1919.

SOURCE C

The Freikorps on parade.

The Weimar Republic

On 19 January 1919 elections were held in Germany to elect deputies to sit in the new National Assembly.

As there was unrest in Berlin, the capital of Germany, the National Assembly first met in the town of Weimar. So the new government became known as the Weimar Republic.

The constitution of the Weimar Republic

The National Assembly drew up a constitution (list of rules) for the Weimar Republic.

1. Germany was to be a **democracy**. All men and women aged 20 and over could vote in elections for the **Reichstag** (parliament). The Reichstag made the laws.

2. Voting was to be by **proportional representation**. For example, a party getting ten per cent of the votes would get ten per cent of the seats in the Reichstag.

3. The head of state was the president. In times of emergency the president had the power to suspend the Reichstag and rule by himself (Article 48).

4. The head of government was the Chancellor.

Weaknesses of the constitution

The system of proportional representation made it hard for one party to win an overall majority in the Reichstag.

Parties had to join together in coalitions in order to form a government. Often, however, the different parties in the coalitions argued and caused the government to collapse.

In addition, many Germans did not like the new democracy. They wanted Germany to have one strong leader, as it had done before the war.

SOURCE D

A German cartoon from July 1919 called 'Clemenceau the Vampire'. It shows Clemenceau, the French Prime Minister, sucking the blood from Germany.

SOURCE E

We were promised that the peace would be based on President Wilson's Fourteen Points. The treaty which is now proposed, breaks that promise. Such a dictated peace will bring fresh hatred and more killing in the future.

President Ebert condemning the proposed Treaty of Versailles in May 1919.

What was the impact of the Treaty of Versailles on the Republic?

Harsh terms

- The Treaty of Versailles (see pages 52-4) was a harsh treaty that punished Germany for its part in the First World War. Germany lost 13 per cent of its territory and 10 per cent of its population. Germany's armed forces were reduced in size and allowed very few weapons.

- The 'War Guilt' clause (Article 231) said that Germany was totally to blame for starting the war and causing all the damage. As a result of this Germany would be made to pay reparations (compensation). In 1921 Germany was ordered to pay the massive sum of £6600 million in reparations.

'Diktat'

- The Germans were furious about the treaty. They had not been allowed to negotiate the terms of the treaty and called it a 'Diktat' (dictated peace). The Germans had believed the treaty would be based on President Wilson's Fourteen Points, which were much fairer than the final treaty.

- At first Philipp Scheidemann, the German Chancellor, said Germany should refuse to sign the treaty. But the Germans had little choice, as the Allies would probably have invaded had they not signed. The treaty was signed, making the Weimar Republic even more unpopular.

The Kapp *putsch* 1920

1. The Freikorps now started to cause the government problems. Among their number was a group of extreme nationalists.

2. They hated communism and said that the best way to stop it spreading was for Germany to have a strong leader and a strong army.

QUESTIONS

1. What weaknesses did the Weimar constitution have?
2. Why did so many Germans hate the Treaty of Versailles?

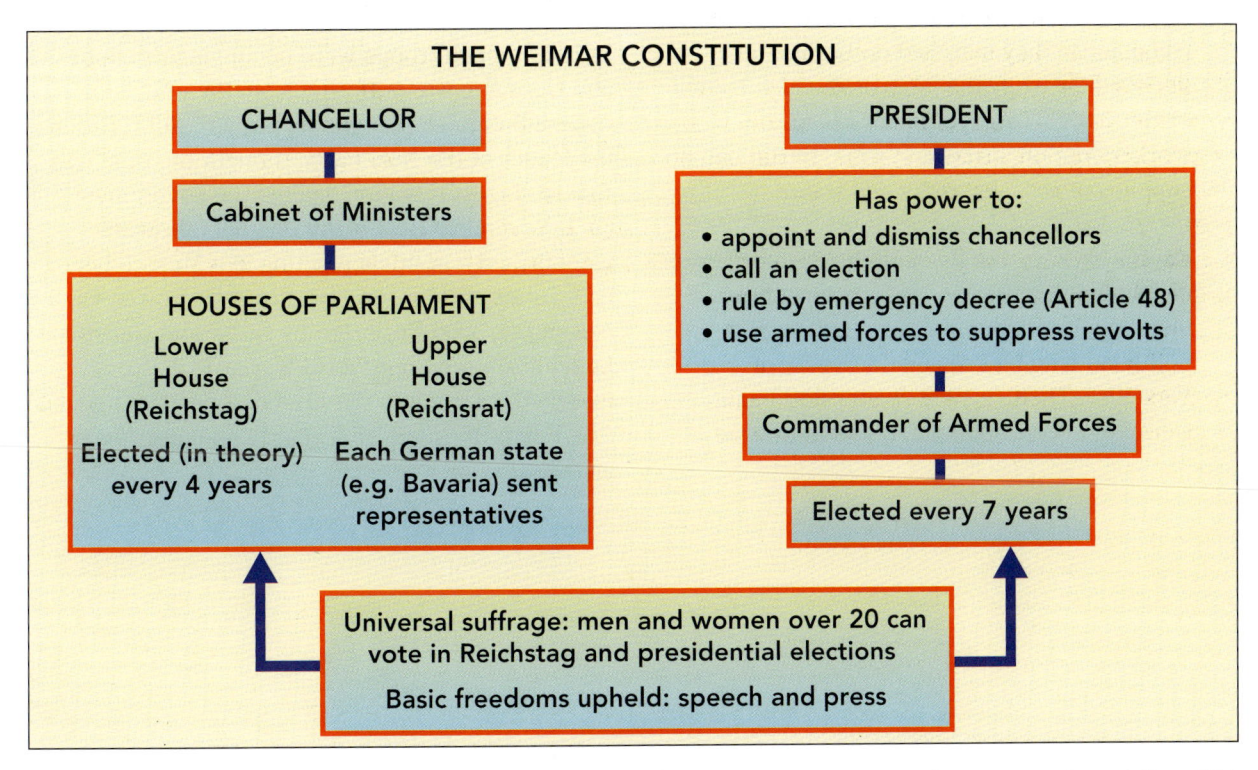

THE WEIMAR CONSTITUTION

CHANCELLOR
- Cabinet of Ministers

PRESIDENT

Has power to:
- appoint and dismiss chancellors
- call an election
- rule by emergency decree (Article 48)
- use armed forces to suppress revolts

Commander of Armed Forces

Elected every 7 years

HOUSES OF PARLIAMENT

Lower House (Reichstag)	Upper House (Reichsrat)
Elected (in theory) every 4 years	Each German state (e.g. Bavaria) sent representatives

Universal suffrage: men and women over 20 can vote in Reichstag and presidential elections

Basic freedoms upheld: speech and press

SOURCE F

The Munich *putsch*. Police in Munich on the morning of 9 November 1923.

3. In March 1920 the Freikorps staged a ***putsch*** (rebellion). They marched on Berlin and declared Dr Wolfgang Kapp as the new leader of Germany. The government called the workers out on strike, and soon, Berlin had no supplies of gas, electricity and water.

4. Kapp was forced to flee and the Freikorps was disbanded. Even so, in 1921, ex-Freikorps members murdered Matthias Erzberger, a politician who had signed the Treaty of Versailles. Then, in 1922, Walter Rathenau, Germany's foreign minister, was murdered.

The Munich *putsch* 1923

In 1923 French troops were occupying the Ruhr and Germany was suffering from the effects of hyperinflation (rapidly rising prices). Adolf Hitler, the leader of the Nazi Party, thought the time was ripe to stage a rebellion against the government. On 8 November 1923 Hitler and his followers gatecrashed a political meeting in a Munich beer hall. Hitler said he was going to seize power. On 9 November, 3000 Nazis, led by Hitler and General Ludendorff, the First World War army hero, marched on Munich. But armed policemen opened fire, killing 16 Nazis. Hitler and Ludendorff were arrested.

Hitler goes on trial

During his trial Hitler made long speeches criticising the government. The trial was widely reported in the newspapers and Hitler became famous throughout Germany. Hitler was sentenced to five years in prison, but he served only nine months. Ludendorff was found 'not guilty'.

In prison Hitler wrote a book called *Mein Kampf* (My Struggle), which told his life story and set out his main beliefs. Hitler also decided that he would now try and get into power by winning more votes than the other parties, rather than using violence.

The economic crisis of 1923

The occupation of the Ruhr

- In 1921 the Allies ordered Germany to pay £6600 million in reparations. This was a ridiculous amount and beyond the means of Germany to pay. At the end of 1922 Germany failed to make a reparations payment. This angered the French and Belgians and, in January 1923, they sent troops to occupy the region of the Ruhr, Germany's largest industrial area.

- The French and Belgians planned to take the value of the reparations payments in goods such as coal, iron ore and factory goods. The German government, however, told the German workers to go on strike. As a result no goods were produced and the French and Belgians were left empty-handed.

SOURCE G

> My daily wage was just enough to buy a loaf of bread and one small piece of cheese or oatmeal. A friend of mine, a priest, came to Berlin with a month's wages to buy a pair of shoes for his baby. He could only afford a cup of coffee.

A German journalist describes the effects of hyperinflation in Germany.

Hyperinflation

- The German government still had to pay the workers and meet its other bills. So more and more banknotes were printed. This led to hyperinflation. In January 1923 a loaf of bread had cost 250 marks. By November the same loaf cost 201 *billion* marks. Paper money in Germany became almost worthless.

- German people who had life savings were very hard hit by the huge increase in prices. All of a sudden their savings would not buy a week's groceries. Wages did not keep up with the rapidly rising prices, so living standards fell. Many people could not even afford to buy food and hunger was common.

QUESTIONS

1. What was the Munich *putsch*?
2. **a** What caused the hyperinflation in Germany in 1923?
   b What were the effects of hyperinflation for the German people?

- The situation was very serious. Thousands of Germans had been financially ruined and it looked as though the government had lost control. This is why Hitler thought the time was right to try and seize power by carrying out the Munich *putsch*.

QUESTIONS

1 Read the text on page 105. How did Stresemann restore Germany's economy?

2 Why were Stresemann's measures in foreign policy so important?

3 What do you think Stresemann meant in Source J?

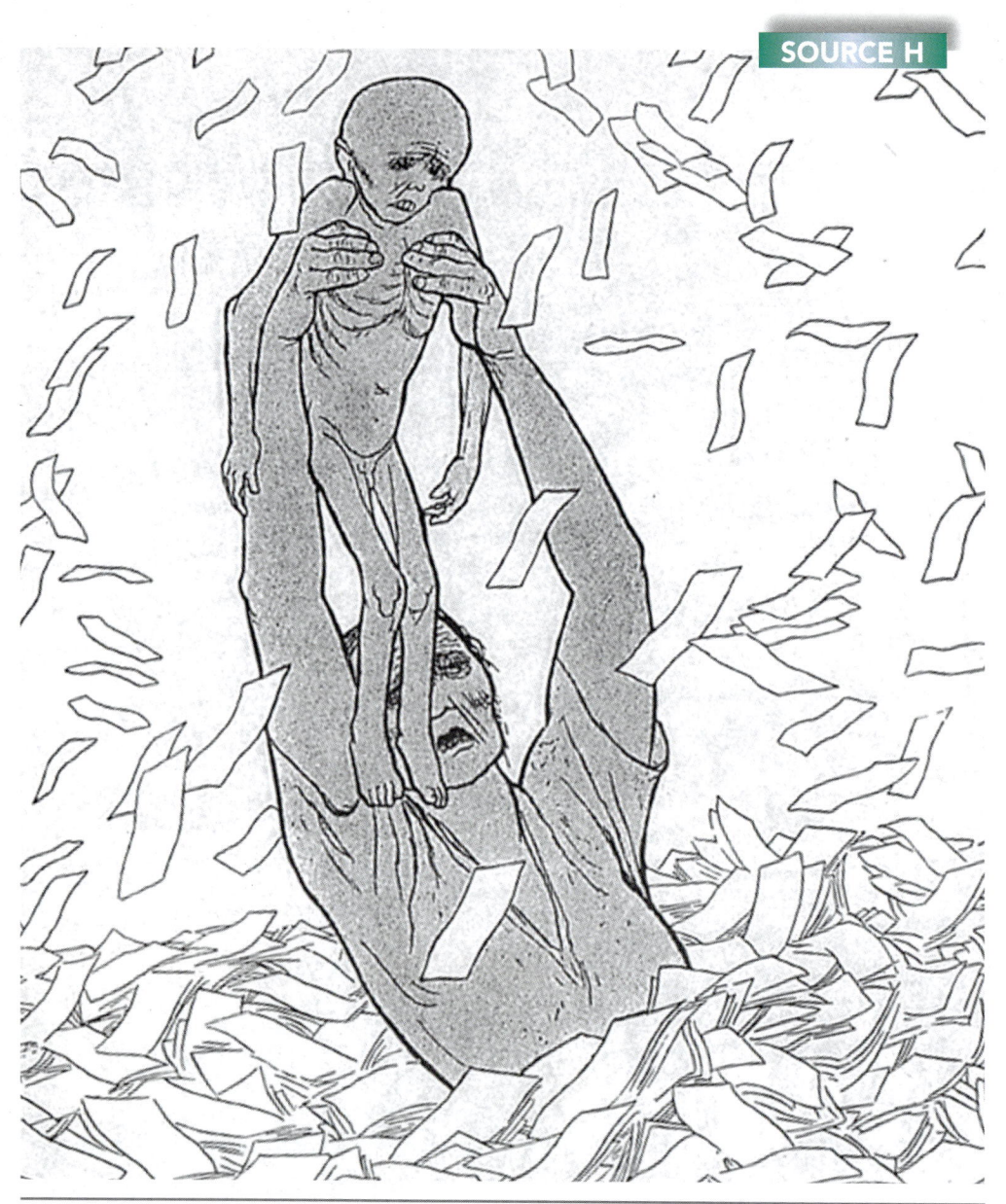

SOURCE H

A German cartoon from 1923. The mother is calling for bread while she and her child drown in a sea of banknotes.

The Stresemann era 1923-9

From August to November 1923 Gustav Stresemann was the Chancellor of Germany. From November 1923 to October 1929 he was the foreign minister.

Stresemann helped to put Germany back on the road to economic recovery and also improved Germany's relations with other countries.

To what extent did the Weimar Republic recover after 1923?

Economic recovery

- **The Rentenmark**
  Stresemann introduced a new type of money called the Rentenmark and cut back government spending. This helped to end the hyperinflation. People began to feel more confident and German industry began to recover.

- **The Dawes Plan**
  In 1924 Stresemann negotiated the Dawes Plan with the Americans. Under the plan the USA agreed to loan Germany 800 million gold marks. It also reduced the annual reparations payments and gave Germany longer to pay. The Young Plan of 1929 gave Germany even more time to pay. (As it turned out Germany stopped paying reparations in 1930.)

Foreign policy

Stresemann wanted to overturn the Treaty of Versailles, but realised it would take time and could only be done by improving relations with other countries. He made a number of treaties with other countries.

- **The Locarno Pact**
  Stresemann signed this treaty with France and Belgium in 1925. The three countries agreed to respect the borders that had been laid down between them at Versailles. Stresemann had shown that Germany wanted to get on with other countries, and in 1926 Germany was allowed to join the League of Nations.

- **The Kellogg-Briand Pact**
  1928 Germany was one of 60 nations that signed this treaty, which said that countries should not settle their differences by going to war.

SOURCE I

Gustav Stresemann.

SOURCE J

A country must not have the attitude of a child who writes down everything it wants for Christmas for the next fifteen years. There is no way the parents could give it all of this. I often have the feeling that the German people have given me such a list.

Gustav Stresemann explaining why the Germans needed to be patient about overturning the Treaty of Versailles.

The Party, painted by George Grosz. It shows the seedy night club life of the Weimar Republic.

SOURCE K

Art and culture under the Weimar Republic

Before 1918, when Germany was ruled by the Kaiser, literature and art had been **censored**. There was much more freedom under the Weimar Republic. People were allowed to criticise the government. Art and culture flourished.

- Berlin became a thriving centre of the arts with over 120 newspapers, 40 theatres and numerous night clubs where jazz was played.

- Erich Remarque's anti-war novel, *All Quiet on the Western Front* sold over half a million copies.

- Artists, such as George Grosz, became famous for their original style of painting (see Source K).

Some Germans did not like the new ideas in art or the many night clubs. They said they were depraved and 'un-German'. They argued that Germany was becoming an immoral and corrupt country.

What were the achievements of the Weimar period?

Right from the start the Weimar Republic faced a number of difficult problems, which it did well to survive. By the mid-1920s most Germans had come to accept the Weimar government. There were fewer calls for a return to the 'good old days' of the Kaiser.

Stresemann helped Germany to become more prosperous. He also improved Germany's reputation with other countries. Despite this, a number of problems remained.

- Germany was heavily dependent on loans from the USA.

- German exports were falling.

- There were arguments between workers and employers.

- Prices for farm crops were falling and many farmers were in debt.

- Many Germans were still angry about the Treaty of Versailles. They blamed the Weimar government for not doing enough to overturn the treaty.

The achievements of the Weimar government were therefore very mixed.

Why was Hitler able to dominate Germany by 1934?

What did the Nazi Party stand for in the 1920s?

- In January 1919 Anton Drexler, a Munich locksmith founded the German Workers' Party (DAP). Adolf Hitler joined the party in September. Hitler was a powerful public speaker and a good organiser. He was put in charge of publicising the party's ideas.

- In February 1920 Hitler helped to write the party's Twenty-Five Point Programme which listed its beliefs. This programme showed that the party was **anti-Semitic** (anti-Jews).

- In April 1920 the DAP was renamed the National Socialist German Workers' Party ('Nazi Party' for short). The Nazis bought a newspaper called the *Volkischer Beobachter* to help spread their views. Support for the Nazis began to grow.

SOURCE A

Goodness! He's got a big gob. We could use him.

A comment made by Anton Drexler on first hearing Hitler speak in public.

SOURCE B

Hitler's membership card for the German Workers' Party. He claimed he was the seventh member of the party, but his card shows he was the 555th. Some historians say that the party started numbering at 500 to make it look better.

QUESTION

1 Look at Source A and read the text. Why did Drexler think that the German Workers' Party could 'use' Hitler?

Hitler's rise to power

SOURCE C

A Nazi propaganda poster showing the SA as a popular movement.

The SA

In 1921 Hitler became the leader of the Nazi Party. In the same year he founded the **Sturm Abteilung (SA)**.

Also known as Stormtroopers or Brownshirts, the SA paraded in full military uniform and wore the Nazi 'swastika'. The military style of the SA attracted many unemployed soldiers. The job of the SA was to break up the meetings of rival political groups.

The SA soon had a reputation for violence.

Why did the Nazis have little success before 1930?

The failure of the Munich *putsch* in 1923 led to Hitler being imprisoned and the Nazi Party being banned. When Hitler was in prison, some of his supporters formed the National Socialist Freedom Party.

It only managed to win fourteen seats in the Reichstag in the 1924 elections. At the time Stresemann was doing well for Germany and people were not interested in extremists such as the Nazis.

108 Germany 1918–45

Hitler reorganises the Nazi Party

- Hitler was released from prison in December 1924, and in 1925 the ban on the Nazi Party was lifted. Hitler now set about reorganising the party. He divided Germany into 34 districts. A leading Nazi was put in charge of getting more support in each district. Hitler also started the Hitler Youth and set up the **Schutzstaffel** (**SS**), as his own personal bodyguard.

- By the end of 1926 the Nazi Party had 50,000 members. In 1927 it held its first annual rally at Nuremberg. The Nazis were now better organised and known throughout Germany, and not just in Bavaria. Despite this, they only won twelve seats in the 1928 Reichstag elections. Things were soon to change.

Why was Hitler able to become chancellor by 1933?

1 The Great Depression

On 3 October 1929, Gustav Stresemann died. Germany had lost one of its best politicians. Then, on 29 October 1929, the Wall Street Crash took place in the USA. Share prices on the American stock exchange fell to rock bottom. Thousands of American businesses went bankrupt and a slump in world trade followed. The Wall Street Crash led to the Great Depression, which had disastrous results for Germany.

- American banks stopped lending money to Germany. German factories could not manage without this money.

- German factories were forced to close and millions of workers lost their jobs.

Most German people blamed the Weimar government for the Depression and began to lose faith with democracy. They thought that the extreme parties, such as the Nazis or Communists, might do a better job.

SOURCE E

- We demand the union of all Germans in a Greater Germany.
- We demand land to feed and settle our surplus population.
- No Jew may be a member of the German nation.
- All citizens shall have equal rights and duties.
- We demand profit-sharing in large industrial companies.

Extracts from the Nazis' Twenty-Five Point Programme, 1920.

SOURCE D

Germany has lost her most able politician. Gustav Stresemann worked hard for the recovery of his shattered country. He worked hard for peace and co-operation abroad. The domestic recovery of Germany and her new standing in Europe give measure to his achievement.

The obituary of Gustav Stresemann from the English newspaper, *The Times*, on 4 October 1929.

QUESTIONS

1. What was the job of the SA?
2. How did Hitler reorganise the Nazi Party?
3. How did the Wall Street Crash affect Germany?

2 Crisis in the government

The Weimar government failed to do anything about the rising unemployment.

President Hindenburg declared a state of emergency and began ruling the country without consulting the Reichstag.

Between 1930 and 1932 the Reichstag met less and less frequently.

During this time Hitler toured Germany, holding huge rallies (meetings). He told people that the Nazis would give them jobs, bring back prosperity and destroy the Treaty of Versailles. It was just the message the people wanted to hear.

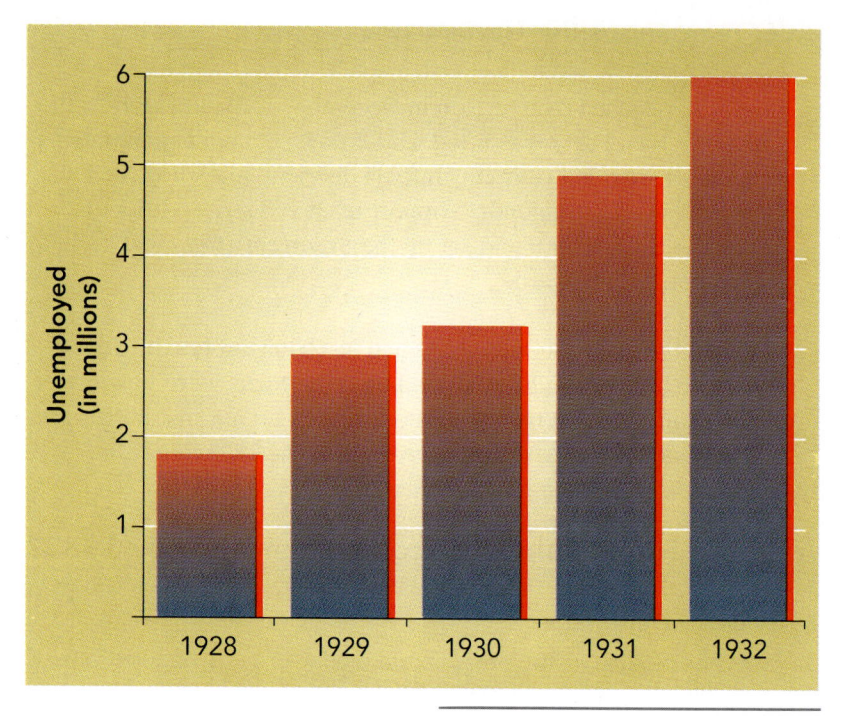

Unemployment in Germany, 1928–32.

As a result the Nazis began to win more seats in the Reichstag, and, in July 1932, they became the largest single party in the Reichstag. President Hindenburg now came under intense pressure to make Hitler chancellor.

Party	1928	1930	July 1932	Nov. 1932
Social Democrats	153	143	133	121
National	73	41	37	52
Centre	62	68	75	70
Communists	54	77	89	100
People's	45	30	7	11
Democrats	25	20	4	2
Nazis	12	107	230	196

Seats won in elections to the Reichstag, 1928-32.

QUESTION

1 Explain why the Nazis became the largest single party in the Reichstag. Use the graph, the table and the text to answer.

> **SOURCE F**
>
> **German women!**
> **Our young people degraded**
>
> In one German Girls' Grammar School, 63 per cent of the girls have had sexual intercourse, and 43 per cent have had some form of sexual disease. This is because our young people have been faced with a flood of filth and muck in books, in the theatre and in the cinema.

An extract from a Nazi election leaflet in 1932.

3 Hitler appointed Chancellor

Hindenburg disliked Hitler, and felt he could not be trusted. But on 30 January 1933, he gave in and appointed Hitler the Chancellor of Germany.

How did Hitler consolidate his power in 1933-4?

The Nazis attracted support from a wide variety of people in Germany (see box). Although they were the largest party in the Reichstag, they did not have an overall majority of seats.

They had to join with other parties to form a coalition government. Out of twelve government ministers only three were Nazis.

The election of March 1933

Hitler wanted the Nazis to rule on their own without having to depend on the support of other parties. He persuaded President Hindenburg to call another election for 5 March 1933.

In the run up to the election, members of the SA beat up anyone who disagreed with the Nazis, especially the communists.

Reasons for Nazi support

- Factory owners were worried that the communists would come to power in Germany, and take over their businesses. They preferred the Nazi Party to the communists and gave money to help the Nazis fight elections.

- The Nazi promise to abolish the Treaty of Versailles and restore Germany to its former greatness appealed to many Germans.

- Millions of unemployed people supported the Nazis because Hitler promised to give them jobs.

- Members of the middle-classes, who had lost their savings in the hyperinflation of 1923, thought the Nazis would provide a strong government.

- Many women liked what the Nazis said about family life being important.

- Hitler gave people a reason for Germany's problems by saying that Jews and communists were to blame, even though there was no truth in this.

- Hitler was a powerful speaker who swayed people into thinking that the Nazis would improve their lives.

Hitler's rise to power

The Reichstag fire

On 27 February 1933 the Reichstag building in Berlin was burned down.

A Dutch communist, Marinus van der Lubbe, was found in the building with matches and firelighters. He confessed to starting the fire, and was later put on trial and executed.

Many historians, however, believe that the Nazis themselves started the fire.

Hitler attacks the communists

Whoever was to blame, Hitler cleverly used the fire to say that German communists were trying to stage a violent revolution in Germany.

President Hindenburg gave Hitler the power to ban communist election meetings and shut down communist newspapers. Thousands of leading communists were arrested and imprisoned by the SA.

In the March election the Nazis won 288 seats out of 647 but this was still not enough for an overall majority. So, Hitler stopped the 81 communist deputies from taking their seats and persuaded the 74 Centre Party deputies to support the Nazis. Germany now had a fully Nazi government.

SOURCE G

A cartoon from the *Daily Express*, 5 March 1933. It shows how Hitler forced people to vote for him in the March election.

SOURCE H

The Reichstag building on fire, 27 February 1933.

SOURCE J

A young Dutchman turned up whom we could use. This Dutch communist, van der Lubbe, was to climb into the Reichstag and make himself seen. Meanwhile, my men and I would set fire to the building.

We prepared a number of fires by soaking carpets and curtains in paraffin. We finished at 9.05 exactly and left. I am writing this confession because the SA has been betrayed by the evil plans of Goering and Goebbels. I shall destroy it when these two traitors have been removed.

An extract from a confession written in June 1934 by Karl Ernst, a leading member of the SA. Ernst was murdered in the 'Night of the Long Knives' (see pages 114-15). His confession was found later and published by a German communist.

SOURCE I

I had to do something on my own. I thought starting a fire was the best way. I did not wish to harm private people, but something that belonged to the country. I acted alone. No one helped me. I did not meet a single person in the Reichstag.

Said by van der Lubbe to the police in March 1933.

QUESTIONS

1. Explain how Hitler used the Reichstag fire for his own ends.
2. How does Source I differ from Source J?
3. What did Hitler do in March 1933 to give the Nazis a majority of seats in the Reichstag?

Hitler's rise to power

How effectively did the Nazis control Germany 1933-45?

The Enabling Law

Hitler did not like democracy and wanted to give himself greater power. On 23 March 1933 the Reichstag met in the Kroll Opera House in Berlin.

Hitler asked the Reichstag deputies to pass the **Enabling Law**, which would give him the power to make laws without consulting the Reichstag.

To make sure the deputies voted for the Enabling Law armed Stormtroopers surrounded the building. Not surprisingly, the Enabling Law was passed by 441 votes to 84. Hitler now had the power to make laws on his own. Between 1933 and 1939 the Reichstag only met twelve times.

A Nazi dictatorship

Hitler used his new powers to turn Germany into a Nazi **dictatorship**. In July 1933 Hitler said that the only legal political party in Germany was the Nazi Party. People's lives were now under the total control of Hitler. Democracy in Germany was dead.

The 'Night of the Long Knives'

- Ernst Röhm, the leader of the SA, demanded that the SA should be joined with the German army and the combined force put under his command. Army generals were horrified by this idea. They looked upon the SA as nothing more than an armed gang of thugs.

- Hitler did not like the thought of Röhm getting more power and he also needed the support of the army. Furthermore, Röhm had left-wing views that would offend the factory-owners who had given the Nazis money. Röhm could even become powerful enough to challenge Hitler as leader of the Nazi party.

- Hitler decided to take action against Röhm and the SA. On the night of 30 June 1934, Hitler ordered the SS to arrest and execute Röhm and hundreds of other SA leaders. The event became known as the 'Night of the Long Knives'.

SOURCE A

The Reichstag has given the Nazi government the power to make own laws on its own.
The laws passed by the Nazi government will be announced by the Chancellor [Adolf Hitler].

Taken from the Enabling Law.

QUESTIONS

1. What was the Enabling Law?
2. What do you think the cartoonist was trying to say in Source B?
3. Why did Hitler carry out the 'Night of the Long Knives'?

Führer of Germany

- Many people were shocked by what had happened to the SA leaders. But Hitler told them that Röhm was a danger to the country. President Hindenburg even thanked Hitler for saving Germany from a possible revolution.

- On 2 August 1934 President Hindenburg died. Hitler now joined the offices of president and chancellor and called himself the '**Führer**' (leader). From 1934 the army swore an oath of loyalty to Hitler rather than to the country of Germany.

SOURCE C

We entered the house and took a number of SA leaders prisoner. With great courage Hitler personally arrested them. I do not want to say much about the filthy scenes of debauchery we saw, but one of our guards said, 'I wish the whole country could see these happenings. Then people would understand how good it is that out leader acts in this way.'

From a radio broadcast by Joseph Goebbels on 1 July 1934. He describes how the SA leaders were arrested during the 'Night of the Long Knives'.

SOURCE B

A cartoon from an English newspaper on 3 July 1934 about the 'Night of the Long Knives'.

How did the Nazis use culture and the mass media to control people?

The Nazis made great use of propaganda and censorship to make sure that the people supported Hitler and his ideas.

The Ministry for People's Enlightenment and Propaganda

- In 1933 the Ministry for People's Enlightenment and Propaganda was set up under **Joseph Goebbels**. Goebbels made sure that Nazi ideas were widely broadcast on the radio. Most German families had a radio, so Goebbels could get the Nazi message over to millions of people at a time.

- Films, plays and books also had to keep to Nazi ideas, otherwise they could not be performed or published. Posters and photographs were put up all over Germany, showing Hitler as a strong leader.

- Goebbels also used censorship, giving out instructions to say what could be written in newspapers and broadcast on the radio. Anything that went against the Nazis was banned. Goebbels made sure, for example, that 'undesirable' music such as jazz or Black American music was not heard by the German people.

SOURCE E

In the next newspaper there must be a main article in which a decision of the Führer is fully described as being the only right one for Germany.

Instructions given to the press by Goebbels in 1939.

SOURCE D

Crowds at the 1936 Nazi Party rally in Nuremberg.

Book burning

The Nazis banned the work of over 2500 writers. In May 1933 Goebbels watched students burn the books of 'undesirable' writers on bonfires in the streets of Berlin.

The work of musicians, poets and playwrights was also banned if they did not fit in with Nazi beliefs.

Rallies

The Nazis put on great public displays to win support. Each year a huge rally was held in the city of Nuremberg. Thousands of soldiers and party officials gathered in a large stadium, which was surrounded by large swastika flags.

Hitler and other party leaders made powerful speeches saying how well the Nazis were ruling Germany. Other processions and marches were held to celebrate 'special' events, such as Hitler's birthday in April.

The Berlin Olympic Games

- In the summer of 1936 the Olympic Games were held in Berlin. The Nazis used the games to show their achievements and the supremacy of the **Aryan** race. A magnificent stadium, holding 100,000 people, was specially built. Visitors from abroad were very impressed with the facilities and organisation of the games. The bad side of Nazism, such as the mistreatment of the Jews, was kept in the background.

- To Hitler's joy, the German team won more gold, silver and bronze medals than any other team. But he was not pleased about the performance of the American athlete, Jesse Owens. Owens was black and was seen as inferior by the Nazis. Yet he won four gold medals and was the star of the games. This made the Nazi's ideas about race look rather stupid, so Hitler refused to shake hands with Owens.

SOURCE F

Jesse Owens in action at the 1936 Olympic Games.

QUESTIONS

1 How did the Nazis get their message over to the German people?

2 Why do you think Hitler refused to shake hands with Jesse Owens?

How much opposition was there to the Nazi regime?

Although many people did not like the Nazis they were frightened to speak out. They were afraid of being arrested by the **Gestapo** (secret police) and sent to a concentration camp (see page 121).

As time went on, however, there was more and more opposition to the Nazis.

1 Opposition from political parties

Hitler had banned political parties other than the Nazis in 1933, but some members of the Social Democratic Party and the Communist Party went on meeting in secret.

During the 1930s they published pamphlets criticising Hitler and the Nazis, but this did not have much effect.

2 Opposition from artists and writers

Many artists and writers did not like being told what they could or could not draw and write by the Nazis. Some spoke out against Hitler but most kept silent. Others chose to leave Germany.

3 Opposition from the Church

- To begin with the Church wanted to get on with the Nazis because the Nazis said family life was important and campaigned against immorality in Germany.

- In 1933 the Nazis signed the **Concordat** with the Catholic Church. The Nazis promised not to tell the Catholic church what to do if it did not interfere in politics. Hitler, however, broke his promise and banned the Catholic Youth Movement. The Pope was angered and criticised Hitler for mistreating people such as Jews, gypsies and the disabled. Hitler reacted by sending nuns and Catholic priests to labour camps.

- Hitler also interfered with the affairs of the Protestant Church. Many Protestant churchmen, including Pastor Niemoller, spoke out against him. They were arrested and sent to concentration camps.

SOURCE G

Two 'swing types'. Pictures like this were meant to shock the German public.

4 Opposition from army generals

Some army generals were suspicious of the Nazis. They disagreed with Hitler using force to take over territory in Europe. Hitler sacked large numbers of generals in 1938.

SOURCE H

Members of the Navajos Gang in Cologne in 1940.

5 Opposition from youth groups

The Hitler Youth Movement was very popular with many young German people. Some young people did not like the control the Nazis tried to have over their lives, though, and opposed the Nazi Party.

- **'Swing' types** were young people who refused to join the Hitler Youth movement. Instead, they were more interested in listening to jazz and dancing to American music. They grew their hair long to show their opposition to the Nazis. The Nazis said these young people were **degenerate** and called them 'swing' types. ('Swing' was the name for a type of American music banned by the Nazis.)

- **The Navajos Gang** and **Edelweiss Pirates** beat up members of the Hitler Youth. During the Second World War they spread anti-Nazi leaflets and helped Allied pilots, who had been shot down, to escape. In 1944 a group of Edelweiss Pirates took part in an attack on the Gestapo in which an officer was killed. The Nazis took revenge by publicly hanging twelve pirates in Cologne.

- **The White Rose Movement** was made up of Munich students. They tried to overthrow the Nazi government when the Second World War began to go badly for Germany after 1943. White Rose members handed out leaflets asking people to oppose the Nazis. The leaders, Hans and Sophie Scholl, were arrested and executed in 1943.

SOURCE I

They are everywhere. There are more of them than the Hitler Youth. They don't go to work and disagree with everything.

A German complaining about the Edelweiss Pirates in the town of Oberhausen in 1941.

QUESTIONS

1. Why were many people afraid to oppose the Nazis?
2. How well did Hitler get on with the Church in Germany?
3. Which youth groups opposed Hitler?

Nazi control of Germany 119

6 Opposition from the upper classes

Upper class people in Germany supported Hitler at first. But by 1940 they had grown tired of Hitler's brutality and thought he was bringing ruin on Germany. Two main upper class groups opposed Hitler.

- **The Kreisau Circle** led by Helmuth von Moltke. This group wanted to see Hitler overthrown but did not favour violence. The Nazis discovered the group in 1944 and executed the leaders.

- **The Beck-Goerdeler Group** led by General Ludwig Beck and Karl Goerdeler. On 20 July 1944 one of their supporters, Count Claus von Stauffenberg, tried to murder Hitler at his military headquarters. Hitler had called a meeting of his generals, and Stauffenberg attended the meeting and placed a briefcase containing a bomb under the table near to Hitler. Stauffenberg then left the room, saying he had a telephone call to make. The bomb exploded but Hitler missed the full blast and escaped with minor injuries. Beck, Goerdeler and Stauffenberg were arrested and executed by the Nazis.

How effectively did the Nazis deal with their political opponents?

There were a number of Nazi groups who dealt ruthlessly with any opposition.

1 The Schutzstaffel (SS)

- The SS was formed in 1925 as Hitler's personal bodyguard. Members of the SS wore black uniforms, so they could be told apart from the SA who wore brown. From 1929 the SS came under the leadership of **Heinrich Himmler** and was the Nazis main security force.

- The SS was responsible for running the concentration camps where 'enemies of the state' were taken. Discipline in the camps was hard and the food was poor. Few people survived a stay in one of these camps. At first most prisoners were communists or trade union leaders, but later people whom the Nazis looked upon as 'undesirable' were sent to the camps. They included Jews, gypsies and homosexuals. After 1942 many concentration camps became death camps (see pages 130-1).

- Some members of the SS were formed into the Waffen SS, a highly skilled group of soldiers who fought alongside the main German army.

SOURCE J

A German cartoon published in 1934 entitled, 'Life in the Third Reich'.

2 The Gestapo
- The Gestapo was a secret state police force set up in 1933 to find people who opposed the Nazi system of government.
- The Gestapo set up a web of spies to tell them of anyone who was acting against the Nazis.
- By 1936 the Gestapo was led by **Reinhard Heydrich**, who was ruthless in dealing with opposition. People were very frightened of being reported to the SS or the Gestapo, and this stopped them from voicing their opposition.

3 The People's Court
- In 1934 Hitler set up the People's Court to try people who spoke out against him. All the judges were Nazis and could be depended on to give the 'right' verdict. The number of people arrested for opposing the Nazis increased rapidly.
- Between 1934 and 1939, 534 people were executed for political crimes. In 1939, 162,734 people were under arrest awaiting trial for daring to criticise the Nazis.

What was it like to live in Nazi Germany?

How did young people react to the Nazi regime?

The Nazis were very keen to teach their ideas and beliefs to young people. If young people were taught Nazi ideas from an early age, they would grow up to be loyal to Hitler.

SOURCE A

KOMM ZU UNS!

DEUTSCHES JUNGVOLK IN DER HITLER-JUGEND

A recruiting poster for the Hitler Youth.

The Hitler Youth

The Hitler Youth Movement was formed in 1926. It had different sections, depending on age (see box). Everyone was taught Nazi ideas and beliefs. Members were told to report their parents and teachers if they heard them saying anything bad about Hitler. The boys did military drill and outdoor activities such as camping and hiking. The girls were taught how to be good mothers.

Boys	Girls
Aged 6-10 Little Fellows	Aged 10-14 Young Girls
Aged 10-14 Young Folk	Aged 14-17 League of German Maidens
Aged 14-18 Hitler Youth	

Life in Nazi Germany 121

Year	Membership	Population of Germany aged 10–18
1933	2,292,041	7,529,000
1934	3,577,565	7,682,000
1935	3,394,303	8,172,000
1936	5,437,601	8,656,000
1937	5,879,955	9,060,000
1938	7,031,226	9,109,000
1939	7,287,470	8,870,000

Membership of the Hitler Youth, 1933–9.

Many young people were keen to join the Hitler Youth because of the sporting activities, camping holidays and marches.

In 1936 membership of the Hitler Youth was made compulsory and other youth clubs were closed down. As a result, membership of the Hitler Youth grew (see chart).

By 1939 most young people were members, although there were still some who were reluctant to join.

Schools and education

In order to try and **indoctrinate** children still further the Nazis laid down what should be taught to schoolchildren.

In History children were taught how successful the Nazis had been.

In Biology and Race Studies they were taught that the Aryan (Germanic/North European) race was better than any other race of people. They were told that black people and Jews were inferior.

Education for boys and girls was different. Girls studied Domestic Science and were taught about housekeeping and being good mothers. Boys had to do military exercises to prepare them to be soldiers in the German army.

SOURCE B

A Nazi poster showing an ideal German family.

Germany 1918–45

Textbooks were rewritten so they contained Nazi beliefs. Teachers were made to join the Nazi Teachers' League otherwise they would lose their jobs.

Children had to give the Nazi salute and sing Nazi songs.

Class exercises were devised to encourage support for Nazi beliefs. In Geography children were taught that the Treaty of Versailles was unfair on Germany, and in Physics they learned about making weapons. In Maths children would have to work out how many bombs could be dropped on Jewish towns.

How successful were Nazi policies towards women and the family?

- The Nazis said that women should stay at home, have children and look after their husbands. They were discouraged from going out to work and having careers. Under the Nazis the number of women teachers and doctors fell sharply. Women were also banned from being judges.

- Hitler was worried that the birth rate was falling in Germany. So he encouraged people to have large families. Mothers who had eight or more children were awarded the golden Mother Cross. Propaganda posters, such as Source B, were put up praising the 'ideal' German family.

- Women were not allowed to wear make-up or smoke in public. The Nazis thought that women should wear flat heels and have plaited hair.

- During the Second World War (1939-45) there was a shortage of male workers in German factories, so the Nazis had little choice but to reverse their beliefs and allow women to work.

SOURCE C

We do not think it is right that women should be part of the world of a man. Men and women have separate worlds. What a man gives in courage on the battlefield, a woman gives in bearing children for the country.

From Hitler's 'Address to Women' at the Nuremberg rally in 1934.

QUESTIONS

1. What was the purpose of the Hitler Youth?
2. What were children taught about Nazi beliefs in school?
3. What did the Nazis say was the role of women in society?

Life in Nazi Germany

Did most people in Germany benefit from Nazi rule?

Unemployment

When Hitler came to power in 1933 the German economy was in a mess. This was because of the Great Depression that set in after the Wall Street Crash. There were six million people out of work. What steps did Hitler take to bring down unemployment?

SOURCE D

- Hitler started to rearm Germany. People were employed to make iron and steel, and weapons such as tanks and aircraft. Others were recruited into the army. Germany had 750,000 more soldiers in 1938 than in 1933.

- More jobs were created by building houses, hospitals, schools and Autobahns (motorways). Between 1933 and 1938, over 3000 kilometres of motorway were built.

By 1938 unemployment in Germany had dropped to less than one million. However, wages did not rise and the working week rose from 45 hours in 1928 to 50 hours in 1939. So, the economy under Hitler was not as strong as it appeared.

Hitler starts off the building of the first German Autobahn in 1934.

The German Labour Front

In 1933 Hitler banned trade unions and replaced them with the German Labour Front. This was made up of two parts.

- **Beauty of Labour**, which set out to improve working conditions in the factories.

- **Strength Through Joy**, which provided workers with holidays and leisure activities.

Despite these new organisations under the Nazis, workers worked longer and for less money. There was also a shortage of consumer goods, such as household appliances. German factories were more geared to making weapons and armaments.

Although Hitler had lowered unemployment this was done at great cost to the German people. Under Hitler they had lost many rights that were taken for granted in other countries. They had to do as the Nazis said, or risk imprisonment.

Why did the Nazis persecute many groups in German society?

The Aryans

Hitler and the Nazis believed that the Germanic race (the Aryans) were superior to all other people.

The ideal Aryan was tall with blond hair and blue eyes. Hitler liked to be photographed with people who looked like this.

The Nazis preached that Jews, gypsies and black people were inferior and not worthy of respect.

Jews' the scapegoat

In his book *Mein Kampf* (My Struggle) Hitler wrote that communists and Jews were to blame for Germany's defeat in the First World War. To begin with people took no notice of Hitler's opinions on race. After all many German Jews had fought bravely in the 1914-18 War.

But Nazi propaganda later led many German people to believe that the Jews were to blame for everything that had gone wrong in Germany since 1918. Once in power Hitler soon began to put his anti-Semitic (anti-Jewish) policies into action.

> **SOURCE E**
>
> All the science and technology we have today is almost entirely the work of the Germanic race.

Adolf Hitler writing in *Mein Kampf*, (My Struggle), 1925.

> **QUESTIONS**
>
> 1 How did Hitler bring down unemployment?
>
> 2 In what ways were German workers *worse off* under Hitler?
>
> 3 What did Hitler say about Aryans and Jews?

Life in Nazi Germany

Persecution of the Jews

- On 1 April 1933 the SA organised a **boycott** of Jewish shops. Members of the SA stood outside Jewish shops to scare people from going in to buy goods (see Source G).

- Also in 1933 the Nazis banned Jews from being teachers, doctors and journalists.

- In 1935 Jews were banned from public places such as swimming pools, parks and cinemas.

- In the same year the Nuremberg Laws were passed, which said that Jews could not be German citizens. Marriages between Jews and non-Jews were banned.

Kristallnacht

The Nazis arrested hundreds of Jews and sent them to concentration camps. Many Jews, frightened for their safety, fled Germany. In the 1930s half the German Jewish population left Germany. Things went from bad to worse. In 1938 a German politician was shot dead by a Jew in Paris. The Nazis reacted by ordering attacks on Jewish shops, homes and synagogues.

On the night of 9–10 November 1938 Nazi thugs went on the rampage in Germany. They burned down 267 synagogues and smashed the windows of over 8000 Jewish shops. This event became known as **Kristallnacht** (The Night of Broken Glass).

Over a hundred Jews were killed during *Kristallnacht* and thousands more were imprisoned.

SOURCE F

The front of a Jewish shop in September 1938.

SOURCE G

My grandmother went to a shop to buy some butter. In the doorway stood an SA man with a gun. He said, 'You don't want to buy from a Jew.' My grandmother shook her stick and said, 'I will buy my butter where I buy it every day.' She was the shop's only customer that day. Everyone else was too scared of the man with the gun.

A Berlin woman remembers an incident on 1 April 1933.

Afterwards, Jews were no longer allowed to run shops and factories and Jewish children were banned from attending school. The Jews had been very badly treated by the Nazis, but even worse was to follow during the Second World War (see pages 128-131).

Other minority groups

The Nazis also **persecuted** other minority groups in Germany.

1 The Nazis hated homosexuals. About 15,000 homosexuals were sent to concentration camps. Nazi doctors later carried out cruel medical experiments on homosexuals.

2 Gypsies were also badly treated. The Nazis said they were lazy and made them live on special sites. If they refused they were sent to concentration camps. Some gypsies were sterilised so they were unable to have children.

3 Disabled people did not fit in with the Nazi view that the Germans were the master race. In 1939 the Nazis put about 75,000 mentally and physically disabled people to death by lethal injection, gassing or starvation.

4 About half a million tramps and beggars were sent to labour camps, and many were sterilised.

SOURCE H

A cartoon of Jews from a Nazi newspaper in 1935. The Jewish butcher is making sausages from rats.

SOURCE I

Are you, German people, ready to work fourteen hours a day and do your utmost for victory? The country is ready for anything. The Fuhrer has commanded and we shall obey him.

A speech by Goebbels in 1943. He asked the audience ten questions and each was answered with loud shouts of agreement.

How did the coming of war change life in Germany?

In the early years of the Second World War, the Germans quickly took over much of western Europe. The German people were overjoyed, and felt they had at last got revenge for their harsh treatment under the Treaty of Versailles. Although food and clothes were rationed in Germany, this seemed a small price to pay for the success of the German army.

Hitler invades the Soviet Union

In June 1941 Hitler invaded the Soviet Union. At first, the German army did well. It pushed deep into the Soviet Union, but then the very cold winter set in. The German advance came to a halt. By early 1943 the Germans had suffered heavy casualties (nearly 200,000 men) and were on the retreat. The British had also defeated the German army in North Africa.

Sacrifices at home

The German people now realised how difficult war was when you were not winning. People were asked to make sacrifices for the war effort. They gave 1.5 million fur coats to the troops in the Soviet Union and worked longer hours in the factories.

Women also went to work in the factories to keep up production. Food rations were cut and the Nazis began a propaganda campaign aimed at making German people believe they could win the war. Goebbels, the head of Nazi propaganda, made a number of speeches in an effort to raise people's morale (Source I).

SOURCE J

DEFENCE OF THE NAZI HOME FRONT

BE CAREFUL TO FIX THEM SO THAT THEY CAN TURN BOTH WAYS

A cartoon in a British newspaper in August 1943.

Germany 1918–45

Bombing raids

In 1942 the Allies began bombing German cities, aiming to break the morale of the German people and force surrender.

Allied bombing raids on German cities killed more than half a million people. In one raid on Dresden in February 1945, 135,000 Germans died.

By early 1945 the German people were tired of the war. There was a shortage of food, major cities were in ruins and over three million civilians had been killed. Hitler refused to surrender and the fighting went on until 7 May. No wonder opposition to the Nazis grew in the last months of the war.

> **QUESTIONS**
>
> 1 How successful were the Nazis in the early years of the war?
>
> 2 Why were German civilians tired of the war by early 1945?

SOURCE K

Victims of the Dresden bombing, February 1945.

Life in Nazi Germany

Case Study: The 'Final Solution'

During the Second World War the Nazis conquered much of Europe. Millions of Jews came under Nazi control. Many Jews were sent to ghettos in the cities. These were areas that were sealed off from other parts of the city. Conditions in the ghettos were so bad that thousands of Jews starved to death.

Einsatzgruppen

When the German army invaded the Soviet Union in 1941, it was followed by four death squads called *Einsatzgruppen*, whose job was to kill communist officials and Jews. By the end of 1941 they had murdered half a million Jews.

The setting up of the extermination camps

In January 1942 the Nazis decided on the **Final Solution** to the 'Jewish problem'. The Jews in Europe were to be rounded up and sent to extermination camps. Here they would be put to death. Six concentration camps were turned into extermination camps (see map on page 131). Huge chambers were built, disguised as showers. Up to 2000 Jews at a time were led into the chambers believing they were to have a shower. Gas was then released and within three minutes everyone was dead. The bodies were then burned in huge ovens.

By 1945, six million Jews had been murdered in what became known as the **Holocaust**.

The need for secrecy

The Nazis kept these events secret. Instead, they made propaganda films that gave the impression the Jews were being treated well in the camps. The Nazis said they were 'resettling' the Jews.

The countries fighting the Nazis had an idea that something terrible was happening to the Jews, but there was little they could do. In 1945 as Allied troops began to liberate Germany they found the extermination camps, and the real horror of what had happened to the Jews became known.

Knowing that they were going to be defeated, the Nazis tried to cover up what had happened in the concentration camps. It was impossible to do this, however, as the Allies found many mass graves. Inside the camps were thousands of Jewish people whom the Nazis had left behind to die of starvation or disease.

Number of Jews killed in death camps and by the Einsatzgruppen.

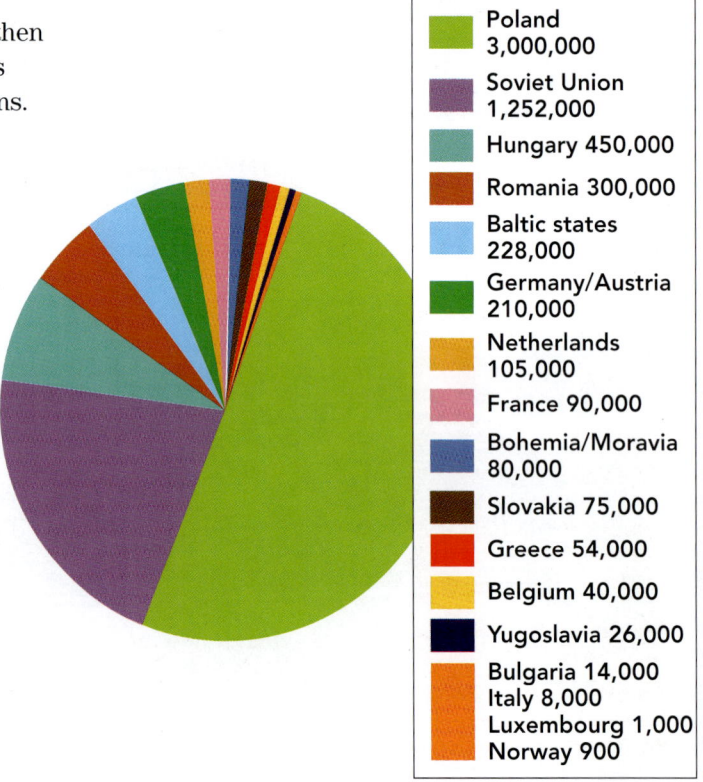

- Poland 3,000,000
- Soviet Union 1,252,000
- Hungary 450,000
- Romania 300,000
- Baltic states 228,000
- Germany/Austria 210,000
- Netherlands 105,000
- France 90,000
- Bohemia/Moravia 80,000
- Slovakia 75,000
- Greece 54,000
- Belgium 40,000
- Yugoslavia 26,000
- Bulgaria 14,000
- Italy 8,000
- Luxembourg 1,000
- Norway 900

The Nuremberg Trials

- Hitler, Goebbels and Himmler committed suicide in 1945. The treatment of the Jews was the main reason why 21 senior Nazis were put on trial for war crimes at Nuremberg in 1946. Eleven were hanged, seven imprisoned and three acquitted. Goering poisoned himself in his cell the day before he was due to be executed.

- At Auschwitz extermination camp over two million Jews were murdered. The head of Auschwitz, Rudolf Hoess, went in hiding at the end of the war but was soon arrested in Poland. At his trial, Hoess claimed he was a good family man and that he had merely obeyed orders. The court found him guilty and he was executed in 1947.

The case of Anthony Sawoniuk, a former British Rail worker, tried for war crimes in Britain in 1999. The trial cost over £1 million. Sawoniuk was found guilty of 18 murders and sentenced to life imprisonment.

The Case of Anthony Sawoniuk

In February 1999 Anthony Sawoniuk was put on trial in Britain. He was charged with murdering 16 Jewish women and 4 Jewish men in 1942.

At the time he was a policeman in the Soviet Union. The Germans murdered 3000 Jews near his village. It was said that Sawoniuk helped the Germans to round up the Jews and that he killed those who tried to escape.

78-year-old Sawoniuk told the court he was deaf in one ear, diabetic and suffering from heart disease and brain damage. The judge said, 'there can be no trial in our history that has been more emotive than this.'

QUESTIONS

1 What were *Einsatzgruppen*?

2 What did the Nazis mean by the 'Final Solution'?

3 Why did it take until the end of the war for people to learn what had happened to the Jews?

4 Some people say there is no longer any point trying to convict those accused of killing Jews in the war.
   a Why do you think they say this?
   b Do you agree?

Use the case of Anthony Sawoniuk to help you answer.

The 'Final Solution'   131

Paper 1-type assessment: Germany 1918-45

SOURCE A

A cartoon from an American newspaper in February 1936.

"In these three years I have restored honor and freedom to the German people!"

SOURCE B

We didn't know much about Nazi ideals. Nevertheless we were politically programmed to obey orders, to cultivate the soldierly virtue of standing to attention and saying 'Yes, Sir', and to stop thinking when the word 'Fatherland' was uttered and Germany's honour and greatness was mentioned.

A member of the Hitler Youth commenting after the war.

QUESTIONS

When answering these questions make sure you answer ALL three parts.

Remember that you should always explain your answer as fully as you can and support it with specific detail where possible.

Section C Questions

1 Study the sources carefully and then answer the three questions which follow.

   a Study Source A. Is this an accurate portrayal of how the Nazis governed Germany? Use the source and your own knowledge to explain your answer. (7)

   b Study Source B. How far does this source explain why the Nazis had the support of the German people? Use the source and your own knowledge to explain your answer. (7)

   c Study Source C. Do you think that the cartoonist supported or opposed the Nazi Party? Use the source and your own knowledge to explain your answer. (6)

2 a Describe the problems faced by the governments of the Weimar Republic in the years 1919-22. (4)

   b Explain why Germany was restored to prosperity in the period 1924-29. (6)

   c Explain how the following together contributed to the rise of the Nazi Party up to 1933:
   i the economic depression from 1929
   ii the Nazi Party's use of propaganda
   iii the weaknesses of the Weimar Republic. (10)

3 a What happened on the 'Night of the Long Knives'? (4)

   b Explain why the Nazis persecuted many groups in German society. (6)

   c Explain how the following together contributed to the success of the Nazis in maintaining themselves in power in the period 1933-39:
   i the Enabling Law
   ii the economic policies of the Nazis
   iii Nazi policies towards the young. (10)

SOURCE C

A cartoon from a British newspaper in 1934 commenting on the 'Night of the Long Knives'.

4 The USA 1919–41

- The USA came out of the First World War as the richest country in the world. During the 1920s industries made more and more products for the Americans to buy. Many ordinary people could afford goods, such as motor cars, radios and washing machines. Americans had more and more money to spend and plenty of leisure time in which to spend it. This was the 'Jazz Age' or the 'Roaring Twenties', a time to party and have fun.

- However, many Americans still lived in poverty during the 1920s. Farm workers in rural areas were particularly poor, with agriculture facing a crisis of overproduction and falling prices. Black people and immigrants faced discrimination in housing, education and employment. The banning of the sale of alcohol led to a growth in organised crime.

- Overproduction and the Wall Street Crash of 1929 brought the party to an end and started the Great Depression. The collapse of the stock market led to high unemployment and thousands of businesses went bust.

- President Hoover failed to deal with the effects of the Depression. He lost the 1932 presidential election to Franklin Roosevelt, who promised a 'New Deal' for the American people.

- The New Deal spent government money to create new jobs. After 1933 unemployment came down, but it took the Second World War to get all Americans back to work.

This topic is examined in Paper 1 of the examination. Paper 1-type exercises are included at the end of the chapter. Mark schemes, sample answers and comments can be found in the accompanying Teacher's Resource Pack.

A map of the USA showing states and major cities

The USA 1919–41

How far did the US economy boom in the 1920s?

- For most Americans the 1920s were boom years. No fighting took place in the USA in the First World War, so American industry was not damaged. American factories had kept going and production went up. The USA was also owed vast sums of money by the Allies, to whom it had lent money to help fight the war.

- During the 1920s the American government cut taxes so people had more money to spend. The government also helped American industry by putting taxes, called **tariffs**, on foreign goods coming into the USA. This made foreign goods more expensive than American goods.

- Farmers and black people, however, did not share in the boom and stayed poor. The economic boom in the USA came to an end at the end of the 1920s.

On what factors was the economic boom based?

1 The USA's wealth
By the early 1900s the USA was the world's leading industrial nation. It was rich in raw materials such as coal, iron ore and oil and also had a lot of fertile farming land.

The American people were hard working and wanted to make the most of their opportunities.

2 New industries
American industrial production increased by about 50 per cent during the 1920s. New industries were set up producing electrical goods such as washing machines, refrigerators, vacuum cleaners and radios. The demand for these products was very high. New materials such as rayon and plastic were also developed. The most important new industry was the manufacture of motor cars.

3 Rising wages and cheaper prices
During the 1920s, goods, such as cars and radios, were produced in large numbers using assembly lines. This made them cheap to make and the price of goods fell.

At the same time wages went up, so people were able to afford all the new products that were coming on the market. Assembly lines were first used to make motor cars by Henry Ford, but it was a method that was soon widely copied by other industries.

4 Government policies
- Throughout the 1920s the Republican Party was in power in the USA. Republicans believed that the government should leave industry alone and allow factory owners to manage their own affairs.

- The Republican president from 1923 to 1929, Calvin Coolidge, said, 'The business of America is business.' The government cut taxes so that industries had more money to invest in new factories and machinery.

- American factory owners told the government they did not want any competition from cheap foreign imports. The government therefore put a tariff on foreign goods entering the USA making them more expensive to buy than American goods.

- By the end of the 1920s, however, other countries were putting tariffs on American goods. This then made it more difficult for the USA to export goods.

5 Hire purchase

People were able to buy goods such as motor cars by **hire purchase**.

They put down a small deposit and then paid the rest off in instalments over a long period of time.

People were also able to buy goods by mail order. For example, Sears, Roebuck and Company of Chicago posted glossy catalogues to people all over the USA, enabling them to buy the latest fashions (see Source A).

6 Weak trade unions

The Republican governments and businessmen did not like trade unions. Employers were allowed to use violence to attack strikers.

Many workers were not allowed to join a trade union. In the car industry, for example, trade unions were banned until the 1930s. As trade unions were weak employers were able to pay low wages, allowing them to make big profits. Only a few employers, such as Henry Ford, were forward-looking enough to pay wages above the going rate and cut the hours of work.

SOURCE A

The front cover of the Sears, Roebuck catalogue for the spring and summer, 1927.

Henry Ford and the motor car industry

- The motor car industry started in the early 1900s.
- The greatest figure in the growth of the car industry was Henry Ford who set up the Ford Motor Company in 1903.
- By 1908 Ford had developed the first 'Model T', a car designed for the masses and not just the rich.
- From 1913 the Model T was manufactured using an assembly line. Before this one worker would carry out a range of jobs in the making of a car.
- With an assembly line workers would do just one job - say, bolting in a seat, as the car moved along the line.
- This meant large numbers of cars could be built more quickly and cheaply than ever before.
- The price of a Model T fell from $850 in 1908 to $260 in 1924. This meant that even ordinary people could afford to buy one.
- Ford stopped making the Model T in 1927, by which time 15 million had been sold.

By 1929 half a million people were employed in making cars, more than any other industry. At this time there were 27 million cars in use in the USA.

The three biggest car firms were Ford, General Motors and Chrysler.

Many more were employed in 'spin-off' industries such as firms making car parts, the oil industry and road building. Hotels and restaurants also sprang up across the USA, as people were able to travel about much more.

SOURCE B

An advertisement for an early Model T Ford.

The social consequences of the motor car

Before the motor car, people depended on railways and horse drawn coaches to travel around. The motor car meant people had the freedom to travel where they wanted, when they wanted.

> ### SOURCE C
>
> It is obvious that the car was faster than the horse and carriage. The Model T car was also cheaper than a horse and carriage.
>
> A car only uses up fuel when it is moving; a horse has to be fed all year round.
>
> The Model T gave mobility and freedom and at a lower cost. This was a product which sold itself. The Model T had a very simple design. There were no doors and no side windows; there was no speedometer or windshield wiper.
>
> There was no choice of colour as they were all black.
>
> The engine of the Model T was so simple it could easily be repaired by the driver himself. No wonder sales rocketed.

A description of the Model T Ford, adapted from a modern American history book.

- Farmers could now drive to the nearest town to buy supplies.
- Young people could drive into town for entertainment.
- People who lived in the cities could go for drives in the countryside.
- People were no longer tied to their home area and could travel around looking for work.

Why did some industries prosper while others did not?

- The most prosperous industries in the 1920s were new industries such as those making cars and electrical goods. Most people could now afford these products when before they had been too expensive. The building industry also enjoyed success. Many tall buildings called skyscrapers were built in American cities.

- Older industries such as cotton textiles and coal mining did not do as well as the new industries. People bought new fabrics such as nylon and rayon rather than cotton. This forced cotton factories to close down. Demand for coal fell because electricity and gas was being used for heating. As a result, many coalmines had to close down.

However, in general, American industry was very prosperous in the 1920s.

QUESTIONS

1. What factors helped American industry to prosper in the 1920s?
2. What part did Henry Ford play in the growth of the car industry?

SOURCE D

Building workers on the Empire State Building in New York. Finished in 1931, this was the highest building in the world at the time.

Why did agriculture not share in the prosperity?

Overproduction

During the 1920s American farmers grew more food than the country could eat or use. Food prices dropped and, with them, farmers' incomes. Only 10 per cent of farmers could afford electric lights or mains water supplies.

Many farmers borrowed money from banks, hoping that prices would go back up. They never did. So they were unable to pay back the money. They had to leave their farms and give them up to the banks. In 1920, 27 per cent of the USA's labour force was employed in farming, but by 1930 this figure had dropped to 21 per cent.

Sharecropping

Worst hit were the southern states of the USA. Farms here depended on a single crop such as cotton or tobacco. Not only were prices at rock bottom, but the crops were often destroyed by pests such as the boll-weevil. Most of the farm workers were black people. They were either paid a very poor wage or employed as **sharecroppers**.

This meant they were not paid any wages but, instead, they were given a share of what the crop made when it was sold. When, as in the 1920s, prices were low they received hardly any money.

140   The USA 1919–41

SOURCE E

Child workers in the cotton fields in the 1920s.

Did all Americans benefit from the boom?

- The USA became richer during the 1920s but the wealth was not shared out equally. In 1929 one third of all income was earned by just 5 per cent of the workforce. In the same year about 60 per cent of American families were still living in poverty.

- Some parts of the USA prospered more than others in the 1920s. Industrial areas were much more prosperous than farming areas. Wheat farmers on the Great Plains, for example, received very low prices for their crops because of falling demand and competition from abroad.

Black people in the USA

- Most black Americans lived in the southern states such as Georgia and Kentucky. During the First World War (1914–18) many moved to the northern cities to work in the factories. After the war there were fewer jobs in the cities, and white people objected to black people still being employed. As a result, there were race riots against black people in many cities during 1919.

- Those black Americans who had stayed in the southern states faced even worse problems. They worked as farm labourers and had to put up with low wages and terrible living conditions.

- Native American people also suffered, being made to live on reservations in poor conditions.

- So, despite the economic boom of the 1920s the USA was a deeply divided society. There were big differences between rich and poor, white and black, city and country.

QUESTIONS

1 Why did farmers do badly in the 1920s?
2 What were living conditions like for black Americans in the 1920s?

How far did US society change in the 1920s?

What were the 'Roaring Twenties'?

- After the First World War people wanted to enjoy themselves. Many had money to spend and plenty of leisure time. The 1920s became known as the 'Roaring Twenties'. Young fashionable women, known as 'flappers' smoked, dated and danced the Charleston. The entertainment industry boomed. People went to the cinema, dances, concerts and listened to jazz music. Although alcohol was prohibited (banned) in the 1920s, this did not stop people from drinking in illegal bars, known as 'speakeasies'.

- But there was another side to the 1920s. Not everyone approved of such 'wild' leisure pursuits. Many of the older generation wondered what the world was coming to. There was also widespread discrimination against black Americans who were not allowed to join in the fun.

The movies

- The popularity of movies (films) soared during the 1920s. By 1929, 95 million people a week were going to the cinema. Hollywood in California was the centre of the movie industry. Here were the studios of the big movie companies, such as MGM and Warner Brothers. All sorts of movies were made in Hollywood, including comedies, romances and westerns.

- Movie stars such as Charlie Chaplin, Clara Bow and Rudolf Valentino became household names. Valentino was such a heart-throb that thousands attended his funeral when he died in 1926. Several fans were so upset they even committed suicide.

The Hays Code

Some people, however, were worried that movies were having a bad effect on the morals of the young. So, in 1922, the Hays Code set out strict rules about what could be shown in films. The Hays Code banned complete nudity in films and said that screen kisses should last no more than seven feet of film. Despite this the Hays Code did little to change what was shown on the screen.

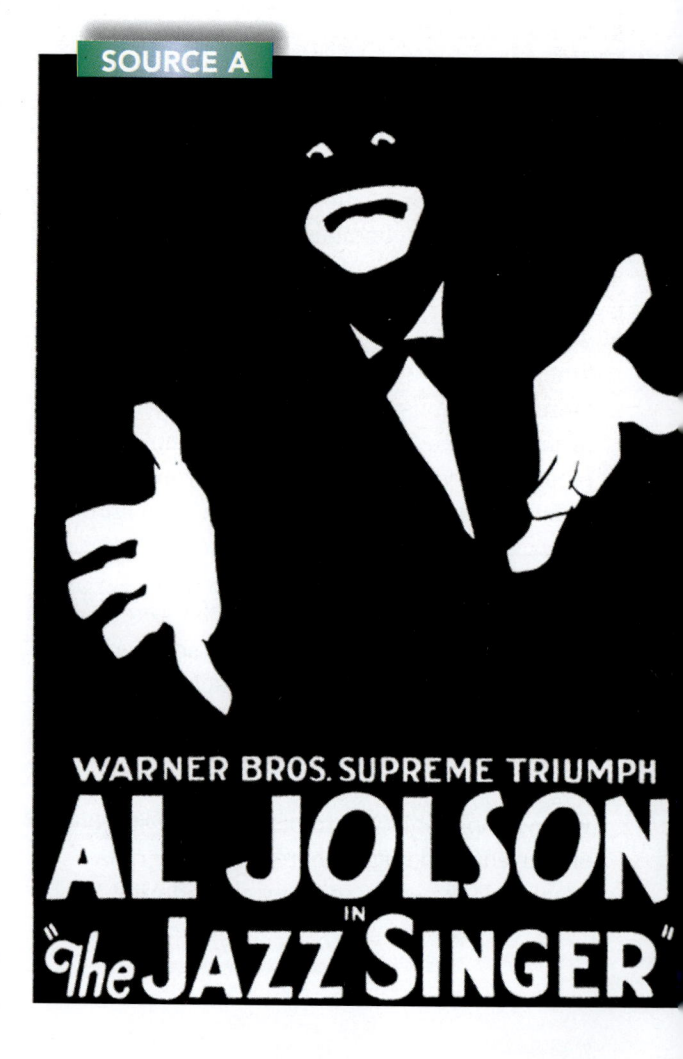

SOURCE A

A poster for the film, *The Jazz Singer*, 1927.

SOURCE B

Babe Ruth in action.

Sport

With plenty of money and leisure time people attended sporting events in great numbers.

- **Baseball** was popular with working class people in the cities. There were many great players. One of the most famous was 'Babe' Ruth of the New York Yankees. In 1927 season he recorded 60 home runs, a record that lasted until 1961. By 1930 Babe Ruth was earning $80,000 a year, a huge amount for that time.

- **Boxing** was also popular. The most famous boxer was Jack Dempsey, who was world heavyweight champion from 1919 to 1926. Dempsey was well known for his powerful punching and was a great favourite with the fans.

- **Golf** had one of the greatest sporting heroes of the time. Bobby Jones was the best golfer in the world, but was also a good sport. He once lost his ball in some trees. While looking for it he accidentally trod on it. No one saw this happen, but Jones told his opponent and accepted a penalty of one shot.

The Jazz Singer

People liked films because they provided an escape from everyday life. The film companies were aware of this, so they built grand and glamorous cinemas that were known as 'picture palaces'. This made going to the cinema a fantastic experience.

In 1927 Warner Brothers released *The Jazz Singer*, starring Al Jolson. It was the first 'talkie' film. Before this all films had been silent. The talkies spelt the end for many film stars who looked good, but had unattractive voices.

American society in the 1920s

SOURCE C

A Chicago night club in the 1920s.

QUESTIONS

1 What entertainment was available to Americans during the 'Roaring Twenties'?

2 Why did some Americans dislike the new forms of entertainment?

Music

- The 1920s were also known as the 'Jazz Age'. Jazz was a new kind of music that grew out of earlier forms of black music such as blues and ragtime. When black people moved from the southern states to the northern cities after the First World War, they took jazz music with them. The most famous jazz musicians, such as Duke Ellington, Louis Armstrong and 'Jelly Roll' Morton were all black.

- Jazz was always being played on the radio and became very popular with white people. The northern cities, such as New York and Chicago, had numerous jazz clubs, but in many of them the only black people allowed were the musicians. Even the famous Cotton Club in New York was owned by white people.

- New dance crazes also took hold in the 1920s. The two most popular were the Charleston and the Black Bottom. These dances were very suggestive and shocked the older generation.

Radio

Music was constantly played on American radio. Sales of records fell as the popularity of the radio increased. Not many people had a radio in 1920 but, by 1929, about 40 per cent of families owned one. Americans listened keenly to music, sport commentaries and comedy programmes.

The first local radio station started in Pittsburgh in 1920 and the first national station was opened in 1926. Radio stations earned money by broadcasting adverts.

How widespread was intolerance in US society?

Immigration

During the 1800s millions of people left Europe to build a new life in the USA. By the early 1900s, however, the Americans began to feel that the country was full up. They felt there was no more room for any more immigrants from Europe.

Immigration into the USA

1821–1880:	10,189,429
1881–1920:	23,465,356
Total	33,654,785

144   The USA 1919–41

The First World War stirred up a hatred of foreigners, especially German people. Many Americans hated the slums of the cities full of immigrants from numerous countries. They decided that they had to limit the number of immigrants allowed into the USA.

In 1924 the American Congress (parliament) passed a law that said only 150,000 immigrants a year would be let into the USA.

The Red Scare

- In 1917 communists took control of Russia. The Americans hated communism. They were frightened that communism would take over the world and thought that immigrants from Europe would bring communist ideas into the USA.

- In 1919 Attorney-General Palmer rounded up thousands of suspected communists after a number of industrial strikes. Those who were recent immigrants were sent back to Europe.

- A wave of anti-communist feeling, known as the **Red Scare**, swept the USA. This reached its height when Palmer's house in Washington was blown up.

The Sacco and Vanzetti case

- In April 1920 there was a robbery at a shoe factory in Massachusetts. The robbers stole $16,000 and shot dead two people. Two Italian immigrants, Nicola Sacco and Bartolomeo Vanzetti were arrested and charged with the crime, even though there was no real evidence against them. The two men were picked on because they were **anarchists** and did not believe in organised government. They were also immigrants and this put the police and judge against them.

- The trial was a **farce**. The two men kept saying they were innocent, but the judge made it clear he wanted the jury to find them guilty. Sacco and Vanzetti were convicted and sentenced to death. For the next six years they both pleaded their innocence and called for a retrial.

- An international campaign called for their release, but without success. Although another man confessed to the crime, Sacco and Vanzetti were executed in the electric chair in August 1927. They were the most famous victims of the Red Scare.

SOURCE D

QUESTION

1 Why were Sacco and Vanzetti executed even though someone else confessed to the crime?

A painting of Sacco and Vanzetti.

American society in the 1920s

Discrimination against blacks

- In the southern states black people lived in poverty. Most black people were farm workers and were very badly paid.

- Black people were kept apart from whites by the 'Jim Crow' laws. These laws made sure that black people lived in separate areas and went to separate schools. They also banned black people from using the same restaurants and buses as white people.

- Many white people formed lynch mobs and murdered black people for no reason at all, other than the colour of their skin. White judges and policemen usually turned a blind eye to these **lynchings**. In the early 1920s there were about 50 lynchings each year but few people were ever brought to justice.

- There were also racism and discrimination in the northern cities. Black people lived in slum areas, found it hard to get jobs and were paid low wages.

- White people looked upon black people as inferior. Bad feeling between the two groups sometimes led to race riots. Although ten per cent of the USA's population was black they did not have equal rights with white people. They were treated like second class citizens in their own country.

SOURCE E

A black family and their home in Virginia in the 1920s.

The Ku Klux Klan

At the end of the American Civil War in 1865, black slaves in the southern states were set free. Some white people did not like this so they formed the **Ku Klux Klan** to terrorise the black people.

Members of the Klan dressed in white robes and wore pointed hoods to hide their faces. They terrified black people, burning down houses and shops. They also tarred and feathered black people. This means that victims were covered in tar and feathers as a punishment.

- The Klan faded away for a time but was restarted in 1915. This time it targeted Catholics, Jews and foreigners as well as black people. The Klan grew in numbers. By 1925, it had 5 million members. The Klan said it stood for 'true American values' – the values of white, Protestant, rural America. Most other Americans looked on the Klan as racist thugs.

SOURCE F

Klansmen marching through a town in New Jersey.

- Although it was a secretive group, the Klan paraded openly in large cities (see Source F). During this time Klan members carried out a number of terrible murders. The Klan's racist views were similar to those later put forward by the Nazis in Germany in the 1930s.

- At the end of the 1920s, membership of the Klan went down. It lost its appeal when a Klan leader was convicted of raping and murdering a woman on a train. After this the Klan was not heard of so much, but it was still a threat to black people in small towns in the south.

QUESTIONS

1 How were black Americans treated in the 1920s?

2 What was the Ku Klux Klan?

American society in the 1920s

The 'Monkey Trial' 1925

The case

Johnny Scopes, a Biology teacher in Dayton, Tennessee was found to be giving lessons on Charles Darwin's theory of evolution. This went against a state law, passed in 1925, which forbade the teaching of the theory of evolution, because it went against the story of creation given in the Bible. People in the southern states were very traditional in their religious beliefs. Scopes was arrested and put on trial.

Two famous lawyers

The issue was whether the fundamental religious beliefs of rural America could be upheld against the advance of science. Two famous lawyers argued the case.

For the Prosecution	For the Defence
William Jennings Bryan, a religious fundamentalist who said that the theory of evolution was wrong.	Clarence Darrow, hired by the American Civil Liberties Union.

Wide press coverage

Journalists flocked to Tennessee to cover the case. They called it the 'Monkey Trial' because Darwin's theory of evolution said that humans evolved from apes. Darrow knew he could not win the case because Scopes had deliberately broken the law. His aim was to show that the anti-evolution law of 1925 was a threat to freedom of thought and speech.

Darrow called Bryan to give evidence and questioned him about his religious beliefs (Source G). Under this questioning Bryan admitted that he did not believe everything that was written in the Bible. As a result Bryan's credibility was destroyed. Scopes was found guilty and fined $100, but the religious fundamentalists had been made to look rather silly. The anti-evolution law was never used again and in 1926 the verdict against Scope was overturned.

SOURCE G

Q: [Darrow] Do you think the sun was made on the fourth day?
A: [Bryan] Yes.
Q: And they had morning and evening without the sun?
A: I am simply saying it is a period.
Q: The creation might have been going on a long time?
A: It might have continued for millions of years.

An extract from Darrow's cross-examination of Bryan. He is asking about the story of creation in the Bible.

SOURCE H

The main people in the 'Monkey Trial' of 1925.

QUESTIONS

1 Why did the 'Monkey Trial' come to court?
2 Why do you think people in the southern states were opposed to Darwin's ideas?
3 Who won the case? (Think carefully.)

Why was prohibition introduced?

In 1919 Congress (the American parliament) passed a law which banned the making and selling of alcohol anywhere in the USA. This was known as **prohibition**. The prohibition of alcohol lasted until 1933, but why was it introduced in the first place?

1 It already existed
Some states already had prohibition laws in place. The law passed by Congress simply made the ban on alcohol nation-wide.

2 Moral reasons
Many people were against the sale of alcohol and said that alcohol caused problems such as violence, poverty, sexual immorality and crime. They said that if alcohol was banned the USA would be a healthier and more moral country in which to live.

3 Campaigners
Many groups campaigned to get alcohol banned.

- The **Anti-Saloon League of America**, founded in 1893, put pressure on politicians to ban alcohol. Politicians listened to what the League said because they did not want to lose votes. The League had a lot of influence and people voted 'dry' politicians (who supported prohibition) into Congress. The most support for prohibition came from people living in rural areas. Prohibition showed the division in beliefs between rural areas and cities. One prohibition campaigner said: 'The USA can only be saved by using the pure morals of the country to flush out the cesspools of cities, and so save our country from pollution.'

- Churches supported the League and said that a ban on alcohol would improve people's behaviour.

SOURCE I
Daddy's in There---

An Anti-Saloon League poster.

4 The First World War
People of German descent owned many of the breweries in the USA. When the USA joined the First World War in 1917, there was a lot of anti-German feeling amongst Americans. They forced breweries to close down, saying that the grain used to make alcohol was needed to feed the USA's allies in Europe.

QUESTIONS
1. What was prohibition?
2. Look at Source I. Explain the message of this cartoon.
3. What other reasons did people have for wanting alcohol banned?

What were the effects of prohibition?

1 More alcohol was drunk

Once alcohol was banned it actually became more attractive to people. Many people ignored the law and illegal bars, known as 'speakeasies', opened in their thousands.

The amount of alcohol people drunk went up. Alcohol was still easy to obtain:

- **Moonshine** Many people made their own alcohol, which was known as 'moonshine'. Much of it was poisonous and many people died from drinking it. Government prohibition agents tried to stop the production of moonshine, but there were so many illegal breweries and distilleries they had an impossible job.

- **Smuggling** Smugglers brought alcohol into the USA from Canada and the West Indies. In four years one smuggler, William McCoy, smuggled $70 million worth of whisky into the USA.

2 Organised crime

Gangsters controlled the speakeasies. They made huge profits from the sale of illegal alcohol.

The gangsters **bribed** judges, politicians and the police into turning a blind eye. This meant that gangsters, such as Al Capone, could operate without fear of being arrested.

Rivalry between the many gangs led to violence in cities such as Chicago. Between 1927 and 1931 over 200 gangsters were murdered in Chicago. No-one was arrested for these crimes!

	1921	1925	1929
Illegal distilleries seized	9,746	12,023	15,794
Gallons of distilled spirits seized	414,000	1,103,000	1,186,000
Number of arrests	34,175	62,747	66,878

Al Capone

- Al 'Scarface' Capone became the boss of the Mafia in Chicago in 1925.
- He used violent methods to attack rival gangs and was involved in dozens of murders.
- The violence reached its peak with the St Valentine's Day Massacre in 1929. Seven members of a rival gang were machine-gunned to death.
- At the end of the 1920s, Capone was making $100 million a year. It was rumoured that he gave $100 dollar tips to waiters.
- Capone's career as the USA's most feared gangster came to an end when Government agents arrested him in 1931. He was imprisoned for eleven years for tax dodging.

QUESTION

Look at the table. Do the figures show that the ban on alcohol was successful?

Explain your answer.

The fight against alcohol production in the USA, 1921-9.

SOURCE J

The murder of Frank Yale, liquor boss of New York, who was killed on Capone's orders in 1928.

SOURCE K

In 1929 just one gang challenged Capone's control of Chicago's underworld: George 'Bugs' Moran's North Side gang. Capone decided he would put a bloody end to the rivalry on St Valentine's Day.

On 14 February, a Cadillac disguised as a police car pulled up outside a garage that was used as Moran's headquarters. Four men, disguised as police officers, got out of the car.

Inside the garage the phoney policemen lined up six gangsters against a wall. Suddenly two opened fire with machine guns. The other two used shotguns to finish off anyone still twitching.

One of Moran's men survived for a few hours. When a real policeman asked who had shot him, he kept to the 'gangster's code'. 'No-one,' he said. Luckily, Moran was not present when the murders took place. When he found out, he shouted, 'Only Capone kills like that!'

A historian's account of the St Valentine's Day Massacre.

Why was prohibition ended?

People soon realised that prohibition was not working and was causing damage. When the Great Depression came millions of people were thrown out of work. It seemed wrong that the government was wasting money trying to enforce prohibition. The money could be better spent on helping the poor.

'Wets' (people who were against prohibition) said that making alcohol legal again would be a good thing.

- It would provide people with jobs in breweries.
- The government could get money by taxing sales of alcohol.

In March 1933 Franklin Roosevelt became the new president of the USA. He ended prohibition in December 1933, joking that it 'would be a good time for a beer!'

QUESTIONS

1. How did people get round the ban on alcohol?
2. Why was prohibition ended?

How far did the roles of women change during the 1920s?

1 More freedom

In 1920 women in the USA won the right to vote. During the 1920s more and more women went out to work. For the first time they earned their own money. They no longer had to stay at home and rely on men to support them.

This meant that some women could make their own decisions about how to live. Labour saving machines, such as washing machines and vacuum machines, also provided women with more leisure time.

2 Changing fashions

- Fashions changed in the 1920s. Some women cut their hair short in the new 'bobbed' style, wore make-up and smoked in public. Skirts became much shorter than they had been before the First World War.

- However, we should not make too much of these changes. Many older people thought it was improper to wear short skirts and wear make-up. Also, the majority of women were not affected by the changes. They were too busy raising a family to go out partying. The new fashions also had a bigger impact on women in cities than those who lived in the countryside. Here women had to keep to old-fashioned values of decency and respectability.

SOURCE L

Women's fashions of the 1920s.

SOURCE M

Think of the modern young American girl. She is the loveliest creature, and has the brightest mind - if only it were used.

Do they ever think, these beautiful young girls? It would seem not. Their aim seems to be to flirt with men, and get money. Has the American girl no self-respect?

What can a man with a mind find in these lovely, brainless, cigarette-smoking girls?

Written by a female English journalist in 1921.

QUESTION

1 Do you agree that the lives of *all* American women changed in the 1920s?

What were the causes and consequences of the Wall Street Crash?

- In 1928 Herbert Hoover, a Republican, was elected President of the USA. At the time the country was still prosperous. Hoover told the people that soon there would be no more poverty in the USA, but he turned out to be completely wrong.

- In October 1929 the Wall Street **stock market** in New York crashed. Share prices started to fall so people began to panic sell their shares. This made prices fall to rock bottom. The Great Depression followed. Thousands of businesses and factories went bankrupt and about 13 million people lost their jobs. Hoover's Republican government did not do enough to help them. This led to Franklin Delano Roosevelt, a Democrat, winning the 1932 presidential election.

How far was speculation responsible for the Wall Street Crash?

The workings of the stock market

- A stock market is where people buy and sell shares in companies and businesses. The American stock market is on Wall Street in New York.

- People buy shares in companies hoping to make money. People who have shares in companies are called **shareholders**. If the company does well, it shares its profits out among its shareholders by paying them a dividend. The price of shares rises and shareholders can, if they wish, sell their shares and make money. If a company does badly, however, its share price falls and shareholders lose money.

Speculating on the stock market

- During the boom of the 1920s most companies were doing very well. People began speculating by buying shares as way of making some easy money. They believed share prices would keep going up, so they would be able to sell their shares at a profit. Like Hoover, they thought the good times would go on forever.

- Many people borrowed money to buy shares. As soon as the price went up they were able to sell their shares, pay back the loan and still be in profit. This was called '**buying on the margin**'. It was a good way of making money, as long as share prices kept going up.

SOURCE A

We, in America, have almost brought poverty to an end. We have not quite done it yet. But if we keep going with the Republican policies of the last eight years, the day is in sight when poverty will be gone forever.

Herbert Hoover, speaking during the presidential election campaign of 1928.

QUESTIONS

1. What is a stock market?
2. Why did Americans buy shares in the 1920s?

The banks were pleased to lend people money as they could charge interest on the loan. Share prices went up and up. People became greedy and did not think about what would happen if the 'bubble' burst.

The American economy slows down

The American economy did well in the 1920s. By 1928, however, there were signs that the economy was slowing down.

- The USA was not selling so many goods abroad.

- Farming was in a bad state.

- Most people had bought washing machines and vacuum cleaners for their homes, so the demand for these products fell. Companies were now making more goods than they could sell.

People slowly came to realise that the boom had been built on debt. Investors and companies owed money to the banks that had loaned money too easily. Shareholders grew nervous. The economic boom was about to come to a sudden end.

What impact did the Crash have on the economy?

- On Thursday 24 October 1929 ('Black Thursday') people began selling shares. Prices dropped and soon panic-selling set in. The big banks were forced to buy shares to stop the prices falling further. By the end of the day prices had recovered a bit, but thousands of people had been ruined by selling their shares at a loss.

- On Monday 28 October share prices fell sharply again. This time the big banks did not step in to buy shares.

- On Tuesday 29 October over 16 million shares were sold at a loss. About $10,000 million were lost during the day. Thousands went bankrupt, including people who had bought 'on the margin', banks that had lent money and companies whose shares were now worthless.

The Wall Street Crash was to have terrible results for both the USA and the rest of the world.

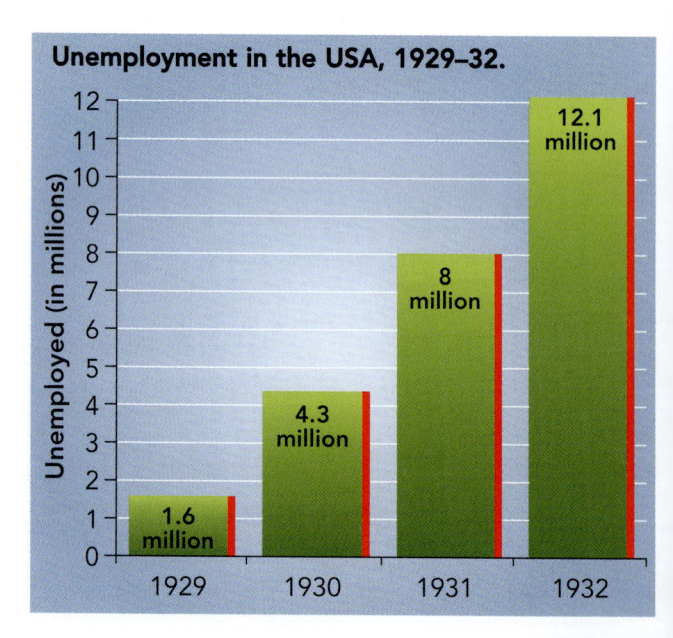

Unemployment in the USA, 1929–32.

Year	Unemployed (in millions)
1929	1.6 million
1930	4.3 million
1931	8 million
1932	12.1 million

SOURCE B

We seem to have stepped through a mirror into a world where everything shrinks, including share prices, the price of goods and employment.

One writer sums up the plight of the USA after the Wall Street Crash.

SOURCE C

A car for sale after the Wall Street Crash, October 1929.

What were the financial and economic effects of the Wall Street Crash?

- The Wall Street Crash sparked off the Great Depression. Factories closed down, production fell and people were thrown out of work. The trading of goods also fell away and, as a result, the Depression spread to other countries.

- People had lost money in the Crash and now had less to spend. Factories could not sell their goods. In 1929, 4.5 million cars were sold in the USA, but only one million were sold in 1932. Factories were forced to close. As a result unemployment went up rapidly.

- Over 5000 banks had closed down because of the Crash so factories were unable to borrow money to keep going.

- By 1932 over 12 million people were out of work. (See the graph on page 154.)

- By 1933 production of goods was down by 80 per cent compared with 1929.

What action was taken by President Hoover?

Hoover failed to deal with the effects of the Crash, believing that the government should keep out of the affairs of companies. He thought everything would get back to normal given time.

But things did not improve and even Hoover came to realise that the government would have to take some action.

- The Reconstruction Finance Commission was set up to lend money to companies in trouble.

- States were asked to use the unemployed to build roads, houses and hospitals.

- The Federal Farm Board was set up to buy surplus crops from farmers.

SOURCE D

Hungry unemployed people in New York queue for food on Christmas Day 1931.

The measures taken by Hoover did not make much difference. In some cases, he made things worse. In 1930 he put higher taxes on goods coming into the USA.

Other countries did the same to American goods, which made it harder for the USA to sell goods abroad.

Hoover became very unpopular with the American people and they made fun of him. Shanty towns built by homeless unemployed people were nicknamed 'Hoovervilles'.

People thought Hoover was heartless and uncaring. This was untrue, but he was not the right man to help the USA to recover.

QUESTIONS

1. What happened on 'Black Thursday' 1929?
2. What were the effects of the Wall Street crash for factories and businesses?
3. What did the Americans think of President Hoover?

What were the social consequences of the Crash?

1 Breadlines
For those who had lost their jobs, life was very hard. Many families lost their homes, or were split up when parents lost their jobs. At the time the American government did not make dole payments. People out of work had to depend on charity. Breadlines (queues of people lining up for handouts of food) became a common sight.

2 Shanty towns
Homeless people roamed the streets looking for food, work or somewhere to stay. In the major cities they built shanty towns for shelter, using wood or scrap metal.

3 The Bonus Marchers
- During the summer of 1932 about 25,000 ex-First World War very poor soldiers and their families marched into Washington DC. They set up camp in Anacostia Field. They had come to demand a bonus payment of $500 that had been promised to them by the government in 1924. Although the bonus was not payable until 1945 the ex-soldiers wanted it now. The demonstrators became known as the **bonus marchers**.

- President Hoover refused to meet the marchers and decided to throw them out of Washington. He called in the army, who attacked the marchers' camps and drove them out of the city (Source E).

This made Hoover even more unpopular with the American people. He tried to defend his actions by saying that many of the marchers were criminals and communists.

SOURCE E

Government troops arrived at Anacostia Field at about eleven at night. Bedlam broke out in the camp.

Men and women tried to gather their possessions quickly and flee.

The troops came with tear gas, bombs and bayonets. They set fire to shacks on the edge of the camp.

Tanks and soldiers guarded the bridge back into Washington. They did not want any politicians to be disturbed. As the marchers fled they jeered at the soldiers.

The next day General MacArthur, one of the leaders of the government troops, said: 'That mob wanted a revolution. If the President had not acted, he would have faced a very serious situation.'

An eye-witness account of the attack on the Bonus Marchers.

QUESTIONS
1. Who were the Bonus Marchers?
2. What did Hoover do about them?

Why did Roosevelt win the election of 1932?

In 1932 the Democratic Party nominated (chose) Franklin Delano Roosevelt to stand for president against Herbert Hoover. Roosevelt accepted the nomination at a meeting of the Democratic Party in Chicago.

Although he had been paralysed by polio, Roosevelt went on to become one of the greatest presidents in the history of the USA.

Roosevelt's early life

1 Schooldays
Roosevelt was born into a rich family at Hyde Park, a small town in the state of New York. He was an only child and was spoilt by his mother. Roosevelt went to a boarding school where he achieved average grades.

On leaving school he attended Harvard University. After this he worked for a law firm in New York City.

2 Into politics
Roosevelt did not like working as a lawyer. He wanted to go into his politics like his cousin, Theodore Roosevelt, who had been president from 1901–9. He joined the Democratic Party and in 1910 was elected to be a state senator in New York.

By 1913 he was the Assistant Secretary to the American Navy and in 1920 he ran as the Democrats' vice-presidential candidate. Unfortunately for Roosevelt, the Democrats were very unpopular with the voters at the time. Warren Harding of the Republican Party easily won the election and became the new president of the USA.

3 Polio
In 1921 Roosevelt caught polio. It left him paralysed from the waist down. He was never able to walk again without help. Luckily, he was rich enough not to have to work and could afford the best medical care. Roosevelt kept cheerful. He was determined that his disability would not hold back his political career.

4 Governor of New York
In 1928 Roosevelt stood for the post of Governor of New York State and won the election by a narrow margin. When the Great Depression came, Roosevelt took action to help the unemployed of New York State.

In 1931 he set up the Temporary Relief Administration. This used tax payers' money to provide jobs, food and shelter for the unemployed. It was clear that Roosevelt's illness helped him to sympathise with the problems of ordinary people.

SOURCE F

Roosevelt before his illness.

The presidential election, 1932

- Roosevelt was up against the unpopular Herbert Hoover in the election. When out making speeches before the election, Hoover was given a bad reception. People pelted him with eggs and tomatoes. Some carried banners that said, 'Hang Hoover'. A popular saying of the time was, 'In Hoover we trusted and now we are busted.'

- When Hoover was speaking about the Bonus Marchers in one city, he told people: 'Thank goodness we still have a government which knows how to deal with a mob.' This remark almost caused a riot.

- Roosevelt came across as a person who would do something to improve people's lives. He was energetic and offered the USA hope. At a time when millions of Americans were down on their luck, Roosevelt made them feel he was on their side.

Result of the 1932 election

Roosevelt won a great victory in the election. He received 22.8 million votes to Hoover's 15.8 million. Out of 48 states in the USA, 42 chose Roosevelt. The election was held in November 1932, but Roosevelt had to wait until March 1933 to take up office.

For four months it left Hoover a 'lame duck' president. He was still in office but with no real power to do anything. The economic crisis grew worse by the day.

SOURCE G

I pledge you, I pledge myself, to a New Deal for the American people.

From Roosevelt's acceptance speech to the Democratic Party, Chicago, 1932.

QUESTIONS

1. Read page 158. What made Roosevelt such a remarkable person?
2. Read page 159. Why did Roosevelt beat Hoover in the 1932 election?

SOURCE H

Roosevelt making a speech about the New Deal.

How successful was the New Deal?

- Roosevelt promised the American people a **New Deal** and as soon as he became the president he introduced laws to deal with the Depression. He used taxpayers' money to put the USA back to work. Most Americans supported Roosevelt in his efforts to cure the problems of the Depression. He remained president until his death in 1945.

- Business people, however, did not like the government interfering in the economy. The Supreme Court even said that some of Roosevelt's laws were illegal.

However, the New Deal did not completely solve the problem of unemployment and it took the Second World War to put all Americans back to work.

What was the New Deal as introduced in 1933?

Roosevelt took up his duties as president on 4 March 1933. Millions of Americans gathered around their radios to listen to his inauguration speech in which he told people about the New Deal. They were reassured by his calm voice and felt sure he was the right man to overcome the Depression (see Source B).

During Roosevelt's first **Hundred Days** in office from 4 March to 16 June 1933, numerous laws were passed by Congress to deal with the Depression.

SOURCE A

THE NEW CHAUFFEUR

An American cartoon from 1933 entitled 'The New Chauffeur'.

SOURCE B

The only thing we have to fear is fear itself. Our main task is to put people back to work.

We can solve this problem if we face it wisely and with courage. We can partly do this by the government providing jobs and reorganising the use of our natural resources.

From Roosevelt's inauguration speech, 4 March 1933.

QUESTION

1 Look at Source A.
   What is the message of this cartoon?
   ['FDR' was Roosevelt's nickname.]

Helping the banks

1 The Emergency Banking Act

- People had lost their confidence in the banks and rushed to take out their money. Soon the banks began to run out of money. On 4 March 1933 hundreds of banks across the USA failed to open for business. The country was on the brink of economic disaster. If the banks stayed closed nobody would have any money to spend. If, on the other hand, they opened they might collapse and go bust.

- Roosevelt solved the problem by passing the Emergency Banking Act. All banks were made to close for four days, so they could be inspected. Those whose finances were poor were ordered to close for good. The rest were given government grants and allowed to re-open.

- Roosevelt made a speech on the radio asking people to stop panicking. He asked people to take their money back to the banks. This worked and the next day people started putting their money back in. Roosevelt had restored people's confidence in the banks.

2 The Securities Act

Roosevelt did not want another Wall Street Crash to happen. So, he decided to introduce rules to control the buying and selling of shares. In 1934 he set up the Securities and Exchange Commission, which had the power to control the activities of the stock market. People investing in shares could now be sure that they would not be swindled out of their money.

Helping the farmers

Farmers had been producing too much food. This meant food prices were low and farmers could not make a decent living. Roosevelt helped farmers by passing the Agricultural Adjustment Act (AAA). Under this act the government paid farmers to cut down on their production. This meant that food prices went up and farmers received a higher income. The government also advised farmers about how much food they could grow in the future.

SOURCE C

An American cartoon about the AAA, 1933.

QUESTIONS

1 How did Roosevelt restore people's confidence in the banks?
2 How did the Agricultural Adjustment Act help farmers?

Helping the unemployed

Roosevelt soon set about helping people who were out of work.

1 The Civilian Conservation Corps (CCC)

The government set up the Civilian Conservation Corps (CCC) which provided work for young men in the countryside. They carried out work such as strengthening river banks against flooding and planting trees.

Members of the CCC were aged between 18 and 25. They were paid a small wage and given a uniform, food and shelter. The CCC provided work for three million young men during the 1930s.

2 The Federal Emergency Relief Administration (FERA)

The Federal Emergency Relief Administration (FERA) gave grants of government money to help out the homeless and hungry. This was an emergency measure only.

Roosevelt did not believe that it was right to make dole payments. He thought people should be put to work. However, so many people were out of work and starving in 1933, the government needed to give them emergency help.

Helping industry

The National Industrial Recovery Act

In 1933 Congress passed the National Industrial Recovery Act, which set up two agencies.

• The National Recovery Administration (NRA)

Companies were asked to agree a code of employment with the NRA. The code would provide workers with a fair wage and conditions. Workers were given the right to join trade unions and bargain for increased wages. Companies would also agree not to employ children. In return companies were allowed to charge a fair price for their goods and display the NRA's logo of a blue eagle. The government rewarded these firms by favouring them when contracts were awarded.

• The Public Works Administration (PWA)

The PWA provided work for unemployed skilled workers on large government funded projects such as building roads, bridges, schools, city halls, court houses and hospitals.

The National Industrial Recovery Act also gave workers the right to negotiate wage increases with the employers.

SOURCE D

An American cartoon about the NRA.

QUESTIONS

1. How did Roosevelt help the unemployed?
2. How did Roosevelt help industry?

The presidential election, 1936

Roosevelt's opponent in the election was Alf Landon of the Republican Party. Landon did not stand a chance. Roosevelt was so popular he easily won the election.

After the election Roosevelt quarrelled with the Supreme Court and, as a result, fewer reforms were passed. He also made a number of mistakes and in 1937-8 unemployment rose again.

Many blamed Roosevelt and for a while his popularity was dented.

Why did the New Deal encounter opposition?

- The New Deal brought in laws that created jobs, fixed prices and provided good working conditions. Many said this was none of the government's business and went against the American way of doing things. Roosevelt, they argued, was trying to make the USA a socialist country.

- Others said that the New Deal was costing the country too much money. They did not like having to pay higher taxes to pay for employment schemes. Despite this, poor Americans were very grateful to Roosevelt for helping them to survive the bad times.

SOURCE G

TRYING TO CHANGE THE UMPIRING

"LISTEN – I DON'T LIKE YOUR 'DECISIONS' FROM NOW ON, YOU'RE GOING TO HAVE TO WORK WITH SOMEONE WHO CAN SEE THINGS MY WAY!"

An American cartoon of 1937, commenting on Roosevelt's quarrel with the Supreme Court.

QUESTION

Why were some Americans against Roosevelt and the New Deal?

Opposition from the Supreme Court

The Supreme Court is the highest court of law in the USA. One of its jobs is to judge if new laws fit in with the constitution (rules) of the country.

In 1935 the nine judges in the Supreme Court said that the National Recovery Administration (NRA) and the Agricultural Adjustment Act (AAA) were illegal.

The judges said that the central government did not have the right to interfere with industry and agriculture. Roosevelt was angry at the court's decision. The New Deal was under threat.

Roosevelt tries to 'pack' the court

- After he was voted back into power in 1936, Roosevelt decided to change the Supreme Court, so that it could no longer block his laws. His plan was to increase the number of judges from nine to fifteen. He would make sure that the six new judges were supporters of the New Deal.

- Roosevelt's plan was a big mistake. People accused Roosevelt of trying to 'pack' the court with judges who would do as he said. There was a huge outcry against Roosevelt and many said he was acting like a dictator. In the end Roosevelt had to back down and withdraw his plan.

Afterwards, however, Roosevelt did not have any more problems with the Supreme Court and they blocked no more of his laws.

Radical critics of the New Deal

The radical critics of the New Deal said that Roosevelt was not doing enough to help poor people.

1 Father Coughlin

Coughlin was a priest from Detroit. In 1935 he formed the National Union for Social Justice. Coughlin said that everyone should have a job and a decent wage. He had a weekly radio programme in which he explained his ideas and criticised Roosevelt. It was so popular that Coughlin had 40 million regular listeners.

Coughlin was nicknamed the 'radio priest', but his ideas were confused and he soon lost his popularity.

2 Dr Francis Townsend

Townsend was a doctor from California and the author of the 'Townsend Plan'. This said that all those over 60 should receive a monthly pension of $200. Townsend formed clubs to promote this idea. In 1935 the Social Security Act introduced pensions, so Townsend's ideas must have had some influence on the government.

QUESTIONS

1 Why did the Supreme Court anger Roosevelt?

2 How did Roosevelt try to change the Supreme Court?

3 Huey Long

- Huey Long was the Governor of Louisiana. He spoke out for the poor and became very powerful. Long improved public services in Louisiana and his popularity soared. However, he was known for using dirty tricks and sometimes broke the law to boost his own power. He also threatened and bribed his opponents into keeping quiet.

- Long criticised Roosevelt, saying the New Deal did not help the poor enough. He started the 'Share Our Wealth' scheme which aimed to take money away from rich people and give it to the poor. Long also wanted the government to provide free education and pensions. He became famous throughout the USA.

- In 1935, however, Long was assassinated. Had he lived he might well have stood against Roosevelt in the 1936 election and may have had a chance of winning.

SOURCE H

Huey Long (left) and his bodyguard in 1935.

Interesting facts about Huey Long

- He was nicknamed 'Kingfish' from a character in a radio show called 'Amos 'n' Andy'.
- He inspired a best-selling political novel called All the King's Men written by Robert Penn Warren.
- He said that the NRA stood for 'Nuts Run America'.
- An estimated 175,000 people went to his funeral.

QUESTIONS

1 Why did the radical critics not like the New Deal?
2 Look at Source H. Why did Long need a bodyguard?

Why did unemployment persist despite the New Deal?

One of the main aims of the New Deal was to put the USA back to work. Millions of Americans were found work by 'alphabet agencies' such as the CCC and the WPA.

Some people, however, criticised the 'alphabet agencies' saying they did not provide 'real jobs'. As soon as the government stopped funding the agencies the jobs would disappear.

Although the government managed to reduce unemployment, they could not make it go away altogether. In 1936 nine million people were still out of work. The government had made a big effort but it was not enough.

The New Deal and workers

Roosevelt believed that workers and employers should trust each other. He wanted workers to have good conditions and the right to join a trade union.

The National Recovery Administration (NRA) did a lot to improve working conditions. When the Supreme Court declared the NRA illegal Roosevelt brought in the Wagner Act, which gave workers the right to be in a trade union. As a result, trade union membership went up during the 1930s.

The Memorial Day Massacre

Some employers did not like the workers having rights and hired thugs to beat up trade union members. In 1937 there were a number of violent strikes, one of which took place in a large steelworks in Chicago.

On 31 May (Memorial Day) police attacked strikers who had gathered for a rally. Ten strikers were shot dead and a further ninety wounded. The violence shocked the public and the event became known as the 'Memorial Day Massacre'.

In 1937 there were 4700 strikes in the USA. With the support of New Deal laws, however, most of these strikes were settled in favour of the workers.

SOURCE I

Hired thugs beat up a union organiser attempting to hand out leaflets to Ford motor workers.

QUESTION

What was the 'Memorial Day Massacre'?

The New Deal and farmers

The New Deal did much to help farmers. Measures were taken to cut down production (so prices went up), and farmers were given loans to buy machinery. Large farmers benefited the most from this help. Small farmers and farm labourers stayed poor, especially in the southern states.

The 'Dustbowl'

In 1934-5 there was a long drought in Kansas, Oklahoma, Texas and Colorado. The soil turned to dust and the area became known as the 'Dustbowl'. When the wind blew large amounts of soil were blown away. It was impossible to grow any crops in these conditions.

Farmers had no choice but to pack up and leave. Many of them, known as 'Okies' (after the state of Oklahoma), travelled to California in search of work.

The plight of the 'Okies' was described in *The Grapes of Wrath*, a famous novel by John Steinbeck that was later made into a very successful film.

The New Deal and the poor

The New Deal could have done more to help poor people. The government provided jobs and food for many poor people and the Social Security Act of 1935 introduced pensions.

But no laws were passed to help black people specifically, even though they suffered the lowest wages and found it hard to get jobs. Roosevelt did little to help black people get equal rights with white people.

This was mainly because he depended on the support of White Democrats in the south, who did not want to see the lives of black people improved. Roosevelt's opponents criticised him heavily for not helping black people.

SOURCE J

Dust storm damage in Oklahoma, 1936.

QUESTIONS

1. How effective was the New Deal in helping farmers?
2. What was the 'Dustbowl'?
3. What did the New Deal do to help black people?

SOURCE K

A migrant mother in California, 1936.

The slump of 1937-8

In 1937 the American economy was showing signs of recovery. Roosevelt therefore decided to cut the amount being spent on New Deal programmes. Without the support of government money, American industry plunged back into a depression. Industrial production fell by 30 per cent and unemployment went up by 3 million.

In 1938 Roosevelt realised his mistake and started spending money again. Even so, by 1940 employment had not recovered to the level it was in early 1937.

Did the fact that the New Deal did not solve unemployment mean that it was a failure?

Historians argue fiercely about whether the New Deal was a success or a failure.

On page 171 you can read the opinions of five modern historians.

When you have read them, decide whether you think the New Deal was a failure or not.

SOURCE L

Black people queuing for food in 1937. Behind them is a government advertisement.

QUESTION

1 Look at Source L. Why do you think the photographer took this picture?

170 The USA 1919–41

SOURCE M

Roosevelt came to power promising he would bring full unemployment. He didn't make it. In 1938 there were still 10 million unemployed. In the next four years the number did go down. This was not Roosevelt's doing but Hitler's [by starting the Second World War]. The war meant American workers were needed in the steel works again to make goods for the British and French.

SOURCE N

By 1937 factories were producing as much as they were before the Depression started in 1929. However, the New Deal gave the federal [central] government a much more important role in areas previously thought not to be its business. Roosevelt deliberately gave central government the power to make a fairer society that offered its citizens more security.

SOURCE O

Without doubt, Roosevelt's biggest achievement was to preserve American democracy. By his energy and warm-heartedness, Roosevelt raised the prestige of the office of president. He also gave people faith in their country, leader and political system.

SOURCE P

Important improvements were made in working conditions, helping the poor and running businesses. But there was no miracle. Instead, Roosevelt's policies were often hesitant and went against each other.

SOURCE Q

The New Deal did not give Americans any brand new values or ideas. But it did make people discuss the values of society and how to make them better. By 1939 Americans were more caring towards poor people.

QUESTIONS

1. For each of Sources M-Q, say whether it thinks the New Deal is a failure or not.
2. Look back over pages 160–70. Use Sources M-Q and your own knowledge to explain whether or not you think the New Deal failed.

Paper 1-type assessment: The New Deal

SOURCE A

An American cartoon of 1933 commenting on the cost of Roosevelt's New Deal.

SOURCE B

A resident of Park Avenue (a rich area of New York) was sentenced to a term of imprisonment for threatening violence to the person of President Roosevelt. This episode was significant as an example of the fanatical hatred of the President which today obsesses thousands of men and women amongst the American upper class.

From an article in an American magazine, published in 1936.

QUESTIONS

Section C Questions

1 Study the sources carefully and then answer the three questions which follow.

  a Study Source A. Do you think that the cartoonist supported or opposed the New Deal? Use the source and your own knowledge to explain your answer. (6)

  b Study Source B. Explain why many Americans opposed President Roosevelt in 1936. Use the source and your own knowledge to explain your answer. (7)

  c Study Source C. Why do you think this photograph was taken? Use the source and your own knowledge to explain your answer. (7)

SOURCE C

President Roosevelt visiting a Civilian Conservation Corps camp in Virginia in 1933.

QUESTIONS

When answering these questions make sure you answer ALL three parts.

Remember that you should always explain your answer as fully as you can and support it with specific detail where possible.

Section C Questions

2 a What happened in the 'Red Scare' in America in the years 1919-20? (4)

b Explain why not all Americans were able to be part of the prosperity of the 1920s. (6)

c 'The Wall Street Crash occurred in America only because of unwise speculation by investors in shares.' Do you agree with this statement? Explain your answer. (10)

3 a What was 'The New Deal'? (4)

b Explain why the New Deal aroused such strong feelings amongst the American people. (6)

c Was the New Deal a failure or a success? Explain your answer. (10)

Assessment: The New Deal 173

5 Russia, 1905–41

- In 1905 Russia was a backward country, run by an absolute monarch, Tsar Nicholas II. It had mainly a rural economy, but industry was growing quickly. Living conditions in the industrial cities were poor and revolutionary groups flourished.

- In March 1917 the Tsar was overthrown. From November 1917 the Bolsheviks (later called communists) ruled Russia.

- Under Lenin, the Bolsheviks beat their opponents in a civil war. Then they began building a new communist Soviet Union.

- When Lenin died in 1924, Stalin emerged as the new leader. He was a ruthless dictator who crushed all opposition.

- Stalin modernised the Soviet Union. By collectivising agriculture, he gained control of the countryside, and his Five-Year Plans increased production in heavy industry.

- By 1939 the Soviet Union was one of the world's great industrial powers, but at great cost.

This topic is examined in Paper 1 of the examination. Paper 1-type exercises are included at the end of the chapter. Mark schemes, sample answers and comments can be found in the accompanying Teacher's Resource Pack.

A map of the Russian Empire in 1905.

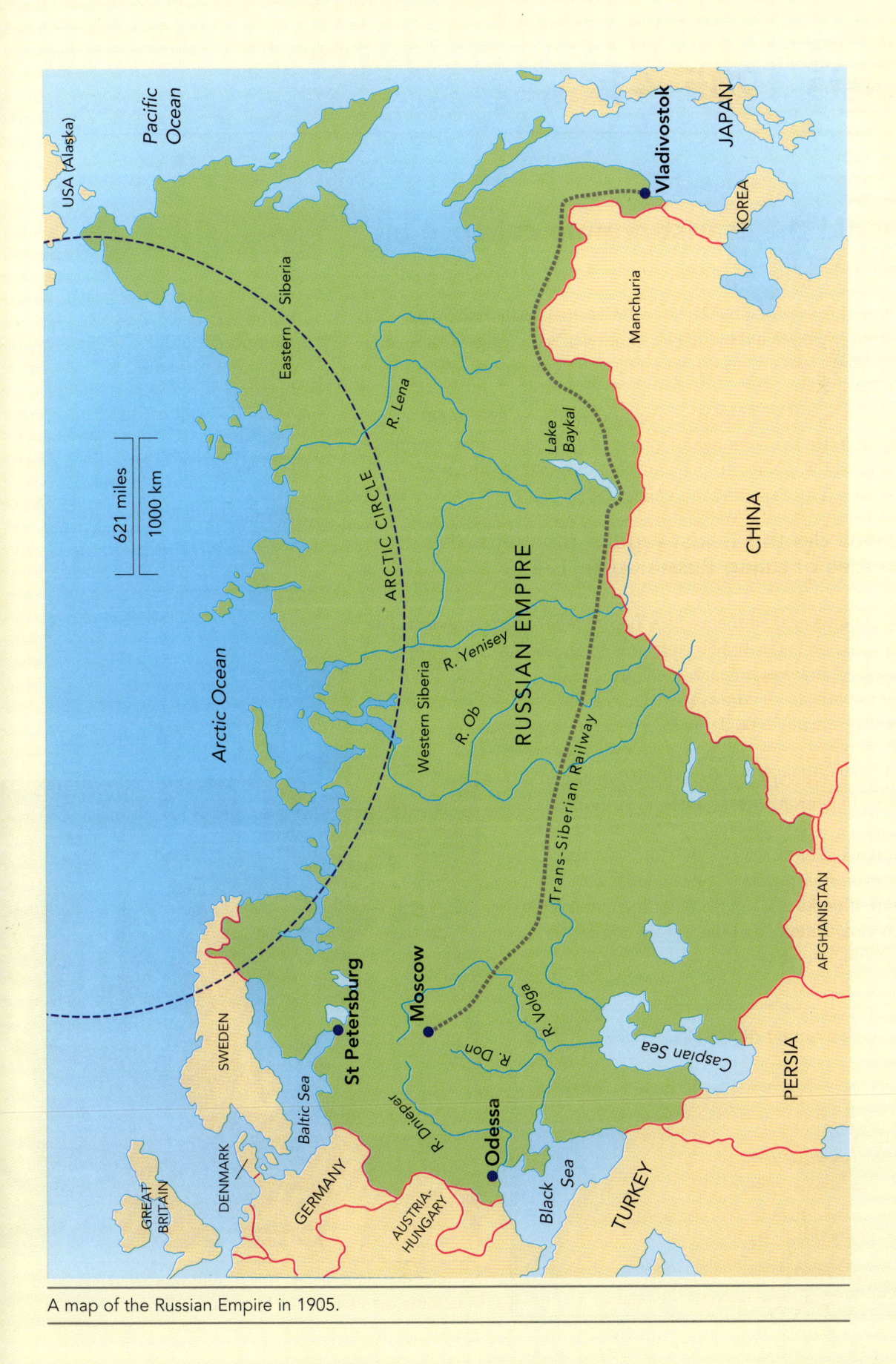

Russia 1905–41

Why did the Tsarist regime collapse in 1917?

- In 1905 Russia was a backward country. Its people had little political freedom and industry had not yet been fully developed. Most Russians were poor peasants living in the countryside.

- Tsar Nicholas II wanted to rule on his own as an **absolute monarch**. He would not share power with a parliament. During the First World War Nicholas became so unpopular that he was overthrown by a revolution in March 1917.

How well did the Tsarist regime deal with the difficulties of ruling Russia up to 1914?

- Russian kings called themselves **Tsar**, which means emperor. The Tsar ruled on his own, helped by a few ministers whom he chose himself. There was no parliament and the people did not have the right to votes in elections. Most Tsars ruled in a harsh manner crushing any one who dared to complain.

- Russian was a very religious, Christian country. The main church was the Russian Orthodox Church, which supported the Tsar. In return, the Orthodox Church was given a lot of power. However, Russia was a huge country with lots of different people. Many were not members of the Orthodox Church, and there were numerous other religious groups.

SOURCE A

What is going to happen to me and all of Russia? I am not ready to be a Tsar. I never wanted to become one. I know nothing about ruling.

The reaction of Nicholas II to his father's death in 1894.

SOURCE B

Nicholas II and his family. This picture was taken just before the outbreak of the First World War in 1914.

The family of Tsar Nicholas II

- Nicholas Romanov (Tsar Nicholas II) married a German princess, Alix of Hesse (Alexandra), in 1894.
- They had five children:
  – Olga (born 1895)
  – Tatiana (born 1897)
  – Maria (born 1899)
  – Anastasia (born 1901)
  – Alexei (born 1904)

- Tsar Nicholas II came to the throne in 1894. Although he was hard working and devoted to his family he had serious weaknesses. He found it hard to make decisions and was unable to concentrate on running the country. Many people wanted Russia to change and modernise, but Nicholas saw this as a threat to his own position. He wanted to make sure that the Tsar's power was not challenged.

Russian society before the First World War

- Russia was more of an empire than a country. It stretched from Europe to the Far East and from the Arctic in the north to the Black Sea in the south. (See map on page 175.)

- Russia had many different nationalities living within its borders. They included Finns, Poles and Ukrainians all of whom wanted their independence. Less than half the population was Russian. As transport was so poor few people travelled outside their own village or town.

The countryside

- Most Russians were poor peasants who lived off the land. Up to 1861 most peasants were **serfs** (slaves) and had to do as they were told by the landowners.

SOURCE C

Russian peasants in their village in the 1890s.

- Then in 1861 they were given their freedom. They were allowed to have some land, but they had to pay for it. Often, however, the peasants did not have enough land to make a decent living.

- Although farming methods had not changed for centuries, Russia could usually grow enough food to feed its people. But if there was a bad harvest people starved.

- With the population growing quickly, people started to realise that farming needed to be brought up to date.

QUESTION

1 Look at Source C.
What does it tell you about life in the Russian countryside in the 1890s?

Landowners

The big landowners in the Russian countryside were very rich. They owned large estates and ran the local councils known as *zemstvos*. Many landowners ran their estates badly and wasted their money.

The peasants, however, started to demand the land for themselves. The better landowners realised that farming had to be improved and began to ask the Tsar for reforms.

The cities

- In the early 1900s Russia began to industrialise. Russian industry grew faster than in any other country in Europe. The Minister of Finance, Sergei Witte, did all he could to help industry develop. Mining, iron and steel, textiles, oil and railways all became big industries.

- Cities grew as people moved from the countryside to work in the factories. Russia now had an industrial working class. The rapid growth of the cities brought problems. Living and working conditions in the cities were terrible.

- The government did nothing to protect the workers in the factories. Children were employed to work in many of the factories and the workers were paid very low wages. Often, workers were injured because the machines did not have any safety guards on them.

- Factory workers were very unhappy. They were ready to listen to anyone who had any ideas about how to improve their conditions.

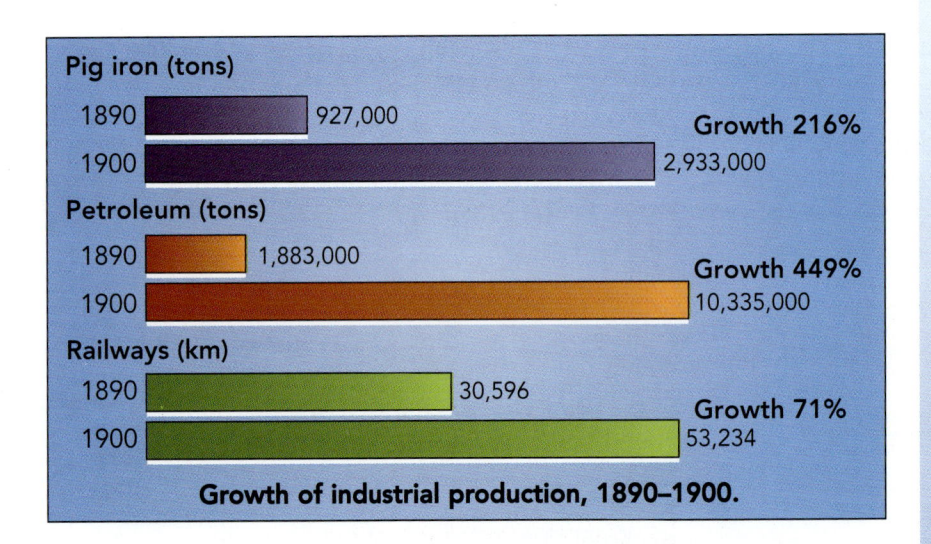

Pig iron (tons)
- 1890: 927,000
- 1900: 2,933,000
- Growth 216%

Petroleum (tons)
- 1890: 1,883,000
- 1900: 10,335,000
- Growth 449%

Railways (km)
- 1890: 30,596
- 1900: 53,234
- Growth 71%

Growth of industrial production, 1890–1900.

A Russian woman remembers the peasants on her grandfather's estate around 1900.

SOURCE D

There were two completely different kinds of peasant in Russia.

Some peasants were well off, with greasy hair, fat stomachs and shiny faces. They were well dressed in embroidered shirts and caftans made of fine cloth.

These peasants were called kulaks. They borrowed money from the bank and built houses out of wood. In their houses were flowers and the smell of buns cooking.

Other peasants were much poorer. They wore sandals, dressed in rags and had sad faces. They often lay in ditches near the wine shop. Their children did not grow because they were underfed.

The windows in their houses were always broken and bunged up with rags. Calves and hens were kept in the corners. There was a terrible smell.

SOURCE E

A boarding house for industrial workers, Moscow 1911.

Opposition to the Tsar

Revolutionary groups began to spread ideas against the Tsar. The most important group were **Marxists**, who were followers of the German writer, Karl Marx (1818-93).

In his book *Das Kapital*, Marx said that capitalism would collapse and communism would replace it.

Although they wanted to improve conditions for the workers, Marxists were middle class. They were often arrested and questioned by the Tsar's secret police and many of them fled Russia.

What Karl Marx said:

- Workers should take over privately owned factories and farms and put them under the control of a communist government.
- To achieve this, violence would have to be used to overthrow existing governments. (In Russia's case, this would be the Tsar.)

QUESTIONS

1 Read Source D.
How did the two groups of peasants differ from each other?

2 Read page 178.
In what ways was Russian changing by the early 1900s?

3 What does Source E tell us about life in a large city such as Moscow in 1911?

4 Read pages 176-179.
Why do you think many people started to oppose Tsar Nicholas II?

The Tsarist regime 179

Bolsheviks and Mensheviks

The main Marxist group in Russia was the Social Democratic Party (SDP). The Social Democrats believed that change in Russia would happen through the efforts of the industrial workers. In 1903 the SDP quarrelled amongst each other at a conference in London. The party split into two groups.

1 The **Bolsheviks** (from the Russian word for 'majority'). The Bolsheviks believed in seizing power at the first chance. Their leader was Vladimir Lenin.

2 The **Mensheviks** (from the Russian word for 'minority'). The Mensheviks believed in working with other groups to improve the lives of working people.

Another revolutionary party in Russia, the **Social Revolutionaries** (SRs), believed that the peasants should rise up and seize land from the big landowners.

Repression

Tsar Nicholas II, however, did not want any changes in the way Russia was run. His secret police, the Okhrana, arrested people who wanted change. Many opponents of the Tsar were tortured, imprisoned and executed. Newspapers were censored and stopped from criticising the Tsar.

The Russo-Japanese War, 1904-5

In February 1904 Russia went to war with Japan over Manchuria, a part of northern China. Both countries wanted control of this area because it was rich in minerals.

Russia had also built the Trans-Siberian railway in the area. People thought that Russia would easily win the war, but the Japanese soon gained the upper hand.

The Russian Baltic Fleet was ordered to sail half way round the world to attack the Japanese navy. When the Russian fleet arrived off the coast of Japan in May 1905, it was heavily beaten by the Japanese fleet in the Battle of Tsushima. The Tsar was forced to ask the Japanese for peace.

SOURCE F

A picture showing the make-up of Russian society in the early 1900s. The workers at the bottom are commenting on each of the classes above them, from top to bottom: 'We work for them while they – get rid of our money – pray for us – eat for us – shoot at us'.

How did the Tsar survive the 1905 revolution?

'Bloody Sunday'

- The Tsar was so shocked by Russia's poor effort in the war that he relaxed his control. This gave the Russian people the chance to demand better living and working conditions.

- In late 1904 a wave of strikes broke out, with the workers demanding better conditions. There was growing anger about the way Russia was being run.

- On 22 January 1905 a large demonstration was organised in St Petersburg. The plan was to march to the Winter Palace (where the Tsar lived). Here the marchers would give the Tsar a petition, asking for higher wages and better living conditions. Father Gapon, a well known priest, led the march.

- The marchers had no weapons and behaved in an orderly manner. When they reached the Winter Palace, soldiers opened fire, killing about 200 people. The event became known as 'Bloody Sunday'. People were shocked and lost all respect for the Tsar. Riots and strikes swept the whole country.

Mutiny

- The Tsar was in danger of being overthrown. In June 1905 sailors on board the *Potemkin*, a warship anchored in the port of Odessa, staged a mutiny.

- About 2000 people, who gathered to support the sailors, were shot. The mutiny showed that the Tsar was losing the support of the armed forces.

The call for reform widened with even doctors and teachers forming groups to demand changes. A middle class political party called the **Constitutional Democrats (Cadets)** was set up to demand reform.

SOURCE G

A French picture drawn shortly after 'Bloody Sunday' in 1905.

SOURCE H

The Cossack [a soldier on horseback] circled round the worker, shrieking and waving his sword in the air. Swooping down on the worker, he slashed him across the face, cutting him open from the eyes to the chin. I remember the murderer's face, his teeth clenched in a grin and the hairs of his moustache standing up on his lip. Brandishing his bloody sword, he let out another shriek and spat at the dead man.

The writer, Maxim Gorky, was in the crowd on 'Bloody Sunday'. Here he describes the death of one of the marchers.

The Tsarist regime

Stolypin

Peter Stolypin was the Prime Minister of Russia from 1906-11. He was a firm leader who gave Russia a sense of direction.

Stolypin allowed the Okhrana (secret police) to crush all opposition to the Tsar. By 1907 many revolutionaries had fled the country or were in prison.

Stolypin encouraged peasants to borrow money to buy land and improve the way the way they farmed.

- As a result by 1917 about one-third of all peasants lived on their own farms. However, most peasants were cautious and opposed these changes.

Stolypin was assassinated while attending an opera in 1911.

The St Petersburg Soviet

During 1905 **soviets** (councils of workers and soldiers) were formed all over Russia. In October the St Petersburg Soviet was formed, which was like an alternative to the city council.

Each factory in St Petersburg sent a representative to the soviet. The St Petersburg Soviet had many revolutionary members and it soon organised a general strike that brought industry to a standstill.

The October Manifesto

- The Tsar realised that he would have to agree to some change. He issued the **October Manifesto**, which said that he would share some of his power with an elected parliament or **Duma**. This gave the middle classes what they wanted. But the industrial workers and peasants were unhappy. They felt that this change did not go far enough. By issuing the October Manifesto, the Tsar had split his opponents.

- The Tsar, however, was not to be trusted. He now tried to recover as much power as he could. He arrested the leaders of the St Petersburg Soviet and then ruthlessly crushed an uprising organised by the Moscow Soviet.

By December the 1905 revolution had collapsed. Now the country wanted to see what would become of the reforms promised by Nicholas.

Attempts at reform before the First World War

Nicholas II had survived the 1905 revolution, but only by agreeing to some reforms. What remained uncertain was how much power Nicholas would give the Duma.

- Working class revolutionaries refused to take part in the elections for the first Duma in 1906, so the Cadets and peasant representatives dominated it.

- When the first Duma met it demanded further reforms. It said that:

  1 large country estates should be confiscated and the land given to peasants;

  2 the Tsar should stop using the death penalty.

QUESTIONS

1 What happened on 'Bloody Sunday' in 1905?

2 What were soviets and what did they do?

3 How did the Tsar bring the 1905 revolution to an end?

- The Tsar hated being told what to do, so he dismissed the Duma. A second set of elections for another Duma were held in 1907 and this time some working class revolutionaries were elected. The Tsar did not like this so he dismissed the Duma once again and then changed the voting rules to suit himself. As a result the third Duma, which met later in 1907, contained mainly supporters of the Tsar. This Duma mostly agreed with the Tsar and did not cause him any problems.

Some progress made

Although the changes were limited in Russia, progress had been made:

1 For the first time some Russians could take part in politics. Matters were discussed and debated. The Tsar's ministers went to the Duma to answer questions.

2 There was more freedom and openness than ever before. Russia was gradually moving towards democracy.

Who knows what might have happened if the First World War had not broken out?

How far was the Tsar weakened by the First World War?

When Germany declared war on Russia on 1 August 1914, everyone thought it would only last for a short time. But the war dragged on and caused Russia many problems.

In autumn 1914 the Russians were beaten by the Germans at the Battle of Tannenberg, where 100,000 soldiers were killed.

In 1916 a Russian attack, led by General Brusilov, recaptured some land before being pushed back.

The Russian army finally collapsed in 1917. This was due to poor leadership, a shortage of supplies at the front and events at home rather than defeat on the battlefield.

SOURCE J

1 Civil freedoms will be granted to the people such as freedom of speech and assembly.

2 All classes of people will have the right to vote in the future.

3 No law can come into force unless it has been approved by the Duma.

The three promises made in the October Manifesto.

SOURCE I

Peter Stolypin in 1909.

Problems created by the First World War

1 Food shortages

About 15 million peasants were made to join the Russian army. Despite this Russia still produced plenty of food. The Russian railways, however, were not good enough to keep the cities and army supplied.

After 1914 there were widespread food shortages throughout Russia, and this was one of the reasons why there was another revolution in 1917.

2 Money problems

Russia was a poor country and could not afford a long war. The Tsar had to borrow money from other countries. He also printed more paper money but this only had the effect of making prices rise quickly (inflation). Wages did not keep up with prices, leaving the workers worse off.

3 Industrial problems

Industry in Russia was geared towards the war. The output of heavy industries, such as iron, steel and weapons went up. But other industries suffered and were forced to close because people could not afford to buy their goods.

The workers grew tired of high prices, job losses and food shortages. The Tsar became very unpopular and there were numerous strikes. Russian workers wanted the war brought to an end.

The middle classes were also unhappy. When the Duma met in 1915, it called for the war to be better organised. The Tsar took no notice and people rapidly lost faith in his ability to rule the country.

SOURCE K

The Russians did not have enough weapons to equip the army. It was usual to have unarmed men behind the action who could take up the weapons of the dead.

Men were sent into battle without rifles. They were armed only with bayonets and bombs. That meant fighting at close quarters. The Russians had to get within range of the enemy to throw their bombs. Then they charged with their bayonets.

An American historian, writing in 1922, describes the shortage of weapons in the Russian army in 1915.

SOURCE L

The Tsar blessing his troops in 1914.

The Tsar takes command of the army

In 1915 the Tsar took over personal command of the Russian army. He had to spend a deal of time away from Petrograd (as St Petersburg was now called). This left the country in the control of Tsarina Alexandra and her favourite adviser, **Grigori Rasputin**. It was a disastrous situation.

A Russian cartoon showing Rasputin with the Tsar and Tsarina.

Rasputin

Rasputin was a holy man from Siberia, who also claimed to be a healer. The Tsar's only son, Alexei, suffered from haemophilia, a disease that stopped his blood from clotting. The slightest accident could kill Alexei. Rasputin seemed able to control this disease and won the friendship of Nicholas and Alexandra.

When the Tsar was away during the war, Alexandra came to rely on the advice of Rasputin. He began to appoint and sack ministers.

There were rumours that he and Alexandra were lovers and they were planning to make peace with the Germans. The story sounded possible because Alexandra had been born in Germany.

A group of nobles decided to get rid of Rasputin. One night in December 1916 he was invited to a nobleman's house for dinner. An attempt to poison him failed. So the nobles shot him and threw his body into a canal.

The police knew who had carried out the murders, but no one was seriously punished. Too many people close to the royal family were involved in the plot.

QUESTIONS

1. Why do you think the Russian army collapsed in 1917?
2. What harmful effects did the war have on Russia?
3. Look at Source M. What does the cartoonist think about Rasputin's friendship with the royal family?

Soldiers in Petrograd supporting the revolution, March 1917.

SOURCE N

Why was the revolution of March 1917 successful?

- By early 1917 the Tsar had totally lost the support of his people. The government had failed to organise the war effort properly and the Russian army faced defeat. In Petrograd the badly paid workers were starving and strikes were common. Russia was on the brink of another revolution.

- By 10 March there were so many strikes that factories were at a standstill in Petrograd. Workers took to the streets to demonstrate against the Tsar. Soldiers were ordered to fire on the demonstrators. However, they did not want to do this because they, too, were hungry and tired of the Tsar.

- On 12 March the soldiers mutinied and joined the protestors. Government buildings were attacked and within hours Petrograd was in the hands of rioting mobs.

- The Tsar was at his country estate a few miles from Petrograd. He was unaware of how serious the rioting was. He made the situation worse when he ordered the Duma to stop meeting. The Duma took no notice and, instead, its middle class members joined the revolution.

- Also on 12 March, the Petrograd Soviet began to meet again. It managed to stop the soldiers' mutiny and brought the army under its control. The Tsar had now actually lost command of his own army.

SOURCE O

It is clear that His Majesty does not realise what is going on. A terrible revolution has broken out, which will not be easy to put down. The troops are dispirited. They are disobeying the officers and even murdering them. Tsarina Alexandra is most unpopular.

Troops everywhere are joining the people and the Duma. They are calling for the Tsar to abdicate [resign].

A telephone conversation in March 1917 between one of the Duma's leaders and one of the Tsar's advisers.

SOURCE P

The roof had already fallen in. The fire crackled throwing ash into the black sky of the night. No one tried to put out the fire. A tall stooping man stopped and asked, 'Well, it means that all justice is to be done away with, doesn't it? Punishments all done away with, is that it?' No one answered him.

The writer, Maxim Gorky, saw the events of the March revolution. Here he describes how the rioters burned down the Palace of Justice.

The Provisional Government

On 14 March the Duma announced that a **Provisional Government** would be set up to run Russia. The Prime Minister was Prince Lvov, with Alexander Kerensky as the Minister of Justice. The Provisional Government would rule until elections could be held for a new parliament.

On 15 March Nicholas finally decided he was in a hopeless position. His generals advised him that bringing troops from outside Petrograd to put down the revolution would only make matters worse. The Tsar abdicated (resigned) the throne. The monarchy in Russia was finished.

The Provisional Government brought in a number of reforms:

- There was to be freedom of the press in Russia.
- All adults over the age of 21 could vote.
- The death penalty was abolished.

But there were still problems. How would the new government cope with the war, the food shortages and the power of the Petrograd Soviet?

QUESTIONS

1. Why did a revolution break out in March 1917?
2. Read Source O. What does this source tell you about the Tsar during the March revolution?
3. What was the Provisional Government?

How did the Bolsheviks gain power, and how did they consolidate their rule?

The Bolsheviks, led by Lenin, overthrew the Provisional Government in the revolution of November 1917. They then defeated their enemies in a civil war that lasted until 1920.

How did a small party like the Bolsheviks seize power and turn Russia into the world's first communist country, when most Russians were against them?

How effectively did the Provisional Government rule Russia in 1917?

The Provisional Government was only meant to hold power for a short time until a new parliament could be elected. But some important questions needed answering straight away.

1 Should Russia make peace or fight on in the war?

2 How could food supplies be increased in the cities, so that the workers had enough to eat?

3 Should land be taken from the big landowners and given to the peasants?

Decisions made by the Provisional Government

- The Provisional Government decided to go on with the war. It was a disastrous decision. When the Russian soldiers were ordered to launch a fresh attack against the Germans, there was a mutiny. Soldiers deserted in their thousands. It was clear that the Russians would lose the war against Germany.

- The Provisional Government tried to improve food supplies into the cities. Rationing was introduced, but there were problems in transporting the food. So the food shortages went on.

- The Provisional Government did nothing about the land question, leaving the problem for the new parliament to deal with when it was elected. This made the Provisional Government very unpopular.

The Russian calendar

Until February 1918 Russia used the old calendar, which was thirteen days behind the rest of Europe. The new Bolshevik government changed the calendar, to bring Russia in line. This means there are two dates for events in Russia before the change. For example, in the old calendar the 1917 revolution took place in October, but in the new calendar it was November. This book uses the new dates.

SOURCE A

The Provisional Government has little real power. Its orders are only carried out if the Petrograd Soviet allows it.

Most power is in the hands of the Soviet. It controls the troops, the railways and the postal services. The Provisional Government will last only as long as the Soviet allows.

From a letter written by a minister in the Provisional Government, March 1917.

QUESTION

1 Read page 188. What disastrous decision did the Provisional Government make in 1917?

188   Russia 1905–41

Kerensky takes over

The problem for the Provisional Government was that it was made up of people from different parties and they argued a great deal.

The middle class Cadets, for example, wanted Russia to be a democracy. But the socialists wanted to take the revolution further and give land to the peasants.

In July 1917, Kerensky replaced Prince Lvov as prime minister, but still the arguments went on.

The soviets

The re-founding of the Petrograd Soviet led to other soviets being set up across Russia. The Petrograd Soviet controlled all the other soviets. It had much more control over the workers and soldiers than the Provisional Government (see Source A).

At first the Petrograd Soviet tried to work with the Provisional Government, but when it fell under the influence of the Bolsheviks, it became very hostile towards the Provisional Government.

The power of the Provisional Government soon began to drain away and it became clear that whoever controlled the Petrograd Soviet would also control Russia.

QUESTIONS

1 What was a soviet?

2 Read Source A. In what ways did the Petrograd Soviet have more power than the Provisional Government?

SOURCE B

A Russian soldier trying to stop colleagues from deserting in 1917.

The growing power of revolutionary groups

The Bolsheviks disliked the Provisional Government. When Lenin returned to Petrograd from Switzerland in April 1917 (see page 192) he said that the Bolsheviks should overthrow the Provisional Government. After this they could set up a communist dictatorship.

To bring this about they needed to get control of the Petrograd Soviet. The Bolsheviks started to push themselves forwards with slogans such as 'All Power to the Soviets' and 'Peace, Land and Bread'.

The July Days

In July 1917, demonstrations against the war, organised by the Bolsheviks in Petrograd, turned into an uprising against the Provisional Government.

The Bolshevik leaders were taken by surprise. Lenin could not decide whether to seize power or not. This gave the government the time to move loyal troops into the city. They put down the uprising and the 'July Days' came to an end.

> **Bolshevik slogans**
>
> 'All power to the Soviets'
>
> 'Peace, Land and Bread'

SOURCE C

Troops open fire on the crowds in Petrograd during the 'July Days', 1917.

190   Russia 1905–41

The Kornilov affair

The government arrested hundreds of Bolsheviks after the 'July Days'. Lenin was accused of being a German spy and was forced into hiding in Finland. The Kornilov affair soon followed.

- In July Kerensky appointed General Kornilov as commander-in-chief of the army. He thought Kornilov would bring back some discipline into the troops. It proved to be a big mistake.

- Kornilov was a supporter of the Tsar and, therefore, wanted to see the Provisional Government overthrown.

- In early September, he sent his troops into Petrograd with the intention of seizing power and bringing back the Tsar.

- Kerensky panicked and asked the Bolsheviks for help. He released many Bolsheviks from prison. They formed a private army called the Red Guard to protect the Provisional Government from attack.

- Kornilov's men did not want to fight. The Red Guard easily persuaded them to lay down their arms and Kornilov was arrested.

- The Bolsheviks had prevented Kornilov from bringing back the Tsar, and as a result their popularity increased.

Bolsheviks in control

By late September the Bolsheviks had won control of most of the soviets, including Petrograd and Moscow. In early October Lenin returned from Finland. Together with Trotsky he began to plan the overthrow of the Provisional Government. It was just a matter of choosing the right moment to seize power.

> **QUESTIONS**
>
> 1 Read page 190.
>   a What slogans did the Bolsheviks have?
>   b What happened in the 'July Days'?
>
> 2 Look at Source D. Why do you think the Provisional Government published this poster?

SOURCE D

A Provisional Government poster. It shows a Russian soldier, backed by workers and soldiers, heroically going on with the war.

Rule of the Bolsheviks 191

Why were the Bolsheviks able to seize power in November 1917?

The Bolsheviks prepare

Lenin believed that if the Bolsheviks could seize power by force no one would have the courage to fight them. The decision was taken to stage an armed uprising, but no date was fixed. However, it was a nervous time for the Bolsheviks, as they could not be certain that the working people of Petrograd would support them.

By now Kerensky was out of touch with the feelings of the workers and soldiers. When he ordered soldiers based in Petrograd to fight the Germans they refused and said they supported the Bolsheviks.

SOURCE E

A painting of Lenin addressing the crowd at the Finland Station in Petrograd, April 1917.

Lenin

Lenin was born into a middle class family in 1870. His real name was Vladimir Ilich Ulyanov. He changed his name to avoid being arrested by the Tsar's police.

Lenin first became involved in revolutionary politics when he was at university. He did not like the way the Tsar ruled Russia and wanted things to change. In 1887 his elder brother was executed for his part in a plot to assassinate the Tsar.

From 1900 Lenin spent most of his time in exile in western Europe. Here Lenin read the works of Karl Marx and became a believer in communism.

When the Social Democrats split in 1903, Lenin became one of the main leaders of the Bolsheviks.

Lenin returned to Russia in 1905, but was forced into exile in Switzerland until 1917. He returned to Russia with the help of the Germans after the March revolution (see Source E).

Lenin set up *Pravda*, the Bolshevik Party's newspaper. He was a very determined person who led the Bolsheviks to power in Russia in November 1917.

After the revolution of 1917, Lenin became the leader of Russia until his death in 1924.

He will be remembered for turning Russia into a communist dictatorship.

> **SOURCE F**

The defenders of the Provisional Government: the Women's Battalion outside the Winter Palace.

The Bolsheviks seize power in Petrograd

- On the night of 6-7 November 1917, Red Guards occupied government buildings all over Petrograd. Most people in the city did not even notice a revolution was happening. Kerensky fled the city while the rest of the government barricaded themselves into the Winter Palace.

- A few thousand soldiers, including 200 women, guarded the palace (see Source F). Gradually the soldiers slipped away. Late in the evening of the 6 November shells were fired at the palace. Then, at 2.00 am on the 7 November Bolsheviks entered the palace and arrested the ministers inside. The Provisional Government had been overthrown.

- The way was now clear for Lenin to form a Bolshevik government. Although the Bolsheviks had control of Petrograd, the capital city, they were not very powerful in other parts of Russia.

- It took the Bolsheviks another ten days to take over Moscow and it was not long before their opponents began to fight back.

What happened to Kerensky?

Kerensky went into hiding in November 1917, before escaping from Russia. He emigrated to the USA in 1940, where he died in 1970 at the age of 89.

> **SOURCE G**
>
> We were under attack. Defence was useless. A soldier rushed in and said, 'We are ready to defend to the last man, if the Provisional Government so orders. What does the Provisional Government command?
>
> 'Surrender!' we shouted. 'Hurry! Go and tell them! We want no blood! We surrender!' The soldier left. The whole scene took no more than a minute.

A member of the Provisional Government describes the surrender of the Winter Palace to the Bolsheviks.

Bolshevik rule

Once in power Lenin moved quickly to help the workers. On 8 November 1917 the new Bolshevik government issued two important decrees.

1. **The Decree on Land** ordered landowners' estates to be confiscated. The land was immediately given to the peasants to farm.

2. **The Decree on Peace** called for Germany to make a fair peace with Russia. The Germans, however, made the peace terms very harsh.

Lenin signed the Treaty of Brest-Litovsk with Germany in March 1918. By this treaty Russia lost half its territory in Europe, including some of its best farming land. Half of Russia's grain and coal production was also lost (see map below).

Industry

Coalmines, factories and banks were taken away from private owners and put under the control of the workers. There were soon problems. High prices and low wages meant people could not afford to buy goods, so production collapsed.

Secret Police

Lenin closed down all the newspapers that opposed the Bolsheviks. In December 1917 he set up the **Cheka** (a secret police force), which tried to find anyone opposed to the Bolsheviks.

The Constituent Assembly

Lenin allowed elections for a new parliament (that had been promised since March 1917) to go ahead. In the elections, the Bolsheviks won only 24 per cent of the vote. The more moderate Social Revolutionaries, however, won 38 per cent.

The new parliament, called the Constituent Assembly, met for only one day. When it refused to accept Bolshevik control, the Assembly was broken up by Bolshevik troops.

In March 1918 the Bolsheviks changed their name to the Communist Party.

Russia's losses in the Treaty of Brest-Litovsk, March 1918.

- Russian frontier in 1914
- Russian frontier after Treaty of Brest-Litovsk
- Russian land lost

QUESTIONS

1. Read page 193. How did the Bolsheviks seize power in Russia in November 1917?

2. Read page 194. What changes did the Bolsheviks introduce once they were in power?

Why did the Bolsheviks win the civil war?

The Bolsheviks started to set up a communist dictatorship in Russia. Many people were opposed to this and wanted to overthrow them.

Reds versus Whites

- In 1918 a bloody civil war broke out in Russia between the Reds (Bolsheviks) and the **Whites**. Fighting on the side of the Whites were Mensheviks, Social Revolutionaries, supporters of the Tsar and a number of foreign countries.

- Three Tsarist generals commanded the White armies: Yudenich, Kolchak and Denikin. The British, French and Americans also sent troops to help the Whites. Trotsky formed the **Red Army** to fight the Whites.

- At first the Red Army was weak, but Trotsky was a good organiser. He soon turned the Reds into an efficient army.

- The White armies seemed to have the Reds surrounded. But the Reds were united and determined to win. They held a central position and controlled Moscow (the new capital) and Petrograd. The Whites did not co-ordinate their attacks, had different aims and were geographically split.

A communist cartoon of 1919. The three dogs are labelled Denikin, Kolchak and Yudenich.

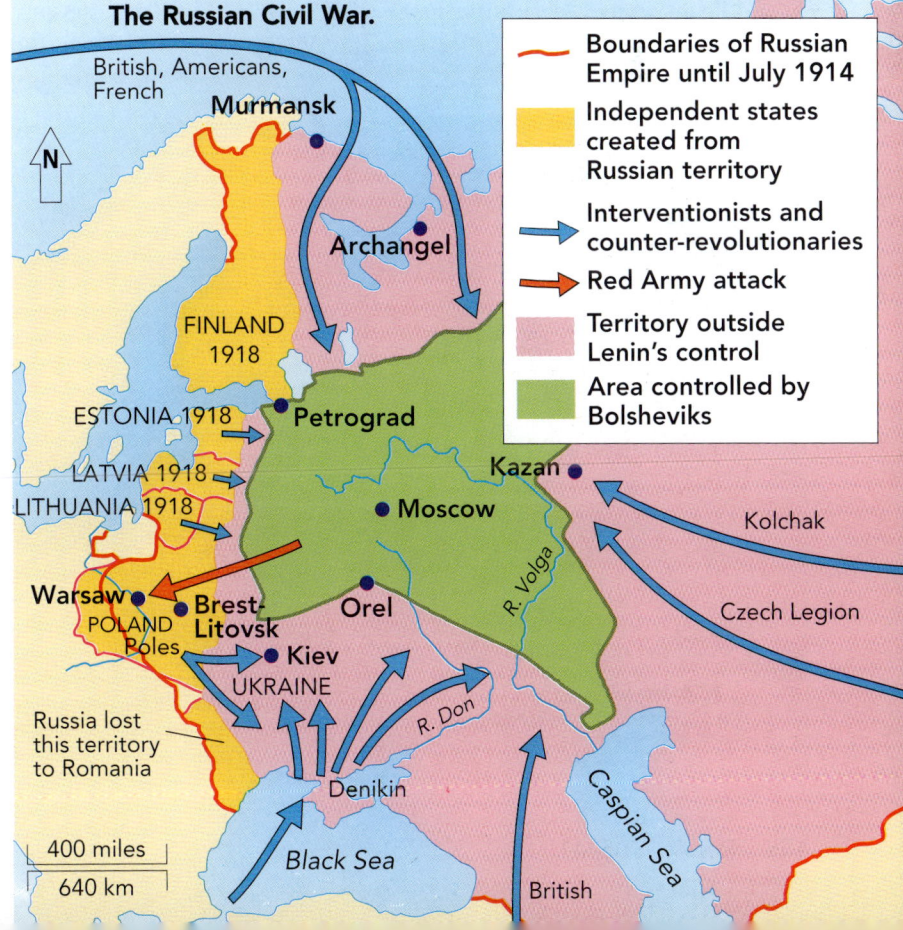

SOURCE H

The Russian Civil War.

Leon Trotsky

Trotsky joined the Bolsheviks in 1917 and quickly rose to become Lenin's second in command. Trotsky was ruthless and determined. He made sure the Red Army was a disciplined force. Anyone who deserted was executed.

Trotsky travelled around Russia by train to meet the troops and spur them to greater efforts. By 1920 the Red Army had five million soldiers.

War Communism and the Red Terror

- To make sure the Red Army was well supplied Lenin introduced **War Communism**. This involved the communist government taking control of factories and the distribution of goods. The Cheka was sent into the countryside to seize grain from the peasants to feed the Red Army. Once the Red Army had been supplied, however, there was not much food left for the people.

- Following an attempt to assassinate Lenin, the 'Red Terror' was unleashed. The Cheka arrested anyone suspected of being an opponent of the Communist Party, especially members of the middle and upper classes. As many as 750,000 people may have been murdered by the Cheka during the Russian Civil War.

Murder of the Tsar

Tsar Nicholas and his family were being held captive by the Reds in a house in Ekaterinburg in the Ural Mountains. With the White armies closing in it was decided to kill the whole family. If the Whites had freed the Tsar, they would have tried to put him back on the throne.

On the night of 16-17 July 1918 the Tsar, his wife, children and servants were taken to the cellar of the house. They were brutally shot by Red soldiers, and their bodies were buried in a nearby forest. The bodies remained undiscovered until 1991.

The end of the civil war

- The fighting in the civil war was bloody and vicious. There were many atrocities on both sides.

- The Whites had some early success in the war, but could not co-ordinate their attacks or agree on a single leader.

- Gradually, the Reds gained the upper hand and were finally victorious in 1920.

- The Russian people suffered terribly during the civil war. Industrial production fell sharply and in 1920 there was a bad harvest. Only 60 per cent of the normal amount of food was grown.

SOURCE I

The cellar in which the Tsar and his family were murdered. The damage to the wall caused by the shots that killed the royal family can be seen clearly.

> ### SOURCE J
>
> In Moscow I asked a colleague, 'Where is the Tsar?'
> 'It's all over,' he answered. 'He has been shot'.
>
> 'And where is the family?'
>
> 'The family has been shot along with him.' 'All of them?' I asked.
>
> 'All of them', he replied. 'What about it?'
>
> 'Lenin believed the Whites would use the Tsar as a live banner to rally around. So he decided to have him killed.'
>
> I did not ask any more questions, but the decision to kill the Tsar and his family was necessary. It was needed to frighten, horrify and dishearten the Whites, and also to show our own side there was no turning back.

In 1935 Trotsky published his diaries. Here he describes how he heard of the Tsar's death.

- There was widespread famine and disease, which killed eight million people. The communist government had become a cruel dictatorship.

The Kronstadt rising

- In March 1921 sailors at the naval base of Kronstadt mutinied. The sailors had supported the communists at first, but they did not like the way they were running Russia. They called for an end to the forced seizures of grain.

- The uprising worried the government. If the sailors were prepared to oppose the government, then anyone could.

- On 16-17 March, 50,000 Red Army soldiers were sent to put down the uprising. More than 2000 of the sailors captured were executed. Thousands were sent to labour camps and a further 8000 fled to Finland. Ending the uprising had also cost the lives of 10,000 Red Army soldiers.

QUESTIONS

1 Read page 196.
   a What was War Communism?
   b What was the 'Red Terror'?

2 Why do you think the Reds won the Civil War?

How far was the New Economic Policy a success?

- During the civil war industrial and agricultural production dropped. War Communism was very unpopular and there were riots in the countryside. Lenin knew he had to do something to put Russia back on its feet. So, in 1921 he introduced the **New Economic Policy (NEP)**, which brought back capitalism and allowed people to trade freely with one another.

1. Peasants were now allowed to sell their crops and keep the profits. This provided them with an **incentive** to grow as much as they could. The peasants stopped rioting.

2. Shopkeepers and small businesses were also allowed to sell their goods on the open market and keep the profits. Only the largest factories were kept under government control. New businesses and market stalls sprang up in the towns. The owners were known as 'NEPmen'.

- Some Bolsheviks thought the NEP was a betrayal of communism. But the NEP was successful in getting Russia back on its feet. By 1926-7, production had returned to the level it was before 1914. The fact that there was peace between 1921-6 also helped industry and agriculture to recover.

Lenin's death

Lenin suffered a stroke in May 1922. This was followed by two further strokes in December 1922 and March 1923.

He eventually died on 21 January 1924. A long struggle for the leadership of Russia then followed.

SOURCE K

The workers and peasants need freedom. They do not want the laws of the Bolsheviks.

We demand freedom of speech, press and assembly. We want free election of factory committees, trade unions and soviets.

Demands of demonstrators in Petrograd, February 1921.

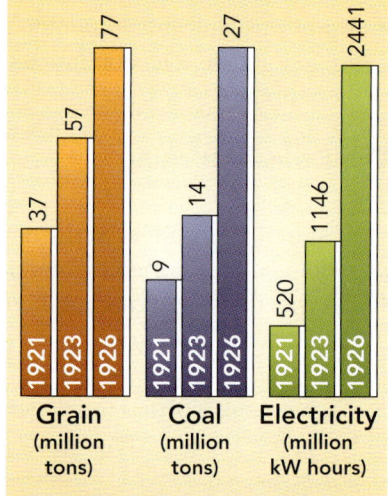

Grain (million tons): 1921: 37, 1923: 57, 1926: 77
Coal (million tons): 1921: 9, 1923: 14, 1926: 27
Electricity (million kW hours): 1921: 520, 1923: 1146, 1926: 2441

The increase of production under the NEP.

SOURCE L

A Soviet cartoon from 1927. A NEPman has become so rich he has to fill in a tax return. Upper class people (who did not pay tax) are laughing at him.

How did Stalin gain and hold on to power?

- In the late 1920s Joseph Stalin emerged as the leader of the **Union of Soviet Socialist Republics** (USSR or Soviet Union for short) as Russia had become in 1922. Stalin was a ruthless dictator. Under him the Soviet Union was to suffer even more. Stalin was determined to make the Soviet Union a modern, industrialised nation. He achieved this by:

1 Taking land from the peasants and making them work on government owned collective farms.

2 Building up industry with a series of **Five-Year Plans**.

- Any opposition to Stalin's plans was crushed by the secret police. In the 'Great Purges' of the mid-1930s Stalin got rid of his opponents in the Communist Party. Most of the 'Old Bolsheviks' were charged with imaginary crimes and arrested. In the **show trials** that followed they were found guilty and sentenced to death.

- By 1939, Stalin had turned the Soviet Union in a great industrial power but at the cost of thousands of lives.

Why did Stalin, and not Trotsky, emerge as Lenin's successor?

After Lenin's death there was a power struggle between Stalin and Trotsky for the leadership of the Soviet Union.

Trotsky

- Trotsky was a brilliant organiser. He helped the Bolsheviks to seize power in November 1917 and won the Russian Civil War by organising the Red Army.

- However, many members of the Communist Party disliked him. They thought he was arrogant and untrustworthy.

- Trotsky was also unpopular because he wanted to carry on with War Communism and was against the NEP. He believed in 'permanent revolution', which meant spreading communism through the world. Some people hated Trotsky simply because he was a Jew.

SOURCE A

Piatakov was very pale and shaken. He poured a glass of water, gulped it down and said, 'You know I have never seen anything like this! This was worse than anything!

'Why did he say this? Stalin will never forgive him.' When Trotsky finally entered the room, Piatakov rushed at him and said, 'Why have you said this?' Trotsky brushed the question aside with the wave of his hand. He had shouted at Stalin, 'Grave-digger of the Revolution'. We realised the quarrel could not be healed.

An account of the moments after the meeting in which Trotsky was sacked from the Politburo in 1926. The author met Piatakov, an important communist, straight after the meeting.

Stalin

- Unlike Trotsky, Stalin had not done anything outstanding. He had none of Trotsky's brilliance. But this did not stop him from steadily gaining in power. When Stalin became the General Secretary of the Communist Party in 1922, he made sure he appointed his supporters to the top positions. Stalin believed in 'socialism in one country', which stressed the need to establish communism in the Soviet Union and make it a powerful country.

- Before he died Lenin noticed that Stalin was becoming over-ambitious. This worried him and the friendship between the two men cooled. In his will Lenin warned that Stalin had too much power and should be sacked as General Secretary.

- Other leading members of the Communist Party ignored Lenin's advice. They preferred Stalin's more cautious policy of 'socialism in one country' to Trotsky's idea of a 'permanent revolution'.

Kamenev and Zinoviev

- After Lenin's death, Stalin ruled jointly with Kamenev and Zinoviev. Gradually, these three men pushed Trotsky out of the top positions. He was sacked from the **Politburo** (the cabinet) in 1926 and in 1927 was removed from the Central Committee of the Communist Party. Trotsky then fled the Soviet Union and went to live in Mexico.

- Stalin now had enough power to turn against Kamenev and Zinoviev. They were sacked from their party and government posts. By 1928, Stalin was the sole leader of the Soviet Union. But the struggle for power had left him very suspicious of his colleagues.

SOURCE B

A Soviet poster from 1927. Kamenev, Trotsky and Zinoviev are shown as part of a 'close' family.

QUESTIONS

1 Read page 199. Why was Trotsky unpopular?

2 Read page 200.
a How was Stalin able to push Trotsky out of power?
b What happened to Kamenev and Zinoviev?

SOURCE C

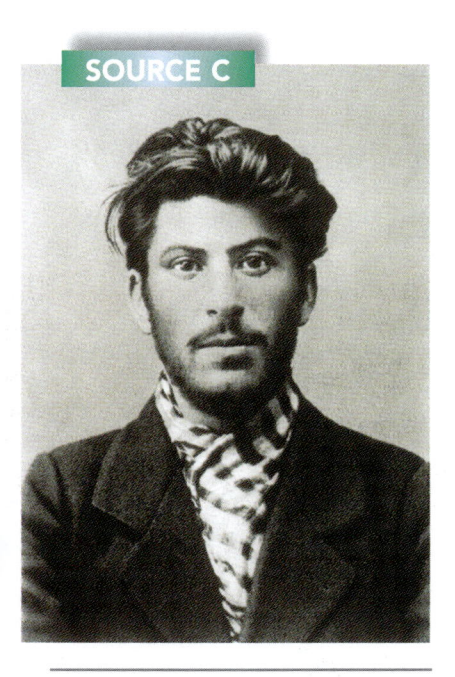

A police photograph of Stalin taken in about 1900.

Stalin

Stalin, the son of a shoemaker, was born in Georgia (see map on page 210). He was one of the few Bolshevik leaders to come from a working-class family.

Stalin's real name was Josif Dzhugashvili. When he became a revolutionary he used false names to avoid arrest and he finally settled on the name of Stalin ('man of steel') in 1913.

Stalin trained as a priest, but was expelled from the priesthood when it became known that he was a revolutionary. He joined the Social Democratic Party in 1898 and was imprisoned several times for committing crimes, including raiding banks to get money for the party.

Stalin became well known in the Bolshevik Party and Lenin made him the editor of Pravda, the party's newspaper. Stalin helped to plan the November Revolution of 1917.

Once the Bolsheviks were in power, Stalin built up a strong position. When Lenin died in 1924, Stalin was well placed to deal with his rivals and he went on to become the leader of the Soviet Union.

Stalin led the Soviet Union during the Second World War and died in 1953.

Why did Stalin launch the 'purges'?

The struggle for power after Lenin's death showed that there were disagreements in the Communist Party. Although Stalin had got the better of Trotsky, Kamenev and Zinoviev, he was still worried that someone else would try to overthrow him.

During the 1930s Stalin decided to **purge** (remove) his rivals once and for all.

Sergei Kirov

- In 1934 Stalin believed his enemies were planning to replace him with Sergei Kirov, a popular party member from Leningrad. Stalin secretly ordered Yagoda, the head of the **NKVD** (secret police), to have Kirov murdered.

- Stalin then used Kirov's murder as a means of removing other opponents. Zinoviev, Kamenev and others were accused of being involved in the murder. In January 1935 they were put on trial and sentenced to imprisonment.

- In 1936 the two men were charged with working with Trotsky and spying for foreign countries. The NKVD provided evidence that friends of Zinoviev and Kamenev had been in touch with Trotsky in Mexico. They both 'confessed' to their crimes in court in August 1936 and were shot.

The Great Terror

- The execution of Zinoviev and Kamenev started the 'Great Terror'. The NKVD was ordered to hunt out Stalin's enemies, both real and imagined. For the next two years no one was safe from arrest.

- Stalin began the terror by sacking Yagoda, the head of the NKVD. Stalin said that Yagoda had not rooted out enough traitors. Yezhov replaced Yagoda.

- There were more show trials during 1937-8. Senior members of the Communist Party were arrested. In court they confessed to committing imaginary crimes against the state. Most of them were found guilty and shot.

- Stalin then turned against the generals in the Red Army. They were made to confess to plotting to overthrow Stalin. So many generals were shot that the Red Army was left short of trained leaders.

The secret police

- The NKVD arrested and shot hundreds of thousands of people. Even official records admit to 700,000 people being shot during the Great Terror of 1937-8. Stalin, himself, played a direct part in the deaths of 40,000 people.

- In the end Stalin turned against the NKVD. Many senior officers were shot and Beria replaced Yezhov, who was arrested and shot in 1940.

SOURCE D

An American cartoon about Stalin's show trials.

The end of the Great Terror

By 1938 it was clear that Stalin had murdered many of the Soviet Union's top people. Managers, engineers, scientists and army officers had all disappeared in large numbers. Factories and other workplaces were grinding to a halt. Stalin therefore called a halt to the Great Terror.

In 1940 Stalin's agents finally hunted down Trotsky in Mexico. Trotsky was murdered with an ice axe. All Stalin's main rivals were now dead.

What methods did Stalin use to control the Soviet Union?

Stalin turned the Soviet Union into a police state. No opposition to Stalin was allowed. All the Soviet people lived in fear of arrest by the NKVD. Prisoners were beaten, tortured or even murdered.

Many people disappeared and were never seen again. Just being suspected of being against Stalin was enough to be arrested. No wonder few people dared to oppose him.

Informers

The NKVD had a network of informers or spies in schools, factories and farms. They reported anyone who criticised Stalin. Even children were told to inform on their parents.

One peasant boy, who reported his father for hoarding grain, was held up as an example to other children.

SOURCE E

Volodya, a young student, noticed that some of his classmates were looking sad. They stood alone in the playground and sat silently in class. Then after a while they disappeared and did not come to school.

Volodya told his father about the vanishing students. His father explained that the NKVD [secret police] was uncovering spies, enemies and traitors. Those found were sent away, along with their families.

One day Volodya saw his father throw some books into the dustbin: the authors had been arrested. Another time his father inked out the photograph of Trotsky in a book about the Russian Civil War.

In school, Volodya's teachers told the class to tear out photographs of people who had been found to be a spy. Volodya thought this was a good thing. Now the spies had been found, people could live in safety.

An account of how the terror affected daily life in the Soviet Union.

QUESTIONS

1 Read pages 202–3. What was the Great Terror?

2 What happened to Trotsky?

3 Look at Source D. Is this cartoon reliable evidence that those accused in the show trials were guilty? Explain your answer.

The Soviet Union under Stalin

Labour camps

- People who were not shot for their crimes were sent to labour camps. These were located in the remotest parts of the Soviet Union. The prisoners were used as slave labour on building projects that were part of the Five-Year Plans.

- Living conditions in the camps were brutal. Prisoners were never given enough food, and were made to work in the icy conditions of the Soviet winter. The camp guards were cruel and beat the prisoners. By 1939 about 3 million people were held in labour camps. Millions died from hunger, cold and exhaustion in these camps.

Propaganda

- Propaganda was widely used to influence the Soviet people. They were not allowed to think for themselves and were told what to do by the state.

- Schoolchildren were taught the communist version of history. Newspapers, radio and films were all controlled by the state. Only material approved by the state could be published.

- Street posters rammed home the message that communism was the best way of running the Soviet Union.

SOURCE F

A French cartoon from the 1930s. The placard says, 'We are very happy.'

QUESTION

1 Study Source F. What did the cartoonist think of Stalin's rule?

The cult of personality

The most important propaganda message was that Stalin was the greatest leader of his time. The Soviet people were taught that Stalin was all-powerful and all-knowing. They came to look upon him as a god. His image was everywhere, in photographs and paintings and on statues. He was always shown as a great person and without any criticism at all.

This flood of pro-Stalin propaganda led to a kind of hero worship known as the **cult of personality**. It helps to explain why so many Soviet people worshipped an evil dictator.

How complete was Stalin's control over the Soviet Union by 1941?

- During the 1930s Stalin destroyed all his opponents, so that he was the unchallenged leader of the Soviet Union. He was the only member of Lenin's government still alive in 1941. All the others had died, been murdered or committed suicide. The Red Army and the secret police had also been purged. Rarely has one leader held such power in running a country.

- Despite this, however, there were limits to Stalin's power. The Soviet Union was so big it was impossible for the government to control everything.

  1 Factory managers sometimes did not obey instructions from the government that they did not agree with. This was why Stalin purged this group in 1937-8.

  2 Crime and hooliganism were common in Soviet cities. Divorce and abortions also increased. It appears that in their private lives many people did as they pleased rather than as the government wished.

Although Stalin dealt ruthlessly with officials who opposed him, it was harder to control the lives of millions of ordinary people.

SOURCE G

The cult of personality: Stalin shown as a father figure. The little girl's father was later shot, a victim of the purges.

What was the impact of Stalin's economic policies?

In 1928 Stalin started to modernise industry and agriculture.

1. **Five-Year Plans** Industry was modernised by a series of Five-Year Plans. Industries were set production targets by the government. The workers made a huge effort to achieve the targets, and within ten years the Soviet Union was a major industrial power.

2. **Collectivisation** The government took land away from the peasants and set up huge collective farms. The peasants were forced to work on these farms. The idea was to increase the amount of food grown. But the peasants resisted the change because they wanted to farm their own land. Stalin used violence to force **collectivisation** on the peasants.

Why did Stalin introduce the Five-Year Plans?

When Stalin came to power the Soviet Union was still a rural, backward country.

Stalin was anxious to make the Soviet Union a great industrial power. He believed that if he did not build up the strength of the Soviet Union, capitalist countries that wished to destroy communism would invade it.

Stalin used **Gosplan**, a government-planning bureau, to organise the Five-Year Plans.

The first Five-Year Plan (1928-32)

This was designed to build up heavy industries such as coal and steel. The workers were encouraged to meet the production targets within four years. The targets were tough, but there was a huge increase in production.

SOURCE A

The Dnieper Dam, built during the Five-Year Plans.

This also made some problems. The roads and railways were not good enough to take all the goods to market, and more houses had to be built in the cities for the increased number of factory workers. The increase in production was paid for by a fall in living conditions. Food rationing was brought back so that the workers had enough to eat.

The second Five-Year Plan (1933-7)
This concentrated on producing machinery, tools and tractors for the collective farms.

The third Five-Year Plan (1938-41)
This focused on the production of household goods such as washing machines and radios. It was interrupted by the outbreak of the Second World War and only lasted about three years. The success of the plan was also hindered by the fact that many factory managers had been killed in the Great Terror.

By 1941, the Soviet Union was the world's second biggest industrial nation.

It was no longer the backward country that it had been when Stalin came to power.

Soviet production figures 1928-38		
	1928	1938
Coal	35 million tonnes	132 million tonnes
Iron and Steel	7 million tonnes	32 million tonnes
Oil	12 million tonnes	29 million tonnes
Tractors	1,000	176,000

The modernisation of Soviet industry

During the 1930s the Soviet Union became a great industrial nation.

- Factories, dams and canals were built.

- Whole new industrial towns sprang up.

- New mining areas were opened up.

The government praised workers who produced more than the targets set for them. The coalminer, Alexei Stakhanov, was held up as an example for other workers to follow. It was claimed that he dug 102 tonnes of coal in 6 hours (his target was 7 tonnes).

How successful were the Five-Year Plans?

- Although the Five-Year Plans increased production, it is not possible to say by exactly how much. The government often lied about the production figures to make the plans look a success. (The figures in the box are an estimation of how much production increased.)

- Factory managers were so concerned about quantity that the quality of the goods was often poor. The workers had to work under tough rules. Those late for work were fined.

- Also, in the rush to increase production, safety was forgotten and accidents were common. As there was a shortage of skilled workers, they were treated better and paid higher wages than unskilled workers.

Why did Stalin introduce collectivisation?

The peasants who farmed the land used old-fashioned methods and did not want to modernise. Stalin wanted to change farming for two main reasons.

- He wanted the peasants' grain so that he could sell it abroad. With the money raised he could buy vital equipment for industry.

- The factory workers in the towns needed cheap food. If the peasants controlled the sale of grain, they would keep the prices high. This would mean that factory workers would need to be paid more.

Collective farms

Stalin made the peasants put their land together to form collective farms that were controlled by the government.

The peasants were paid to work on the collective farms, which were called **kolkhoz**. Stalin's aim was to produce more food by using modern methods.

Rebellion

Most peasants, especially the **kulaks**, hated the collective farms and refused to sell or give their produce to the government.

Stalin forced them to co-operate. He sent the army and secret police into the countryside to terrorise the peasants. By 1930 about 14 million peasant households had been forced to join the collectives. Other peasants were forced off the land to work in factories.

They hid their grain from the soldiers. Many peasants killed their livestock and burned their crops rather than hand them over to the government.

Famine

The amount of food produced actually went down for a time (see chart). Soon there was a shortage of food and it looked like there might be a famine.

Peasants demonstrating against the kulaks. The banner says, 'We demand collectivisation and the extermination of all kulaks.'

SOURCE B

In 1932-3 three million peasants in the countryside died of hunger. Despite this, Stalin still sold grain to foreign countries.

Stalin was ruthless in crushing the resistance of the kulaks. About five million of them were sent to labour camps. As a class they were stamped out.

> ### SOURCE C
>
> Collective farms were absolutely necessary for the Soviet Union, if we were to avoid famines and plough the land with tractors. We needed to mechanise our farming. We took a lot of trouble to explain this to the peasants. But it was still a struggle to set up collective farms. It was all very bad and difficult, but necessary.

Stalin talking to Winston Churchill in 1942.

Food production in the Soviet Union 1930–5			
	1930	1933	1935
Grain	83 million tonnes	68 million tonnes	72 million tonnes
Cattle	52 million	38 million	48 million
Pigs	14 million	12 million	22 million

How successful were Stalin's economic changes?

- To begin with the effect of collectivisation on production was catastrophic. The resistance of the peasants meant that production fell. But, once all the collective farms had been set up, Stalin had control of agricultural production and was able to sell grain abroad. This brought in money to build new factories. Machine tractor stations were set up to help mechanise farming.

- Farms began to specialise in certain crops, which made it easier for new methods to be adopted.

- From the late 1930s the amount of food produced in the Soviet Union went up slowly. Not until the 1950s, however, did food production reach the levels that had been seen before the First World War.

QUESTIONS

1. 1 Read pages 206-7.
   a What were the Five-Year Plans?
   b Why were they introduced?
   c Who was Alexei Stakhanov?

2. Read pages 208-9.
   a What was collectivisation?
   b What effects did it have on Soviet farming?

3. Look at Source B. Why do you think this photograph was taken?

How were the Soviet people affected by these changes?

1 Ethnic minorities in the Soviet Union

- The Soviet Union was made up of many different nationalities. The Russians were the largest group. But there were also, for example, Georgians, Armenians and Ukrainians (see map below). At first Stalin allowed the non-Russian peoples of the Soviet Union to keep their own cultures and traditions.

- From 1934 this changed when Stalin adopted a policy of **Russification** throughout the Soviet Union. Russian was made the main language in schools and the army. Stalin wanted the separate nationalities to forget their own cultures. He was aiming to turn them into loyal Soviet citizens.

- During the purges ethnic minorities were a target for persecution. Muslims, for example, were made to close down the mosques where they worshipped.

2 Women in the Soviet Union

- Under Stalin the government encouraged women to marry and have children. Women who had more than ten children were awarded medals.

- Women were expected to work in factories (see Source E) doing similar jobs to men. But they were also expected to run the house, do the housework and bear children.

- Government propaganda posters showed women as equals with men. But, in reality, Soviet life was still male-dominated. Not one woman held an important position in the government during Stalin's years in power.

The national republics of the Soviet Union (USSR).

3 Social groups in the Soviet Union

There were three major social groups in the Soviet Union in the 1930s.

1. **Peasants** were made to work on collective farms (*kolkhoz*). They were paid a low wage, and would have starved had they not been given a small plot of land to grow food.

   The peasants were angry at the way they had been treated. Life in the countryside under Stalin was very grim.

2. **Industrial workers** also led tough lives. Wages were low, although more people were working and most families had some money to spend.

   Housing was poor in the cities, but many people had free schooling and medicine.

3. **The social elite** was made up of scientists, managers and important people in the Communist Party. They had a much higher standard of living than the workers, earning more and enjoying 'perks' such as special shops and holidays at government-run resorts.

   This trend was most obvious in the Soviet (Red) Army, which went back to using ranks and titles. Even members of the social elite, however, were not safe from the secret police. Many managers and scientists were murdered during Stalin's purges of 1937-8.

SOURCE D

During the 1930s the government raised the living standards of those who had proved their usefulness. A number of privileged people came into being, with large houses in the countryside and cars.

But during the purges they found they could have everything taken away from them, and without any explanation.

N. Mandelstam, the wife of the poet Osip Mandelstan, writing in 1971.

QUESTIONS

1. Read page 211 and Source D.
   Were members of the social elite safe from Stalin's purges?

2. Look at Source E.
   What does this poster tell us about the role of women in the Soviet Union?

SOURCE E

A Soviet propaganda picture from 1927 encouraging women to work.

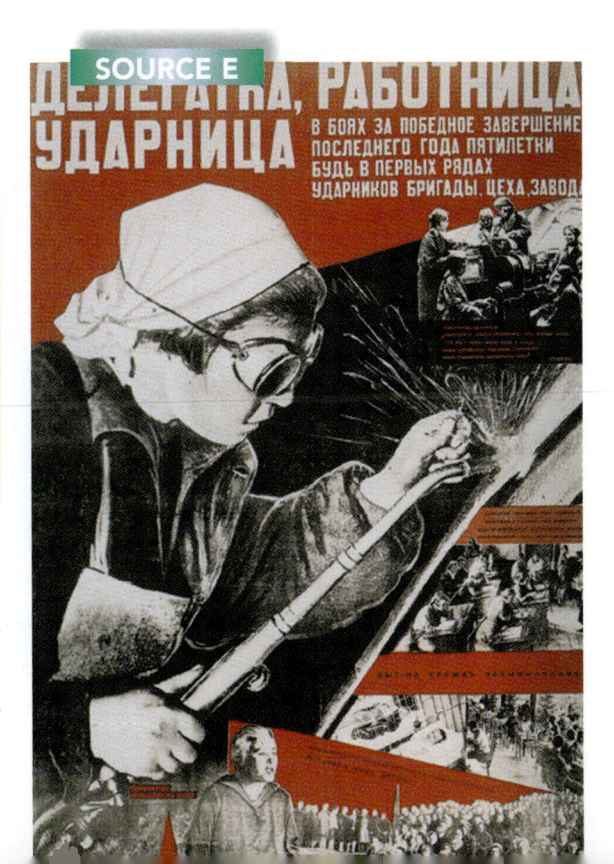

Paper 1-type assessment: Stalin's rule

SOURCE A

His fingers are fat as grubs
And words, final as lead weights, fall from his lips

His cockroach whiskers leer
And his boot tops gleam

Around him a rabble of thin-necked leaders –
Fawning half-men for him to play with

They whinny, purr or whine
As he chatters and points a finger

One by one forging his laws, to be flung
Like horseshoes at the head, eye or groin

As every killing is a treat
For the broad chested Stalin

From a poem written about Stalin in the 1930s. The poet later died in one of Stalin's labour camps.

QUESTIONS

Section C Questions

Study the sources carefully and then answer the three questions which follow.

1 a Study Source A. Why do you think people wrote poems like this in the Soviet Union in the 1930s? Use the source and your own knowledge to explain your answer. (6)

b Study Source B. Why do you think this poster was produced? Use the source and your own knowledge to explain your answer. (7)

c Study Source C. This source shows that Stalin treated the Soviet people badly. Why then did they continue to support him? Use the source and your own knowledge to explain your answer. (7)

SOURCE B

A Soviet poster of Stalin planning shelter belts to alter the climate.

212 Russia 1905–41

SOURCE C

A French cartoon of the 1930s calling on people 'to visit the pyramids of the Soviet Union'.

QUESTIONS

When answering these questions make sure you answer ALL three parts.

Remember that you should always explain your answer as fully as you can and support it with specific detail where possible.

Section C Questions

2 a What were the main weaknesses of the Tsar's government in early 1917? (4)

b Explain why the Provisional Government could not maintain itself in power in 1917. (6)

c 'The most important reason for the success of the Bolsheviks in the period 1917-22 was Trotsky's work in creating an effective Red Army.' Do you agree with this statement? Explain your answer. (10)

3 a What were 'The Five Year Plans'? (4)

b Explain why Stalin introduced collectivisation into the Soviet Union. (6)

c Were Stalin's economic measures in the Soviet Union a failure or a success? Explain your answer. (10)

Core Part II:

International relations 1945–c.1989

6 International relations 1945–c.1989

- As the Second World War came to a close, the alliance between the Soviet Union and the Western Allies (the USA, Britain and France) began to break up. The distrust which East and West felt for each other led to the Cold War (a war of words and propaganda).

- By the end of 1948 Europe was divided by an 'iron curtain' separating the democratic, capitalist West from the communist East. Over the next 40 years each side tried to score diplomatic and tactical victories over the other. The United Nations, formed in 1945 to keep world peace, could do nothing to prevent the bad feeling between the USA and the Soviet Union.

- The USA put huge sums of money into western Europe to bring about economic recovery and stop the spread of communism. The Soviet Union tried to assert its authority by blockading Berlin in 1948-9 and building the Berlin Wall in 1961. It also kept communist east Europe firmly under control, as Hungary and Czechoslovakia found to their cost.

- The Americans were also keen to stop the spread of communism in Asia. They went to war in Korea and Vietnam to do so. In 1962 the Cuban Missile Crisis almost brought about the world's first nuclear war.

- The Cold War came to an end in 1989. Reforms introduced by Mikhail Gorbachev in the Soviet Union started protest movements across eastern Europe. One by one communist governments were overthrown. The communist control of eastern Europe came to and end and so did the Cold War.

This topic is examined in Paper 1 of the examination. Paper 1-type exercises are included at the end of each section. Mark schemes, sample answers and comments can be found in the accompanying Teacher's Resource Pack.

Who was to blame for the Cold War?

- From 1941 the USA and the Soviet Union were allies in the Second World War, fighting against Nazi Germany and Japan. But this alliance hid the distrust each country had for the other. At the end of the war in 1945 the two countries began to fall out.

- By 1949 the USA and the Soviet Union were involved in a **Cold War** – a war fought with words and propaganda. Winston Churchill, the British Prime Minister, said that Europe was divided by an **iron curtain**. On one side of the curtain were the Soviet-led eastern powers. On the other side were the American-led western powers. For the next 40 years the two sides were bitter rivals.

SOURCE A

WHAT, NO CHAIR FOR ME?

A cartoon from a British newspaper in September 1938. Stalin is complaining about being left out of the Munich talks.

Why did the USA-USSR alliance begin to break down in 1945?

Why did the USA and Soviet Union begin to fall out in 1945? How did they become bitter enemies involved in a Cold War? The answer is that the two sides simply did not trust each other.

Reasons for the distrust

1 Different political systems

- **Communism** Since 1917 the Soviet Union had been a communist country. Communists believed that the government should own industry and agriculture (see page 179). Any profits made should be used for the good of all the people. No individual was allowed to own a business and keep the profits for himself.

There was also no political freedom in the Soviet Union. The Communist Party was the only party allowed. In elections people chose from different candidates in that party. People in the Soviet Union were not allowed to criticise the government and the newspapers were told what they could print.

CAPITALISM

Wealthy people (capitalists) invest their money in land and industry. They employ the workers and keep all the profits that are made. A democratic system is followed with a number of political parties.

COMMUNISM

There is a classless society with no individual profit making. Land and industry are owned by the state and profits used for the good of all. There is only one political party.

Capitalism versus communism – a summary.

- **Capitalism** The USA was a capitalist country. Private individuals owned industry and agriculture. They employed the workers and kept the profits they made. There was also more personal freedom in a capitalist country. There were many different political parties and people voted in free elections for the party of their choice. People were allowed to criticise the government and newspapers had the freedom to print what they wished.

2 A history of mistrust

- Both sides thought that their political system was the way that all governments should run their countries. The USA and its western allies, such as Britain, hated communism. They thought that the Soviet Union was trying to spread it across the world.

- Politicians in the Soviet Union, however, thought they were under threat from the West. They said they had a right to take defensive measures to protect themselves from western aggression.

- The Soviets pointed to events in the past that suggested the West was out to destroy communism.

1. The USA, Britain and France had sent troops to help the Whites against the Reds (communists) during the Russian Civil War of 1918-20.

2. Hitler, the leader of Nazi Germany, hated communism. During the late 1930s Stalin tried to get France and Britain to help him against Hitler. But both countries did not appear to want an alliance with the Soviet Union. Stalin thought this meant that Britain and France were supporting Hitler because they wanted him to destroy the Soviet Union. Stalin's suspicions were strengthened by the Munich Conference in 1938. The conference agreed to Hitler taking part of Czechoslovakia. Stalin was not invited to the conference, even though Czechoslovakia was on the Soviet border.

The Cold War

3 When Hitler invaded the Soviet Union in 1941, the USA, Britain and France fought on the same side as the Soviets. Stalin asked his allies to open a second fighting front in Europe. This would draw German troops out of the Soviet Union. It took until 6 June 1944 (D-Day) for a second front to be opened. Stalin thought the allies purposely delayed things to give the Germans more time to weaken the Soviet Union.

The Yalta Conference

- In February 1945 President Franklin Roosevelt of the USA, Stalin and Churchill met at Yalta in the Soviet Union. The war was drawing to a close and the three leaders talked about how Europe was to be run in the future. The following decisions were made:

1 Germany was to be divided into four 'zones of occupation', one each to be controlled by the USA, the Soviet Union, Britain and France.

2 As Berlin, the capital, would be in the Soviet zone, it too was divided into four similar parts. (See the map on page 219.)

3 When Nazi Germany was finally beaten, the Soviet Union would join in the war against Japan.

4 The United Nations Organisation would be set up to keep world peace in the future.

5 As the Nazis were driven out of each eastern European country, free elections would be held to set up democratic governments.

The problem of Poland

The three leaders, however, failed to agree about Poland. Germany had invaded the Soviet Union twice within 30 years and Stalin wanted to make sure this did not happen again.

He wanted to make sure that Poland had a government friendly to the Soviet Union. This would make Poland a **buffer zone** between the Soviet Union and Germany.

SOURCE B

Churchill, Roosevelt and Stalin at Yalta.

SOURCE C

I didn't say it was good, I said it was the best I could do.

President Roosevelt commenting on the Yalta Agreement to one of his advisers.

SOURCE D

So far there has been no progress made in carrying out the decisions made at Yalta about Poland. I am puzzled by this and do not understand the attitude of your government.

President Roosevelt writing to Stalin in April 1945.

The division of Germany in 1945.

In January 1945 the Red Army drove the Nazis out of Poland and Stalin placed a communist government in power. Roosevelt and Churchill were against this. They made Stalin promise to include some 'London Poles' in the government. (The London Poles wanted Poland to be a democracy.) Stalin was also made to agree to hold free elections in Poland.

Stalin, however, did not wish Poland to be democratic. He wanted to keep a communist government in power. Free elections were never held and Roosevelt wrote a letter of complaint to Stalin (see Source D).

The Potsdam Conference

- A second conference was held in Potsdam in Germany starting in July 1945. Roosevelt had died in April 1945 and was replaced at Potsdam by the new American president, Harry S. Truman. Also, Clement Attlee had replaced Churchill as the British Prime Minister.

- By now the Soviets had freed all countries in eastern European from the Nazis. The USA and Britain wanted democratic governments set up, but Stalin ordered the Red Army to stay in eastern Europe. Truman distrusted Stalin and said, 'We have to get tough with the Soviets, they do not know how to behave.'

QUESTIONS

1. What is a Cold War?
2. Why was there so much mistrust between the East and West in 1945?
3. What was agreed about Germany at Yalta?

The Cold War 219

- When the Potsdam Conference started Truman told Stalin that the USA had recently developed an atomic bomb. Truman was sure it would be a long time before the Soviet Union had one, and this would allow him get tough with the USSR. He was not prepared to let Stalin have his own way. The following points were agreed at Potsdam:

1. Germany would be divided as agreed at Yalta.

2. Nazi leaders were to be tried for war crimes.

3. Germans living in Poland, Czechoslovakia and Hungary would be sent back to Germany.

But there were also big disagreements.

1. The Soviet Union demanded to share in the occupation of Japan, but Truman refused.

2. The USA and Britain said they wanted to have more say in eastern Europe. They did not want Stalin to set up communist governments in these countries, but Stalin ignored them.

Further divisions

The atomic bomb

The Potsdam Conference showed how divided the wartime allies were. The gap widened further after 1945. Stalin was afraid that the USA would use the threat of the atomic bomb to stop the spread of communism. He ordered his scientists to produce a Soviet atomic bomb as soon as possible.

SOURCE E

"IF WE DON'T LET HIM WORK, WHO'S GOING TO KEEP HIM?"

A cartoon from a British newspaper in July 1946. The foreign ministers of the wartime allies are arguing over what should be done to Germany now that the war was over.

SOURCE F

From Stettin in the Baltic to Trieste in the Adriatic, an iron curtain has descended across the continent. Behind that line lie all the capitals of the states of central and eastern Europe – Warsaw, Berlin, Prague, Vienna, Budapest, Bucharest and Sofia. All these famous cities lie in the Soviet sphere and are subject to control by Moscow.

Adapted from Churchill's speech at Fulton, Missouri, on 5 March 1946.

Churchill making his speech at Fulton on 5 March 1946.

SOURCE G

Germany

The wartime allies also fell out over Germany. Britain and France accused the Soviets of taking too much in reparations (compensation) from Germany. They said this would prevent Germany from recovering from the war. They also called for democratic elections in Germany, but Stalin refused.

Churchill's 'iron curtain' speech

On 5 March Churchill made his 'iron curtain' speech in the USA at Fulton, Missouri.

He said that Europe was being divided by the Soviet Union's policy. In the West there were free democratic countries. But in the East, behind an 'iron curtain', were communist countries under the control of the Soviet Union (see map on page 222).

Stalin was angered by Churchill's speech and said he was trying to stir up a war against the Soviet Union.

How had the USSR gained control of eastern Europe by 1948?

- By 1948 Stalin had made sure that every country in eastern Europe had a communist government and was friendly towards the Soviet Union. Stalin said this was a defensive measure to stop the Soviet Union being invaded from the west again.

- The USA, however, felt that the Soviet Union was trying to take over the world, and the western way of life was under threat. The spread of communism had to be stopped.

SOURCE H

Mr Churchill takes the stand of the warmongers. He has friends in the USA. As a result of the German invasion, the Soviet Union loss of lives has been several times greater than that of Britain and the USA put together. So, the Soviet Union, anxious for its future, is trying to see to it that governments loyal to the Soviet Union exist in the countries through which the Germans made their invasion.

How can anyone describe these peaceful hopes of the Soviet Union as expansionist?

Stalin's reply to Churchill's speech, 1946.

The Cold War

Soviet expansion, 1945–8.

- Estonia
- Latvia
- BALTIC STATES
- Lithuania
- SOVIET UNION
- Berlin
- EAST GERMANY
- POLAND
- CZECHOSLOVAKIA
- HUNGARY
- ROMANIA
- YUGOSLAVIA
- BULGARIA
- ALBANIA
- GREECE
- TURKEY
- Black Sea

Legend:
- Land taken by USSR at the end of Second World War
- Soviet-controlled communist countries
- Non-Soviet-controlled communist country

250 miles / 400 km

The Baltic States
At the end of the war, the Soviet Union extended its border some 500 kilometres west. It did this by formally annexing Latvia, Lithuania and Estonia, which it had occupied during the war with Finland in 1939–40. It also kept control of the eastern half of Poland, which it had occupied as part of the Nazi–Soviet agreement in 1939 (although the Germans had occupied this area from 1941 to 1945).

Poland
At the request of Britain and the USA at the end of June 1945, Stalin included a few London Poles in the new Polish government. In January 1947, however, fresh (rigged) elections saw the return of a totally communist government. The leader of the London Poles, Mikolaczyk, fled from Poland, fearing for his life.

Romania
After the expulsion of the Nazis, a coalition government dominated by communists was set up. In February 1945 the Soviet Union forced the king of Romania to appoint a communist prime minister. By the middle of the year, communists were in control, and in 1947 the monarchy was abolished.

Greece
Here the communists were not successful. They fought a civil war against royalists supported by Britain and the USA. Stalin stuck by his promise to the western allies not to provide support for the Greek communists, who were finally defeated in 1949.

Bulgaria
In late 1944 a communist-dominated coalition government was set up. In November 1945 the communists won rigged elections, and in 1946 they abolished the monarchy.

Czechoslovakia
Following the war, a coalition government ruled Czechoslovakia. From 1946 the communists were the largest party in the coalition. In 1948 the communists used the army to seize control. Many non-communists were arrested and the non-communist foreign secretary, Jan Masaryk, was murdered. Rigged elections were held in which the communists won a landslide victory. Other political parties were then banned.

East Germany
The Soviet Union controlled the eastern section of Germany after the war. In 1949 it became a separate communist state, the German Democratic Republic (East Germany).

Hungary
In November 1945 free elections were held and the non-communist Smallholders' Party won the most seats. In August 1947 fresh (rigged) elections were held and the communists won total control. All other political parties were then banned.

Yugoslavia
In Yugoslavia the communist resistance had fought bravely against the Germans, and in 1945 its leader, Marshal Tito, was elected president. At first, Tito and Stalin got on well, but relations deteriorated as it became clear that Tito did not intend to follow orders from Moscow. Yugoslavia was expelled from the Communist Information Bureau (Cominform), and economic sanctions were applied against it by other communist countries. Tito countered this by taking aid from the West – much to the annoyance of Stalin.

How did the USA react to Soviet expansion?

The Truman Doctrine 1947

In February 1947 the British told Truman that they could no longer afford to keep troops in Greece and Turkey. Truman knew that if British troops pulled out of these countries, they would be taken over by the Soviet Union.

He decided that the USA would pay for British troops to stay in the area. This was the start of the policy of **containment** – stopping communism from spreading further. Truman announced the policy, called the **Truman Doctrine**, in a speech on 12 March 1947 (Source I). He said that the USA would help any country that was threatened by communism.

The Marshall Plan 1947

- Truman said that communism tended to take root where there was misery and want.

- At the time Europe was struggling to repair the damage caused by the war, so there was plenty of misery. There was still food rationing and shortages in many countries.

- In June 1947 the American Secretary of State, George C. Marshall, made a speech in which he said that the USA would provide money to help Europe recover. This financial aid was called the **Marshall Plan**.

- Marshall said that any country could have American money to end hunger and poverty.

- But the Soviets were suspicious and would not accept Marshall Aid. They believed the Americans were trying to take over Europe.

SOURCE I

I believe it must be the policy of the USA to support people who are resisting subjugation [control] by outside pressures. I believe we must help free peoples to work out their own destiny.

Taken from President Truman's speech on 12 March 1947.

A cartoonist's view of the Marshall Plan, drawn in 1947.

SOURCE J

NEIGHBOURS
"Come on, Sam! It's up to us again."

224   International relations 1945–c.1989

- Between 1948 and 1952 the USA gave $13 million to 16 countries in western Europe. Stalin stopped the communist countries in eastern Europe from receiving money under the Marshall Plan. He did not want any the USA to have any influence in eastern Europe.

Cominform

In September 1947 the Soviet Union formed the Cominform to strengthen the ties between communist countries in eastern Europe.

Comecon

In January 1949 Stalin set up the Council for Mutual Economic Aid (Comecon) to rival the Marshall Plan. The communist countries, however, did not have enough money to give financial aid to each other.

What were the causes of the Berlin blockade?

- Germany was in ruins after the Second World War. The western powers wanted to end poverty in Germany by helping it to rebuild its industry.

- The western part of Germany therefore was given Marshall Aid. Stalin, however, refused to let the Soviet zone in eastern Germany receive American money.

SOURCE K

The Marshall Plan was seen as the Americans wanting to impose their influence over the countries to which they gave aid. This is why it was never accepted by our country.

A senior Soviet politician of 1947, commenting in 1988 on the Marshall Plan.

- In 1947 the USA and Britain decided to introduce a new, stronger currency, the Deutschmark, into their zones. Stalin was worried about this. He wanted the occupied zones of Germany to stay poor. He also did not want a rich western Germany next to a poor Soviet-controlled eastern Germany.

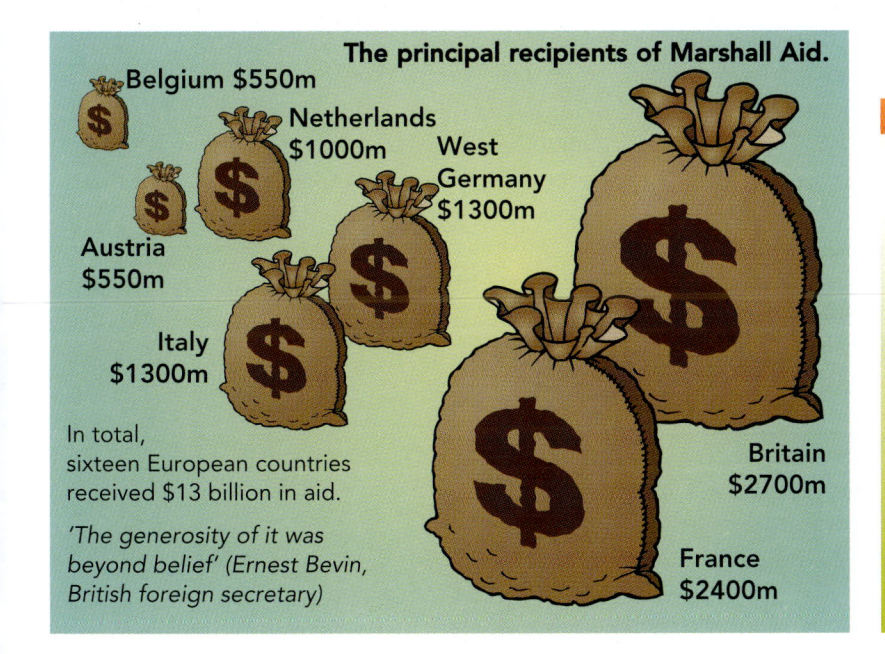

The principal recipients of Marshall Aid.

- Belgium $550m
- Netherlands $1000m
- West Germany $1300m
- Austria $550m
- Italy $1300m
- Britain $2700m
- France $2400m

In total, sixteen European countries received $13 billion in aid.

'The generosity of it was beyond belief' (Ernest Bevin, British foreign secretary)

QUESTIONS

1. What was the Truman Doctrine?
2. What was the Marshall Plan?
3. Look at the diagram. Which countries benefited most from Marshall aid?
4. Look at Source J. What is the message of this cartoon?

The Cold War 225

What happened during the Berlin blockade?

- Stalin decided to try and force the western powers out of Berlin. Berlin was situated in the middle of the Soviet-controlled East Germany.

- On 24 June 1948 Stalin ordered Berlin to be blockaded. Roads and rail links to West Berlin were cut off by the Soviets.

- To break the blockade the western powers would have to smash through the blockades with tanks. Stalin did not think they would do this. He hoped they would abandon their zones, leaving all of Berlin in Soviet hands.

- The Americans, British and French decided to airlift (fly) supplies into West Berlin, a massive task. It took non-stop flights to deliver the large amounts of food and fuel to keep two million people supplied in West Berlin.

- The only way Stalin could have stopped the airlift was to shoot down the planes. Had he done this it might well have led to another war.

- Over the next eleven months over two million tons of supplies were flown into West Berlin. Stalin realised the western powers were determined to hold on to West Berlin and he called off the blockade on 12 May 1949.

The results of the blockade

- Stalin's blockade had meant to win West Berlin for the Soviets, but the western powers stood up to Stalin and then took measures to strengthen their position in Germany.

SOURCE L

A painting by an American artist showing US planes landing supplies at Templehof Airport in West Berlin.

- In May 1949 the Americans, British and French joined their zones together to form the German Federal Republic (West Germany). Part of this new country was West Berlin.

- In October 1949 the Soviet zone was renamed the German Democratic Republic (East Germany).

SOURCE M

Supplies being unloaded from American planes in West Berlin in June 1948.

NATO

The western powers also confirmed their opposition to the Soviet Union by setting up the North Atlantic Treaty Organisation (**NATO**) in 1949.

This was an alliance of western European countries together with the USA and Canada (see box below).

Members of the alliance agreed to help each other if any of them was attacked. By joining NATO the USA had shown it was determined to stop the spread of communism.

The Warsaw Pact

In 1949 the Soviet Union developed its own atomic bomb and in 1955 set up its own military alliance called the **Warsaw Pact** (see box below).

SOURCE N

Planes were taking off every 30 seconds, soldiers were loading trucks [and] the maintenance shops were a beehive of activity. It was a 24-hour operation. To most people it seemed an impossible task to meet the needs of two million people by airlift. But except for water, Berlin was supplied with everything by air.

An American stationed at a base in the American zone of Germany describes the frantic activity of the Berlin airlift.

The two alliances
- **NATO:** USA, Britain, Belgium, Canada, Denmark, France, Iceland, Italy, Luxembourg, Netherlands, Norway and Portugal. Greece and Turkey joined in 1952 and West Germany in 1955.
- **The Warsaw Pact:** Soviet Union, Albania (expelled 1968), Bulgaria, Czechoslovakia, East Germany, Hungary, Poland and Romania.

The Story of 'Operation Little Vittles'

The Americans called the Berlin airlift 'Operation Vittles' ('vittles' is a word meaning food and supplies). But there was another operation, which some American pilots called 'Operation Little Vittles'.

'Operation Little Vittles' was the idea of Lieutenant Gail S. Halvorsen. He was so impressed with the friendliness of the children at a West Berlin airfield that he promised to air drop sweets for them. Halvorsen attached bags of sweets to small parachutes made from scraps of cloth, and dropped them to the children. When they heard what Halvorsen was doing, American firms sent huge amounts of free sweets to Germany. By January 1949 more than 250,000 'candy parachutes' had been dropped.

The Soviets poured scorn on what Halvorsen had done. They spread a story saying that excited children had badly damaged a graveyard while chasing sweets dropped from American planes.

Who was more to blame for the start of the Cold War – the USA or the Soviet Union?

By 1955 the Cold War was well under way.

- Europe was divided. To the east of the 'iron curtain' were the communist countries of eastern Europe under the control of the Soviet Union. To the west were the capitalist and democratic countries of western Europe

- The two superpowers (the USA and the Soviet Union) and their allies were grouped into two alliances, each with the atomic bomb.

- The USA said that the Soviet Union was to blame for the Cold War, because it was trying to spread communism across the world. The Soviet Union argued that it needed to defend itself from attack from the West. This was why friendly communist governments in eastern Europe had been set up as a buffer zone.

Whoever was to blame, the main cause of the Cold War was that each side thought it was right and each totally distrusted the other.

QUESTIONS

1. What was the Berlin blockade?
2. Why did the western powers decide to airlift supplies into Berlin?
3. What were the consequences (results) of the Berlin airlift?
4. 'The USA and the USSR were both to blame for the Cold War'. Do you agree?

Paper 1-type assessment: Causes of the Cold War

SOURCE A

THE BIRD WATCHER

A cartoon published in July 1948. The birds are carrying supplies into Berlin.

QUESTIONS

Section A Questions

1 **a** Study Source A. Do you think this cartoon was published in western Europe or in eastern Europe? Support your answer by referring to details of the cartoon and your own knowledge. (6)

   b Explain why the Soviet Union decided to gain control of eastern Europe after the Second World War. (9)

Section B Questions

2 **a** What was agreed at the Potsdam Conference in July 1945? (4)

   b Explain why the Soviet Union was unhappy at the outcome of the Potsdam Conference. (6)

   c 'The most important cause of the Cold War was the Soviet Union's fear of the West'. Do you agree with this statement? Explain your answer. (10)

How effectively did the USA contain the spread of communism?

Events in Europe after 1945 had led to bitter tension between the USA and the Soviet Union. The two sides were also hostile to each other in other parts of the world.

1. In 1962 the USA and the Soviet quarrelled about Soviet missiles being placed on the island of Cuba. This almost caused a nuclear war.

2. In the 1960s and 1970s the USA fought a costly war in Vietnam to stop the spread of communism.

The Cold War, 1949-61

American fears about the spread of communism were increased in 1949 when China became a communist country. It was lucky that the Soviet Union and China were on bad terms with each other. If they had joined together they would have been a huge threat to the West.

The arms race

- The USA and the Soviet Union began to build up their weapons so as to be able to 'outgun' the other. Both sides had developed the atomic bomb by 1949. Then in 1952 the USA developed the more powerful hydrogen bomb (H-bomb).

> **SOURCE A**
>
> Here in Asia we fight Europe's war with arms. Politicians in Europe still fight it with words. If we lose the war with communism in Asia, Europe will also fall.

General MacArthur, commenting in 1951 on the importance of the Korean War.

It took the Soviet Union just a year to develop a similar bomb.

- By 1958 both sides had Intercontinental Ballistic Missiles (ICBMs), which could fire nuclear warheads thousands of kilometres. The two sides had huge stocks of nuclear weapons, but they were careful not to get involved in a direct conflict with each other.

The arms race between the USA and the Soviet Union.

USA
- ICBMs: 450
- Medium-range missiles: 250
- Bombers: 2260
- Tanks: 16,000
- Submarines: Nuclear 32, Conventional 260
- Battleships and carriers: 76

USSR
- ICBMs: 76
- Medium-range missiles: 700
- Bombers: 1600
- Tanks: 38,000
- Submarines: Nuclear 12, Conventional 495
- Battleships and carriers: 0

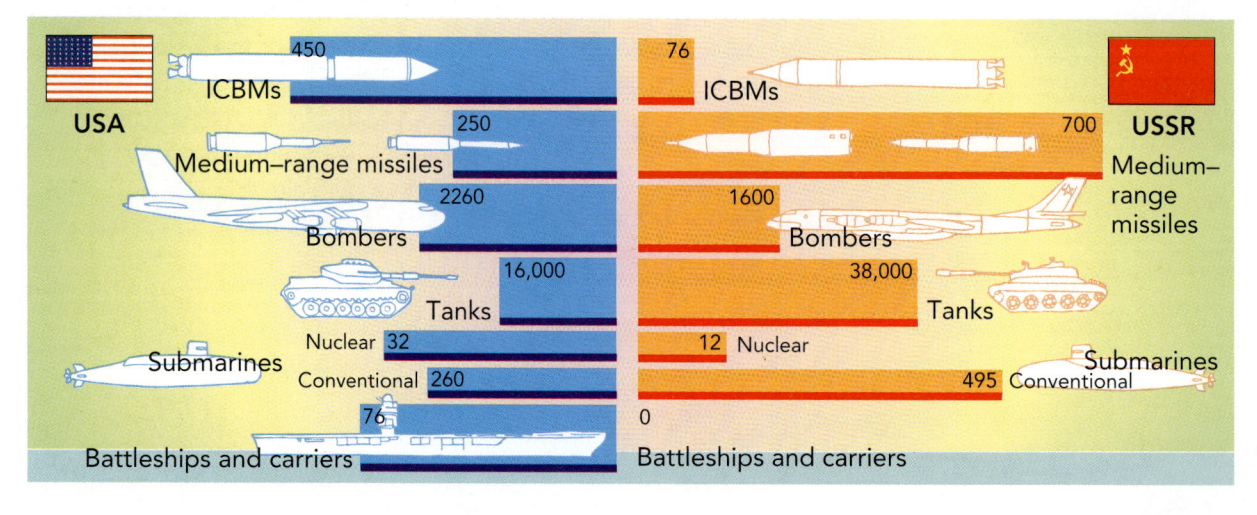

The Korean War, 1950–3.

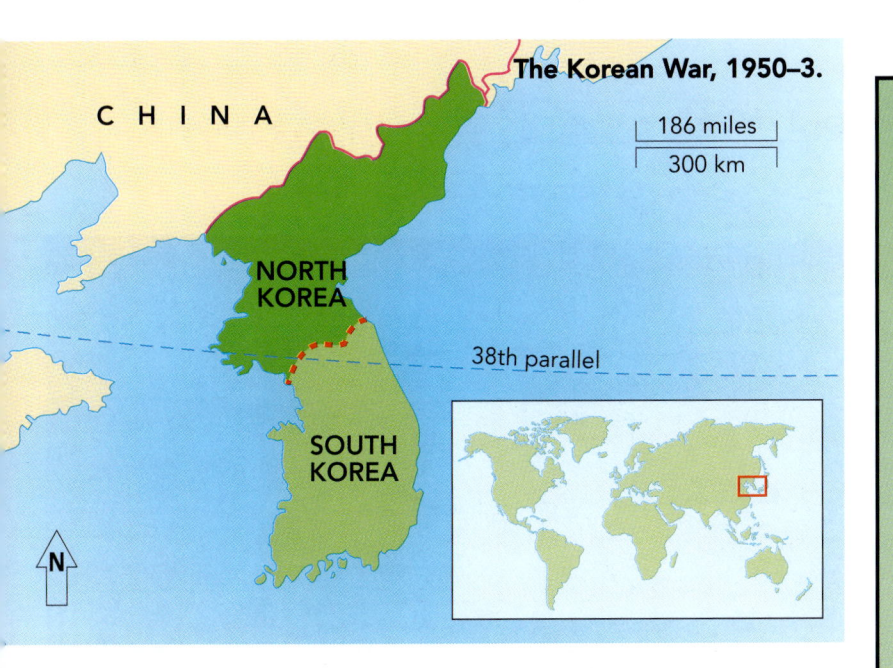

The Korean War 1950-3

- In 1950 communist North Korea invaded non-communist South Korea. President Truman believed that the Soviet Union had told North Korea to invade. A United Nations force, under General MacArthur of the USA, was sent to help the South Koreans. The North Koreans were pushed back and South Korea was saved from communism.

- In 1953 Stalin died and was replaced by Nikita Khrushchev. Khrushchev wanted improved relations between East and West. Talks were held between the USA and Soviet Union and the tension eased a little. However, more problems soon followed that prevented better relations:

1. **The U2 spy plane** In 1960 an American U2 spy plane was shot down over the Soviet Union. Khrushchev was so angry he walked out of a summit meeting with the Americans. Relations grew very tense once more.

2. **The Berlin Wall** In 1961 Khrushchev ordered the **Berlin Wall** to be built, cutting West Berlin off from East Berlin. The only gap in the iron curtain had been closed.

McCarthyism

Anti-communist feelings ran high in the USA after 1945. A law was passed banning communists from having American passports. Senator Joe McCarthy did his best to stir up anti-communist feeling. He said had evidence that over 200 communists were working for the American government. No one dared to question McCarthy. A 'witch hunt' to find suspected communists soon followed. Between 1950 and 1954 hundreds of Americans were accused of being communists and were sacked from their jobs.

In 1954 McCarthy's 'evidence' was proved to be nothing more than rumour. His influence came to an end.

QUESTION

1. What were the main events in the Cold War from 1949-61?

The USA and the spread of communism

The USA and events in Cuba, 1959-62

Fulgencio Batista

- In 1898 the Americans helped the Cubans to win independence from Spain. The USA then invested in Cuban industry. Americans owned many Cuban companies.

- In 1934 the Americans helped to bring Fulgencio Batista to power in Cuba. His government became corrupt and unpopular.

Fidel Castro

- In 1959 Fidel Castro overthrew Batista. Castro began appointing communists to his new government. He signed an agreement with the Soviet Union in which Cuban sugar would be exchanged for Soviet machinery and oil. The Soviet Union also said it would give financial aid to Cuba.

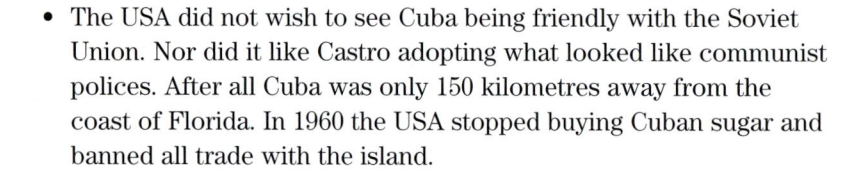

- The USA did not wish to see Cuba being friendly with the Soviet Union. Nor did it like Castro adopting what looked like communist polices. After all Cuba was only 150 kilometres away from the coast of Florida. In 1960 the USA stopped buying Cuban sugar and banned all trade with the island.

- The American president, John F. Kennedy, knew that the Soviet Union was giving weapons to Cuba. In April 1961, a group of Cubans exiles living in the USA decided to invade Cuba. They wanted a return to the days of Batista and had the support of Kennedy.

SOURCE B

Fidel Castro.

SOURCE C

What is the reason for all this silliness about the Soviet presence in Cuba? The Soviet Union does not need to shift its weapons to any other country. Our nuclear rockets are so powerful that we do not need to look for sites outside the Soviet Union.

A statement made by Khrushchev in September 1962.

The Bay of Pigs.

The Bay of Pigs invasion

The Cuban exiles were given weapons and training by the American Central Intelligence Agency (CIA). They aimed to invade Cuba at the Bay of Pigs (see map above).

The invasion turned out to be a disaster. The 1400 exiles found 20,000 Cuban troops waiting for them. Those exiles who were not killed were taken prisoner. Castro and Khrushchev knew that the Americans had helped to plan the invasion. The event was a humiliation for Kennedy.

Results of the invasion

1 Castro took action against the Americans. In July 1961 he took over control of all the American companies in Cuba. He also announced he was now a communist.

2 The invasion made Castro believe he needed more help from the Soviet Union to defend Cuba from possible future American attacks. In September 1961 Khrushchev said he would provide Cuba with weapons. Soon Castro's army had the latest military equipment including tanks and missiles. The Americans were alarmed at what was happening.

3 Tension continued to build up. Kennedy was worried that the Soviets would station nuclear weapons on Cuba. He warned Khrushchev that the USA would not allow Cuba to become a base for Soviet nuclear missiles. Khrushchev assured Kennedy this would not happen (see Source C).

SOURCE D

- Spread false pictures of Castro looking fat sat at a table full of food besides two buxom women. The caption would say, 'My ration is different.'
- Prepare to blame Castro if the 1962 manned space flight carrying John Glenn crashed.
- Prepare a poisoned scuba suit as a gift for Castro.
- Blow up a US warship and blame Cuba.

American ideas to disgrace Castro. None of them was carried out.

QUESTIONS

1 Why was the USA worried when Castro came to power in Cuba?

2 What were the results of the Bay of Pigs invasion?

The USA and the spread of communism

SOURCE E

A photograph of the missile sites in Cuba with labels added by the American government.

SOURCE F

The 1930s taught us a clear lesson. Aggressive conduct if allowed to go unchecked leads to war. We will not unnecessarily risk the costs of world-wide nuclear war. Neither will we shrink from that risk at any time it must be faced.

President Kennedy broadcasting to the American people on 22 October 1962.

Missiles discovered on Cuba

- On 14 September 1962 an American spy plane took photographs from the air of nuclear missile sites being built on Cuba.

- The Americans then heard that Soviet ships were heading for Cuba carrying missiles for the sites.

- Kennedy was very worried. Nearly the whole of the USA would be in range of nuclear missiles based on Cuba. But how could he stop it?

- If he bombed the missile sites or invaded Cuba it would probably lead to a nuclear war between the USA and the Soviet Union.

Kennedy meets his advisers

- On 16 October Kennedy and his advisers met to decide what to do (see Source G). The meeting went on for thirteen days and nights.

- By 22 October Kennedy had decided to place a naval blockade around Cuba. This would stop the Soviet ships from landing their missiles on Cuba.

- Kennedy went on national television to tell the American people about the blockade and to appeal to the Soviets to remove the missiles from Cuba.

- On 23 October Khrushchev replied. He said there were no Soviet missiles on Cuba and he would ignore the blockade.

- The world held its breath. If the Soviet ships tried to break through the blockade they would be fired on and war would follow.

SOURCE G

Tuesday 16 October 1962

President's Kennedy's advisers discuss if the USA could be under threat from Cuba.

General Maxwell Taylor: We are very vulnerable [open] to a conventional bombing attack [from Cuba] in the Florida area.

Douglas Dillon: What if the planes carry nuclear weapons?

The President: Well if they carry a nuclear weapon…

Rusk: We could be just utterly wrong – but we've never really believed that Khrushchev would start a nuclear war over Cuba.

Bundy: What is the impact on the balance of power of these missiles?

The President: What difference does it make? They've got enough to blow us up now anyway.

Thursday 18 October 1962

The groups discusses how they would feel if they started a nuclear war.

Robert Kennedy: I think it's the question of assuming you survive.

Ball: Imagine having to live the rest of your life knowing what you have done.

Robert Kennedy: It's a hell of a burden to carry.

Friday 19 October 1962

The American military chiefs show that they support tough action

General Le May: If we don't do anything to Cuba then the Soviets are going to push on Berlin because they have us on the run … I just don't see any other solution except direct military action. A blockade would be considered by our friends and neutrals as being a pretty weak response to this. And I'm sure a lot of our citizens would feel that way too.

Monday 22 October 1962

The President discovers that American nuclear weapons could be used without his knowledge – and he does not like it.

The President: We may be attacking the Cubans and a reprisal (retaliation) may come. I don't want nuclear weapons fired without our knowing it.

Nitze: The military chiefs will object to new orders because it will change existing ones. A Soviet nuclear attack requires the European Defense Plan to be put into action.

The President: What's the European Defense Plan?

Nitze: Nuclear war.

The President: No … What we've to do is to make sure that the military chiefs don't fire off (nuclear) weapons and out the United States under attack. I don't think we ought to accept the chiefs' word on that one, Paul.

Unknown to the people involved in the discussions about Cuba, President Kennedy taped most of the talks. They give us an understanding of the thinking at the time.

Who's who?

Political advisers: Robert Kennedy (the president's brother), Robert McNamara (Secretary of State for Defense), Paul Nitze (Assistant Secretary of State for Defense), Douglas Dillon (Treasury Secretary), Dean Rusk (Secretary of State), George Ball (Under Secretary of State), McGeorge Bundy (president's aide).

Military advisers: General Maxwell Taylor (Chairman, Joint Chiefs of Staff), General Curtis Le May (Air Force Chief of Staff).

A cartoon from the *Daily Express* in October 1962. President Kennedy and Khrushchev are seen as gunslingers, waiting to see who will draw his gun first. Castro is seen riding on a donkey.

SOURCE H

The crisis unfolds

- On 24 October the Soviet ships reached the American blockade off the coast of Cuba. The Soviet ships turned back and nuclear war was therefore avoided.

- The crisis, however, was not over. Soviet nuclear missiles were still on the island and needed removing.

- On 26 October Khrushchev sent a letter to Kennedy. Khrushchev said if the USA lifted the blockade and promised not to invade Cuba, he would take the nuclear missiles away. It was the first time he had admitted that there were nuclear weapons on Cuba.

- On 27 October a second letter arrived. Khruschev said he would only remove the missiles on Cuba if the USA removed its missiles based in Turkey. These missiles were within easy range of the Soviet Union, but the USA did not want to remove them just because Khrushchev had demanded it.

- Kennedy decided to ignore Khrushchev's second letter and reply only to the first one. He said he agreed to Khrushchev's terms, but if the missiles were not removed an attack would follow.

- Kennedy's brother, Robert, went to see the Soviet ambassador in Washington. He told him the Americans would think about removing their missiles in Turkey 'within a short time'.

Krushchev gives in

On 28 October Khrushchev finally agreed to remove the missiles on Cuba. The crisis was over.

The results of the crisis

1 Kennedy had come out on top. Soviet missiles were removed from Cuba, but the USA did not remove theirs from Turkey.

2 Soviet politicians were angry and felt that Khrushchev had been forced to back down. In 1964 he was dismissed as leader of the USSR.

236 International relations 1945–c.1989

Soviet missile bases
----- US naval blockade

American cities that could be reached by missiles fired from Cuba.

3 Steps were taken to reduce the threat of nuclear war in the future:

- A telephone **hot line** was set up between Washington and Moscow, so that the leaders could speak directly.

- The **Nuclear Test Ban Treaty** was signed in 1963 to stop the testing of nuclear weapons in the atmosphere.

SOURCE I

We sent the Americans a note saying that we would remove our missiles if the President assured us that there would be no invasion of Cuba. Kennedy agreed to such an assurance. It was a great victory for us, a spectacular success without having to fire a single shot.

From Khrushchev's memoirs, written in the 1960s.

The Cuban missile crisis – a summary

14 October	Soviet missile spotted.
16 October	President Kennedy informed.
22 October	US blockade set up. Kennedy broadcasts to the nation.
24 October	Soviet ships agree to turn round.
26 October	Khrushchev's first letter arrives.
27 October	Khrushchev's second letter arrives. Kennedy replies to the first letter. Robert Kennedy visits the Soviet ambassador.
28 October	Khrushchev agrees to remove the missiles on Cuba.

QUESTIONS

1 How big a threat was the Cuban missile crisis to world peace?

2 Read Source I.
Was the Cuban missile crisis a 'great victory' for Khrushchev? Explain your answer.

The USA and the spread of communism

American involvement in Vietnam

Why did the Americans fight in Vietnam?

- Vietnam was a French colony but in 1941 it was captured by the Japanese. When the Japanese were defeated by the Allies in 1945 France tried to get Vietnam back. They sent troops to Vietnam but they were defeated by the Vietnamese in 1954.

- Vietnam was then divided into two separate countries:

    1 **North Vietnam** was a communist country led by Ho Chi Minh.

    2 **South Vietnam** was anti-communist and led by Ngo Dinh Diem.

- Diem treated the South Vietnamese people badly. Many peasants in South Vietnam started to support a group of communist fighters called the **Vietcong** who wanted to overthrow Diem. It was given weapons and arms by the government of North Vietnam.

- The Americans were worried that the Vietcong was trying to spread communism into South Vietnam. They believed that if South Vietnam fell to communism then other countries in Asia would also fall, rather like a row of dominoes (see diagram on page 239). This was known as the **domino theory**. The Americans decided to support the government of South Vietnam to stop it falling to communism.

American help for South Vietnam

The USA sent military advisers and equipment to South Vietnam. Meanwhile, China and the Soviet Union supplied the Vietcong and North Vietnam.

Despite the help of the Americans the Vietcong had taken over about 40 per cent of South Vietnam by 1963.

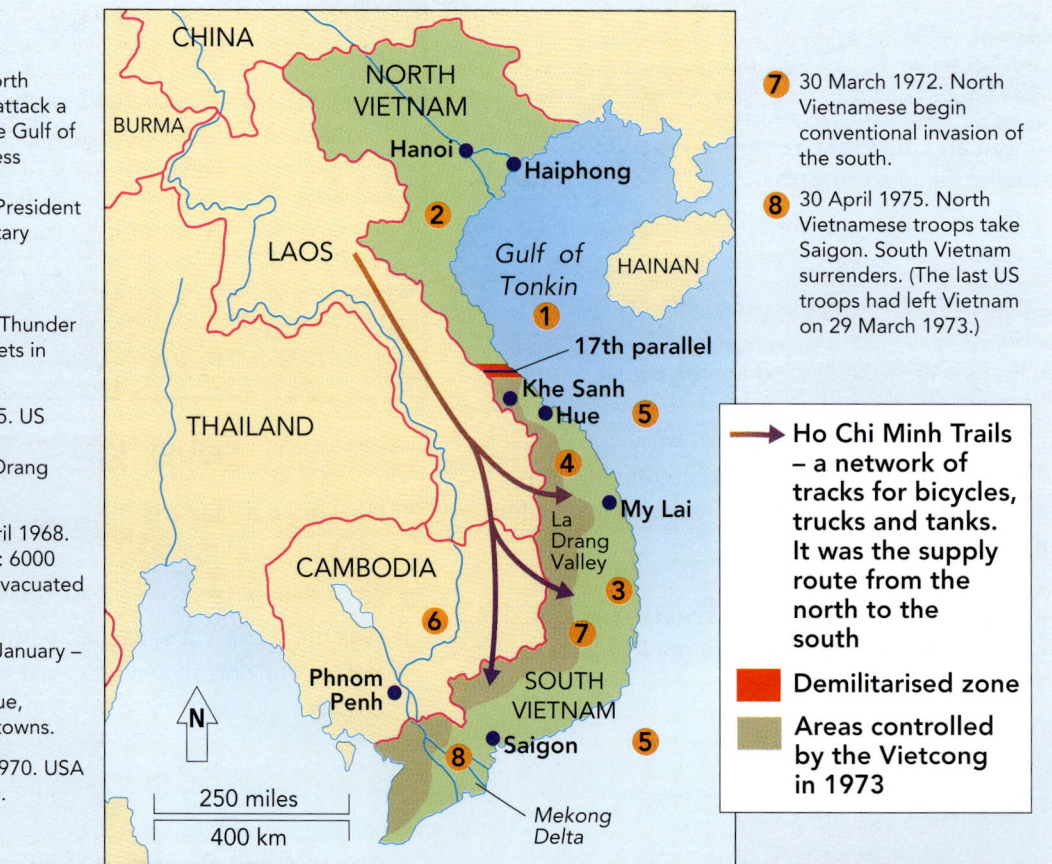

War in Vietnam

1. 2 August 1964. North Vietnamese ships attack a US destroyer in the Gulf of Tonkin. US Congress passes the Tonkin Resolution giving President Johnson wide military powers.

2. 7 February 1965. Operation Rolling Thunder – bombing of targets in North Vietnam.

3. 14 November 1965. US Army fights North Vietnamese in La Drang Valley.

4. 22 January – 7 April 1968. Siege of Khe Sanh: 6000 American troops evacuated after 77 days.

5. Tet Offensive, 30 January – 26 February 1968. Vietcong attack Hue, Saigon and other towns.

6. 1 May – 29 June 1970. USA invades Cambodia.

7. 30 March 1972. North Vietnamese begin conventional invasion of the south.

8. 30 April 1975. North Vietnamese troops take Saigon. South Vietnam surrenders. (The last US troops had left Vietnam on 29 March 1973.)

→ Ho Chi Minh Trails – a network of tracks for bicycles, trucks and tanks. It was the supply route from the north to the south

■ Demilitarised zone

■ Areas controlled by the Vietcong in 1973

The domino theory.

SOURCE J

An aerial view of American bombing in North Vietnam.

Johnson steps up the war

In 1964 North Vietnamese gun boats attacked an American warship in the Gulf of Tonkin. After this, the American Congress gave President Johnson the go ahead to use force to defend South Vietnam.

'Operation Rolling Thunder'

In February 1965 the Americans launched **Operation Rolling Thunder**, bombing factories and military bases in North Vietnam. The aim was to stop the North from supplying the Vietcong, but the bombing did not work.

In July 1965 President Johnson started sending in troops and before long there were 500,000 American soldiers in Vietnam. Meanwhile, the bombing of North Vietnam went on.

SOURCE K

We must fight if we are to live in a world where every country can shape its own future. We are in Vietnam because we have a promise to keep. Since 1954 every American president has offered support to the people of South Vietnam. Over many years we have made a national pledge to help South Vietnam defend its independence. To leave this small and brave nation to its enemies would be an unforgivable wrong.

President Johnson talking to the American people in 1965.

The USA and the spread of communism   239

Guerrilla warfare

The American army was much better equipped than the Vietcong, yet they still could not beat them.

The reason for this was that the Vietcong used **guerrilla tactics**. They would carry out quick attacks on American targets and then disappear into the jungle. As the Vietcong did not wear uniforms, the Americans could not tell them apart from ordinary peasants. The Vietcong's guerrilla tactics outwitted the Americans.

The My Lai massacre

- The American soldiers grew frustrated. They saw their comrades being ambushed or booby-trapped and yet they could not find the enemy who had done it. Sometimes their frustration led them to carry out terrible acts.

- In March 1968 a group of American soldiers, under Lieutenant William Calley, went into the village of **My Lai** to look for members of the Vietcong. When they could not find any, they rounded up the villagers and shot them.

- Calley was later put on trial for the murder of 109 civilians. He was found guilty and sentenced to life imprisonment, but was released after just three days on the orders of President Nixon.

New tactics

The Americans tried a number of new tactics to beat the Vietcong guerrillas.

1. **Strategic villages** The Americans moved peasants into new villages, which were surrounded by barbed wire. They carefully controlled who entered and left the village.

SOURCE L

A Chinese poster showing the Vietnamese people fighting the Americans in South Vietnam.

QUESTIONS

1. Why did the Americans send troops to Vietnam?
2. Why couldn't the Americans beat the Vietcong?
3. What new tactics did the Americans use to try and beat the Vietcong?

An American soldier taking a member of the Vietcong prisoner.

SOURCE M

2 **Defoliation** The Americans dropped Agent Orange (a strong chemical) on jungle areas. This made the trees lose their leaves making it harder for the Vietcong to hide.
3 **Napalm** The Americans also dropped napalm, a petroleum jelly, in an effort to burn jungle or villages. Thousands of innocent people suffered terrible napalm burns.

No success

The new tactics did not work.

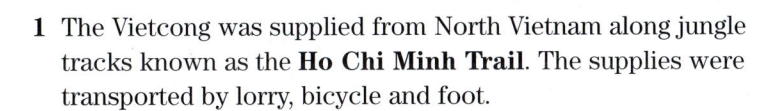

1 The Vietcong was supplied from North Vietnam along jungle tracks known as the **Ho Chi Minh Trail**. The supplies were transported by lorry, bicycle and foot.

2 The Vietcong built a network of tunnels where they had stores, workshops and hospitals. No amount of Agent Orange or napalm could destroy such tunnels.

The Americans began to wonder what they were doing in Vietnam.

SOURCE N

Throughout the war the North Vietnamese were able to absorb more pain than the Americans could deal out. For the Americans the war was a 'limited one' far from home. For the North Vietnamese it was total: they were fighting to defend their homeland.

A modern historian's view of why the Americans did not win the Vietnam War.

SOURCE O

One day a sergeant of mine said, 'You know, Lieutenant, I don't see how we are ever going to win this.'
And I said, 'Well, Sarge, I'm not supposed to say this as your officer -but I don't either!'
So there was this sense that we just couldn't see what could be done to defeat these people.

A Marine Corps lieutenant remembers a conversation with one of his sergeants in Vietnam in 1966.

The USA and the spread of communism

The Tet Offensive

In 1968 the Vietcong launched the **Tet Offensive**, when they attacked towns and American bases in South Vietnam.

At first the Americans were pushed back but they soon regained the towns and bases that had been captured.

By the end of the offensive 50,000 Vietcong troops had been killed.

Time to get out

By 1968, 300 Americans a week were being killed and the war was costing $30,000 million a year.

Despite the cost in money and lives, the Vietcong were still able to mount a major attack such as the Tet Offensive. The Americans realised that they were not going to win the war and decided to get out of Vietnam.

Protests at home

Television changes attitudes

In the beginning most Americans supported the war but as the war dragged on attitudes changed. The American public saw terrible television pictures of innocent Vietnamese civilians and young American soldiers being killed. There were stories of American soldiers taking drugs. The American public was shocked when the My Lai massacre was reported and asked how their own troops could do such a thing.

Demonstrations

There were demonstrations in American cities calling for an end to the war. Thousands of men burned their **draft cards** that called them up to fight. Some fled abroad so they would not have go to Vietnam.

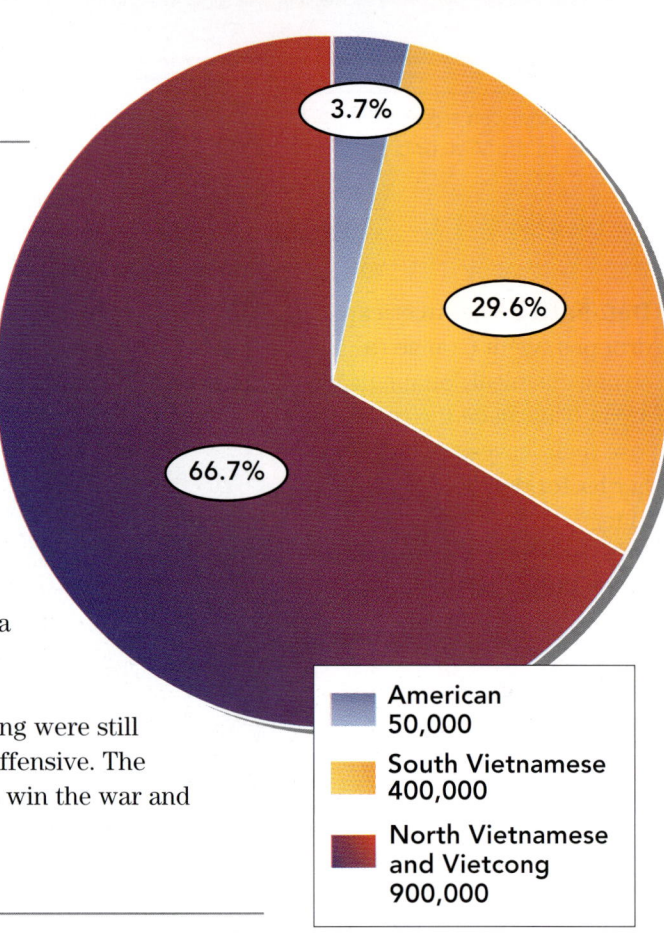

3.7%
29.6%
66.7%

- American 50,000
- South Vietnamese 400,000
- North Vietnamese and Vietcong 900,000

Deaths in Vietnam.

The human costs of the Vietnam War.

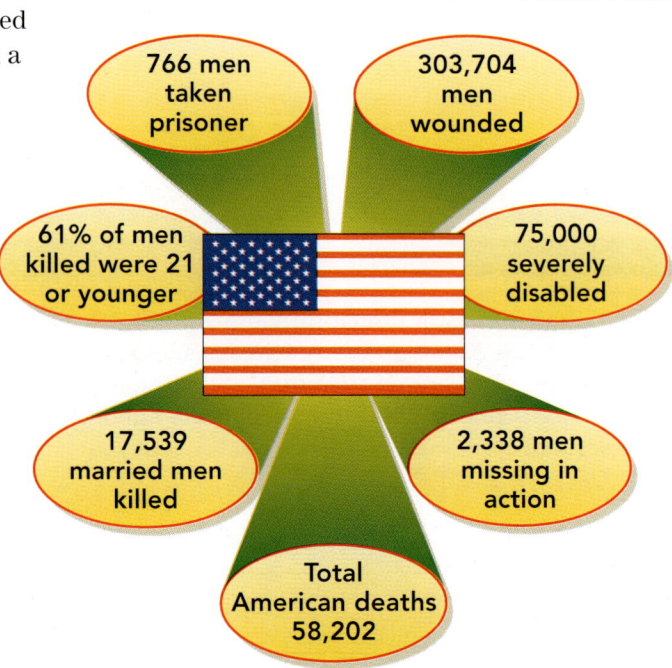

- 766 men taken prisoner
- 303,704 men wounded
- 61% of men killed were 21 or younger
- 75,000 severely disabled
- 17,539 married men killed
- 2,338 men missing in action
- Total American deaths 58,202

242   International relations 1945–c.1989

SOURCE P

An American anti-Vietnam war poster. Uncle Sam is wounded and wants to get out of the war.

Johnson criticised

President Johnson was criticised by many people. People chanted, 'Hey, hey, LBJ, how many kids did you kill today?' Johnson called off the bombing of North Vietnam and decided not to stand for re-election in 1968.

Vietnamisation

The new president, Richard Nixon, could not just take the troops out. Thousands of Americans had died fighting a bloody war. It would be an insult to them to admit defeat and bring the troops home.

Instead, Nixon introduced a policy of **Vietnamisation** as a means of bring the war to an end.

SOURCE Q

On 4 May 1970, 3000 students at Kent State University in Ohio held an anti-war protest. National Guardsmen fired tear gas to break up the crowd. Some of the students threw stones at the troops, who opened fire. Four students (none of whom had been protesting) were killed. President Nixon later called the student protestors 'bums'.

SOURCE R

I don't give a damn
For Uncle Sam
I ain't going
To Vietnam.

An anti-war protest chant from the late 1960s.

The USA and the spread of communism

The policy of Vietnamisation meant that the Americans would train and equip the army of South Vietnam. This would make them strong enough to fight the Vietcong. After which, the Americans would leave.

Victory for the communists

- The South Vietnamese army began to grow, so the Americans gradually withdrew their troops.

- In February 1973 the USA agreed a cease-fire with North Vietnam and the Vietcong. The USA promised South Vietnam it would send troops back if the Vietcong broke the cease-fire.

- When fighting started again in 1974, the USA sent supplies, but no troops.

- In 1975 communist troops from North Vietnam took over much of South Vietnam. The communists captured Saigon, the capital of South Vietnam, in April.

- In 1976 North and South Vietnam were joined together once more into a single country, under a communist government. The USA had failed to contain communism in south-east Asia.

QUESTIONS

1 Why did the Vietnam war become so unpopular in the USA?

2 What was Vietnamisation?

3 What happened in 1975 and 1976?

SOURCE S

I saw villages and fields destroyed. Every time the Americans increased their destruction of our land, more and more men and women joined our side in our fight for freedom.

A Vietcong soldier explains the effects of the American tactics in Vietnam.

SOURCE T

A British cartoon showing the problems facing President Nixon in 1969.

Paper 1–type assessment: US policy in Cuba and Vietnam

SOURCE A

'If this boy of yours *is* real, how come we gotta wind him up all the time?'

A British cartoon commenting on Nixon's policy of Vietnamisation in 1969.

QUESTIONS

Section A Questions

1 a Study Source A. Explain the message of this cartoon. Support your answer by referring to details of the cartoon and your own knowledge. (6)

b Explain why the USA decided to go to war in Vietnam. (9)

Section B Questions

2 a What happened in the 'Bay of Pigs Incident' in April 1961? (4)

b Explain why the Soviet Union wanted to station nuclear missiles in Cuba. (6)

c 'The most important outcome of the Cuban Missile Crisis was that President Kennedy's position as a world leader was improved'. Do you agree with this statement? Explain your answer. (10)

Assessment: US policy in Cuba and Vietnam   245

How secure was the USSR's control over eastern Europe 1948–c.1989?

By 1948 all the countries of eastern Europe had communist governments and were under the control of the Soviet Union.

Hungary (in 1956) and Czechoslovakia (in 1968) tried to break free from the Soviet Union, but failed.

In 1989 communism collapsed dramatically in eastern Europe and there was nothing the Soviet Union could do about it.

Khrushchev and the countries of the Warsaw Pact

Stalin died in 1953 and was replaced as Soviet leader by Nikita Khrushchev. Stalin had ruled the countries of the Warsaw Pact with a rod of iron. Would Khrushchev be the same?

- In 1953 and 1956 Khrushchev used the Red Army to crush demonstrations in East Germany and Poland.

- But he then did an about-turn and publicly criticised Stalin for treating east European countries so badly.

- Khrushchev ended the Soviet Union's quarrel with Tito's communist Yugoslavia. Khrushchev told Tito that the Soviet Union believed in, 'equality, non-interference and respect for sovereignty and national independence.'

- Some countries in eastern Europe took this as a sign that Khrushchev would let them have more say in running their own affairs. But they soon found out that this was not to be the case.

Why was there opposition to Soviet control in Hungary in 1956?

- Before 1956 Matyas Rakosi, a hard line communist, ruled Hungary. He made sure that Hungary stayed loyal to the Soviet Union. The Hungarian people hated Rakosi's policies:

  1 He introduced the AVO (secret police) which terrorised anyone who dared oppose the government.

  2 There was no freedom of speech; radio, newspapers and the arts were censored.

  3 Schoolchildren were taught about the history of communism, rather than the history of Hungary.

  4 Hungarians were very religious people, but the communist government stopped them from worshipping.

- Rakosi was so unpopular he was forced to resign in July 1956. But to the dismay of the people Erno Gero, another hard line communist, replaced him.

Gero soon began to lose control and the people took to the streets to voice their opposition to Moscow. Trouble was brewing.

What Khrushchev said about Stalin

At the twentieth Congress of the Communist Party in 1956, Khrushchev said: 'Stalin was a very distrustful man, sickly and suspicious!'

The speech was supposed to be kept secret, but it leaked out and caused amazement in eastern Europe.

The reforms of Imre Nagy

On 23 October there were riots in Budapest, the capital of Hungary. Fighting broke out between protestors and the AVO.

Khrushchev tried to calm the situation by making Imre Nagy the new prime minister. Nagy was in favour of introducing reforms into Hungary.

Once in power Nagy announced that parties, other than the Communist Party, would be allowed in Hungary and said he would take Hungary out of the Warsaw Pact.

How did the Soviet Union react?

The reforms went too far for Khrushchev. There was no way he would allow one of the Soviet Union's **satellites** to leave the Warsaw Pact.

On 4 November, 2500 Soviet tanks supported by 200,000 troops arrived in Budapest.

The Hungarians fought against the Soviet troops. Nagy asked the United Nations for help and radio messages broadcast from Budapest begged the West for support.

The western powers, however, did nothing to help the Hungarians. At the time the USA, Britain and France were too busy quarrelling about who should control the Suez Canal.

SOURCE B

A member of the hated AVO murdered by protestors in Budapest in October 1956.

SOURCE A

Hungary wishes to leave the Warsaw Pact and declares its neutrality. It turns to the United Nations for help in defending the country's neutrality.

Imre Nagy appealing to the United Nations for help against the invading Soviet troops.

QUESTIONS

1 Look at the map on page 222. List the countries in eastern Europe that were under the control of the Soviet Union.

2 Why did the Soviet Union invade Hungary?

Hungarian rebels in the streets of Budapest in November 1956.

SOURCE C

Hungarians crushed

Although the Hungarians fought bravely, they stood no chance against the might of the Soviet Red Army. About 27,000 Hungarians were killed in the fighting. Within two weeks Soviet control was restored.

Results of the Hungarian uprising

- Nagy was sacked and later hanged by the Soviets.

- Khrushchev had shown that he would not allow any of the eastern European countries to break away from Soviet control.

- People in the West had an even stronger dislike of communism.

- The Hungarians were angry that the United Nations had not helped them.

SOURCE D

There is no stopping the wild onslaught of communism. Save our souls! Save our souls! We beg you to help us in the name of justice and freedom.

A broadcast from a Hungarian radio station on 4 November 1956.

Why was there opposition to Soviet control in Czechoslovakia in 1968?

Leonid Brezhnev became the new Soviet leader in 1964. He continued to be very strict with eastern European countries.

The Czechs were unhappy with the communist system of government:

1 There was no freedom of speech. The government censored radio, television and newspapers.

2 Only the communist party was allowed to exist in Czechoslovakia. The Czechs wanted the right to form other parties.

3 The Czechs were tired of being under Soviet control.

4 Czech factories mainly produced heavy goods for the Soviet Union. There were few consumer goods made and the standard of living was low.

Dubcek's reforms

- In 1968 Alexander Dubcek became the leader of Czechoslovakia. He said he wanted 'socialism with a human face' and a better standard of living for the Czech people.

- Dubcek introduced a number of reforms into Czechoslovakia.

  1. He allowed people to criticise the government. Censorship was relaxed and public meetings could be held to discuss politics.

  2. Factory managers and workers were given a say in running industry.

  3. Czechs were allowed to travel abroad.

- Dubcek's reforms were called the **Prague Spring** because they relaxed the harsh laws of communism.

- Dubcek told Brezhnev, the Soviet leader, that Czechoslovakia would not leave the Warsaw Pact and that his reforms would not threaten the Soviet Union.

- Brezhnev was worried that other satellite countries in east Europe would also want to introduce changes. Czechoslovakia had to be brought back into line.

SOURCE E

Czech citizens attacking a Soviet tank in Prague in August 1968.

How did the Soviet Union react?

- In July 1968 Brezhnev warned Dubcek that his reforms were a threat to the rule of the Communist Party in Czechoslovakia. Dubcek, however, stood firm.

- On 20 August Soviet and Warsaw Pact forces invaded Czechoslovakia and took control. The Czech people took part in street fighting, but there was little bloodshed.

- The Soviet troops were shocked at the attitude of the people. The Soviet government had told them they had been invited to restore order and the Czech people would welcome them!

QUESTIONS

1. What changes did Dubcek make in Czechoslovakia?
2. a Why did the Soviet Union oppose Dubcek's changes?
   b What did the Soviet Union do?

SOURCE F

A drawing on a wall in a Prague street in 1968. In 1945 the Soviet Union had freed Czechoslovakia from Nazi rule.

Jan Palach

Jan Palach, a student, protested against the Soviet invasion by setting fire to himself. His funeral was attended by thousands of Czechs who turned out to show their opposition to the Soviet Union.

There were also huge celebrations when Czechoslovakia beat the Soviet Union in the world ice hockey championships in 1969.

Results of the Czech uprising

- Dubcek was removed from office in 1969.

- The Soviet Union had again shown it would clamp down hard on any attempt to reform communism.

- The Soviet Union said that in future the countries in the Warsaw Pact should act together to stop any member from trying to reject communism. This policy was called the **Brezhnev Doctrine**.

How similar were events in Hungary in 1956 and in Czechoslovakia in 1968?

- The Hungarians had wanted to break completely free from the Soviet Union. The Czechs wanted change but wanted to stay in the Warsaw Pact.

- The Soviet Union used force to put down the uprisings in both countries. It did not want the unrest to spread to other communist countries because it would have threatened the unity of the Warsaw pact.

Why was the Berlin Wall built in 1961?

- Since 1945 Berlin had been a divided city. **West Berlin** was under the control of the Americans, British and French. They put money into West Berlin and made it prosperous, There were plenty of things to buy in the shops. **East Berlin** was under the control of the Soviet Union. Life in East Berlin was drab and the people were poor.

- Many people were crossing from East Berlin into West Berlin where they would have a better standard of living. Many who crossed were skilled workers, teachers and lawyers.

- The Soviet Union needed to find a way of stopping this flood of refugees, which was resulting in East Berlin losing many of its top people.

- The Soviets saw West Berlin as a capitalist 'boil' in the middle of East Germany. In June 1961 Khrushchev, the Soviet leader, met President Kennedy in Vienna. He demanded that the western allies withdraw from Berlin. Kennedy refused and said he would stand by West Berlin.

The wall goes up

On 13 August 1961, Soviet troops put up barbed wire barricades all around West Berlin to stop people moving between East and West Berlin. Gradually, a brick wall replaced the barbed wire. Berlin was now a divided city.

The wall was very unpopular. It cut across streets and even houses. It split families and friends.

Many people from East Berlin tried to escape across the wall to the West (see Source G). Between 1961 and 1989, about 86 people were shot by border guards trying to cross the Wall.

The Wall stopped the flood of refugees to the West (see graph below). Now the Soviets could develop East Berlin as they wanted.

SOURCE G

The body of Peter Fechter, an eighteen-year-old bricklayer in East Berlin. On 17 August 1962 he tried to escape to West Berlin to join his sister. As he climbed the Wall, border police shot him. He fell back on the eastern side bleeding heavily and shouting his sister's name. Crowds on the western side saw what had happened. They begged the American border guards to rescue Fechter. But the guards were told not to do anything by their officers. Fechter died and an hour later East German guards took his body away.

Refugees from East Berlin to West Berlin, 1949–61.

The USSR and eastern Europe 251

What part did 'Solidarity' in Poland play in the decline of Soviet influence?

- The Polish people hated being under the control of the Soviet Union.

  1 Many Poles were strong Catholics. They were very proud of their culture and history.

  2 The Poles said that the Red Army had killed many people in Poland during the Second World War.

- In the late 1970s there was a slump in Polish industry and the standard of living fell.

- In July 1980 the government put up food prices. The Polish workers formed trade unions and went on strike in protest.

- One of the new trade unions, formed in the shipyards of Gdansk, was called **Solidarity**.

Solidarity versus the government

Solidarity, led by Lech Walesa, provided people with the chance to protest against the harsh communist government in Poland. It grew quickly and by the end of 1980 had over 9 million members.

In August 1980 Solidarity demanded greater political and religious freedom in Poland. This put the government in a difficult position as Walesa was very popular, and many members of the Polish Communist Party had joined Solidarity.

> **QUESTIONS**
>
> 1 Why did so many Polish people dislike the Soviet Union?
>
> 2 What demands did Solidarity make in 1980?
>
> 3 Why did the Polish government find it difficult to deal with Solidarity?

Lech Walesa addressing a Solidarity meeting.

SOURCE H

Solidarity worries the Soviet government

Leonid Brezhnev, the Soviet leader, ordered the Polish government to stop the growing power of Solidarity. He was worried that its influence would spread to other communist countries.

In February 1981 General Jaruzelski was made prime minister and told to bring Solidarity into line.

Solidarity then said it wanted to be part of the Polish government. The union went on strike and the Polish economy suffered even more. Unemployment and prices were rising quickly and food was in short supply.

Jaruzelski acts

Jaruzelski took action in an effort to crush Solidarity:

- Walesa and 10,000 Solidarity members were arrested.
- Solidarity was banned.
- Brezhnev sent troops to the Polish border, threatening to invade if order was not restored in Poland.
- Jaruzelski formed his own trade union and forced government workers to join it.

These tough measures only served to increase the popularity of Lech Walesa and Jaruzelski was forced to free him in November 1982.

SOURCE I

A cartoon from the *Sunday Times*, August 1980. The face of the Soviet Union is that of Brezhnev, the Soviet leader.

Jaruzelski attacks the Catholic Church

Next Jaruzelski turned on the Catholic Church, which had been criticising his government. A leading priest was beaten to death by the secret police.

People were outraged and about 250,000 attended the funeral as a way of protesting against the government. Jaruzelski was not having much success in his efforts to stop the influence of Solidarity.

SOURCE J

I was called to the Soviet Union on three occasions. I was shown Soviet troops ready along the Polish border. The Soviet army leader said that what was happening in Poland was too much to bear.

General Jaruzelski describing how the Soviet Union put pressure on him to deal with Solidarity in 1981.

The USSR and eastern Europe

The end of communism in Poland

- In 1986 the government said it was going to put up prices. Solidarity threatened to call a general strike and the government backed down. General Jaruzelski was losing his authority. Foreign leaders came to Poland to speak with Lech Walesa as if he were the Polish leader rather than Jaruzelski.

- In 1989 Jaruzelski was forced to hold free elections in Poland. In the elections Solidarity won massive support and became part of the government.

- Shortly after this Jaruzelski resigned. In 1990 Walesa became the president of Poland's first non-communist government since 1945.

The significance of the Solidarity movement

Solidarity became a mouthpiece for opposition to the communist government and became so powerful even the Soviet Union could not stamp it out.

Solidarity had shown people in other communist countries that if they stood together it was possible to beat the communist authorities.

How far was Gorbachev responsible for the collapse of Soviet control over eastern Europe?

The Soviet Union in crisis

In 1985 **Mikhail Gorbachev** became the leader of the Soviet Union. By this time both the Soviet Union and communism were in crisis. The Soviet people had lost faith in the government.

1. They were angry that they had a much lower standard of living than the West. There was a lack of good quality consumer goods such as clothes, televisions and video recorders. Many goods made in Soviet factories did not even work properly.

2. Soviet farmers could not produce enough grain for the country.

3. The Soviet Union was spending too much money on arms and weapons, while many of its people lived in poverty.

4. Since 1979 Soviet troops had been in Afghanistan fighting a war to protect its communist government. The war was costing the Soviet Union $8 billion a year.

SOURCE K

Mikhail Gorbachev.

Gorbachev's solutions

- Gorbachev said he would bring in **perestroika**. This meant the Soviet economy would be restructured.

- Gorbachev said there should be **glasnost** (openness), so that people's faith in the government would be restored. People should also be allowed to discuss politics and, if they wished, criticise the government.

- Money spent on arms and defence should be cut back.

- The Soviet Union should pull out of Afghanistan.

Gorbachev's actions

After 1987 Soviet people were allowed to make and sell goods for profit.

Gorbachev made agreements with the USA to reduce nuclear weapons and in 1988 he announced the end of the Brezhnev Doctrine. Countries in eastern Europe now had to be responsible for their own defence. They could not expect support from the Red Army.

The reaction to Gorbachev's changes

Hard-line communists were horrified by Gorbachev's changes. They said they were bound to stir up trouble. Allowing individual people to make profits went against communism. More openness was raising the expectations of people. There was little chance of providing them with what they wanted.

They also said that Gorbachev's changes would encourage people in eastern Europe to abandon communism. This is exactly what happened in 1989. One by one, communist governments came to an end in Europe. The map on page 256 shows how communist control of eastern Europe came to an end in 1989.

SOURCE L

A cartoon from a British newspaper in January 1990, showing the communist hammer and sickle in tears.

The break-up of the Soviet Union

In the rest of the world, however, Gorbachev was looked upon as a hero. He was awarded the Nobel Prize in October 1989.

In December 1989 he met President Bush of the USA to announce the end of the Cold War.

What Gorbachev said about perestroika

'Perestroika aims to satisfy the Soviet people's needs for good living and working conditions, for good rest, recreation, education and health care.'

The fall of communist Europe, 1989

1 Hungary
In May, the government dismantled the border with non-communist Austria. There was now a hole in the Iron Curtain. In December, free elections were announced for 1990.

2 Poland
In June, Solidarity won free elections, and by the end of the year it had formed the government. In December, Lech Walesa became president.

3 East Germany
In September, thousands of East Germans escaped to Austria and West Germany. In November, the Berlin Wall was pulled down. Free elections were held in March 1990, and East and West Germany were reunited in October 1990.

4 Czechoslovakia
In November, mass demonstrations led to the opening of the border with the West. In December, the communist government resigned.

5 Romania
In December, there was a revolution and the communist dictator, Ceauşescu, and his wife were executed.

6 Bulgaria
In November, Todor Zhirkov, the communist leader since 1954, resigned. A non-communist government was elected in April 1990.

Gorbachev becomes unpopular

But inside the Soviet Union, Gorbachev was unpopular.

- The hard-liners said his policies had brought the end of communism in eastern Europe.

- Liberal minded people said his reforms did not work.

- The problems in the Soviet economy were not cured. There were still long queues to buy basic goods such as bread and meat. People became restless. They wanted a better standard of living.

- The fact that people could now criticise the government only made them see how deep the problems were. This made them even more unhappy.

- Boris Yeltsin, the ex-mayor of Moscow, said that Gorbachev had failed to introduce reforms to make the Soviet Union more democratic.

The fall of Gorbachev

With the fall of communism in eastern Europe and the failure of his reforms at home, Gorbachev's position came under threat.

In February 1990, there was a huge demonstration against communism in Moscow. Gorbachev was shouted at by crowds in Red Square in Moscow during the annual May Day parade.

In August an attempt by hard liners to overthrow Gorbachev failed. After this he lost his authority.

Yeltsin then made Gorbachev suspend the Communist Party and in December 1991 the Soviet Union was broken up. It was replaced by the Commonwealth of Independent States. In the same month Gorbachev resigned.

SOURCE M

'My life's work has been accomplished,' Mr Gorbachev said last Thursday. Not quite. He did not set out to abolish the Soviet Union or the Communist Party. This happened in spite of his resistance. Mr Gorbachev's career is proof of how powerful historical forces sweep aside the efforts of one man to resist them.

From an English newspaper on 15 December 1991, shortly before Gorbachev's resignation.

QUESTIONS

1. Read page 254. Why were there problems in the Soviet Union in 1985?

2. What did Gorbachev say should be done to solve these problems?

3. Why did Gorbachev become unpopular in the Soviet Union?

4. What happened to communism in eastern Europe?

SOURCE N

What was my reaction the other night? I'll tell you. I had tears in my eyes. To see people standing on the wall, where once they would have been shot, I could hardly take it in.

Said by Gail S. Halvorsen, the American pilot who organised the 'Little Vittles' campaign in 1948. He is talking about how he felt when the Berlin Wall came down in 1989.

Paper 1-type assessment: Soviet control over Eastern Europe

SOURCE A

A drawing on the wall of a Prague street in 1968.

QUESTIONS

Section A Questions

1   a   Study Source A. Do you think the cartoonist supported or opposed the Soviet invasion of Czechoslovakia in 1968? Support your answer by referring to details of the cartoon and your own knowledge. (6)

   b   Explain why the Soviet Union invaded Czechoslovakia in 1968. (9)

Section B Questions

2   a   What policies were followed by the government of Matyas Rakosi in Hungary up to 1956? (4)

   b   Explain why the West did not come to the aid of Hungary in 1956. (6)

   c   'The most important reason for the collapse of Soviet control in eastern Europe in 1989 was the weakness of the Soviet economy'. Do you agree with this statement? Explain your answer. (10)

Glossary

anarchists people who do not believe in organised authority and who take action against it

Anschluss the joining together of Austria with Germany

anti-Semitic anti-Jewish

appeasement agreeing certain terms with an enemy so that confrontation and war are avoided

armistice an agreement to stop fighting so that peace terms can be discussed

Aryan according to the Nazis, the 'master race', meaning people with fair hair, white skin and blue eyes

Blitzkrieg German for 'lightning war', meaning a surprise attack

Bolsheviks a political party in Russia, led by Lenin, which led the Russian revolution in 1917

capitalism an economic and political system where industry and trade are owned and controlled by private individuals or groups, not the state

Cheka Lenin's secret police

coalition a government formed by more than one political party

Cold War the conflict between communist East and capitalist West from 1945 until around 1990, where no actual fighting took place

collectivisation the joining together of individual farms in Russia to form large state-owned farms which peasants farmed together

communism a system of government where all industry and trade is owned by the state and the public, and where people share all work and property equally

conscientious objectors men who refuse to fight because of their anti-war beliefs

conscription military service which all people (usually men) of a certain age are required to do

demilitarisation the removal of military forces from an area

democracy a system of government where leaders are voted in to office by the people

dictatorship government by a leader with complete power over the government and the people

Duma the Russian parliament

Enabling Law a law giving Hitler the power to make laws without consulting the Reichstag

Final Solution the Nazi term for the policy of killing Jews

Five-Year Plans economic plans which set targets for all industrial factories and workers in the Soviet Union

Freikorps semi-official right-wing bands of soldiers in Germany after the First World War

Führer German for 'leader' and the title given to Hitler

glasnost a Russian term meaning 'openness', and one of Gorbachev's policies for ending communist rule over the Soviet Union

Great Depression the economic slump following the Wall Street Crash in the USA, 1929

Holocaust the mass murder of Jews between 1941 and 1945

humanitarian for the good of the human race

hyperinflation a time of rapid price rises

idealist a person who has ideas of perfection which are usually unrealistic or impractical

iron curtain the imaginary boundary separating the capitalist West from the communist East

Kristallnacht German for 'the night of the broken glass' – the event of 9 November 1938 when Nazis attacked Jews and their property

Ku Klux Klan the violent and racist group that terrorised black people, foreigners, Catholics and homosexuals in southern USA

kulaks wealthy peasants in the Soviet Union

Lebensraum German for 'living space', and when Hitler tried to gain more territory in Eastern Europe

Marshall Plan a scheme set up in the USA, in 1947, to provide economic aid to European countries and stop the spread of communism

Mensheviks a political party in Russia, formed after the split of the Social Democratic Party in 1903

munitions military weapons and ammunition

NATO North Atlantic Treaty Organisation – a group of countries made up of the European powers, Canada and the USA, formed in 1949 against the threat of the Soviet Union

New Deal President Roosevelt's programme of legislation to help the USA recover from the Great Depression

NKVD Stalin's secret police in the Soviet Union

October Manifesto the Tsar's promise during the 1905 Revolution to give Russians a constitutional monarchy and an elected parliament

perestroika Russian for 'restructuring' and one of Gorbachev's policies for ending communist rule over the Soviet Union

plebiscite a referendum, or vote, when the public can vote on an important issue

Prague Spring reforms in Czechoslovakia in 1968 before the Warsaw Pact forces took control of the country

prohibition the banning of something, such as the banning of the manufacture, sale and transport of alcohol in the USA after 1920

propaganda information that is presented in a way which is meant to influence how people think

putsch an attempt to gain political power by using force

Red Army the army created by Trotsky to defeat the Whites in the Russian Civil War, 1918-20

Red Scare a period of time in the USA when suspected communists were persecuted and the public was encouraged to act against communists

Reichstag the German parliament from 1871 until 1933

reparations payments made in compensation, for example by Germany to compensate countries after the First World War

sanctions measures taken against a country, such as stopping trade, in protest against the country's political actions

sharecroppers agricultural workers in southern USA who were not paid money but instead received some of the produce they grew

soviets councils of workers and soldiers in Russia

Spartacists a communist group in Germany after the First World War

suffrage votes for all adult men and women

Suffragettes women who campaigned for votes for women, often using violence

Suffragists members of the National Union of Women's Suffrage Societies, an organisation which used peaceful means to campaign for votes for women

Tsar the title given to Russia's absolute monarch

Vietcong South Vietnamese communist guerrillas (small groups of fighters who organise surprise attacks on their enemy)

vietnamisation the policy of withdrawing American troops from Vietnam while preparing the South Vietnamese army to fight on its own

Wall Street Crash the sudden collapse of the US stock market in October 1929

Warsaw Pact an agreement between the communist countries of Europe to become allies, set up in 1955, in response to NATO

welfare state a system of benefits and services set up by the government to make sure that everyone has a basic minimum standard of living

Whites anti-communist forces in the Russian Civil War

Index

Abyssinia 64, 74–5, 77–9, 80
Agricultural Adjustment Act 1933 161, 166
alphabet agencies 163, 168
Anglo-German Naval Treaty (1935) 84, 90
Anschluss 52, 85–6, 90
Anti-Comintern Pact (1936) 85
appeasement 83–92
atomic bomb 220, 227
Austria 55, 68–9, 85–6, 90
Austria-Hungary 50, 54–5, 59, 60, 61

Bay of Pigs 233
Beck-Goerdeler Group 120
Berlin 218, 219, 225–7, 228, 231, 250–1
black Americans 140, 141, 146–7, 169
Bloody Sunday (1905) 180–1
Bolsheviks 180, 189, 190–7
Bonus Marchers 157, 159
Booth, Charles 12
Brest-Litovsk, Treaty of (1918) 55, 62, 194
Brezhnev, Leonid 248–9, 253
Bulgaria 59, 61, 69, 223, 256

Capone, Al 150, 151
Castro, Fidel 232–3
Cat and Mouse Act (1913) 24–5
CCC *see* Civilian Conservation Corps
Chamberlain, Neville 83, 87–91
Children's Charter (1908) 13
China 73, 75–7, 230
Churchill, Winston 9, 16, 218–20, 221
cinema 142–3
Civilian Conservation Corps (CCC) 162
Clemenceau, Georges 50–1, 53, 56

Cold War 216–44, 255
communism
   appeasement 91
   Cold War 216–44
   Germany 99, 101, 109, 111–12, 118
   Russia 179–211
   USA 145
concentration camps 126, 127, 130–1
conscientious objectors 30, 31
Corfu 68–9
Coughlin, Father 166
Cuba 232–7
Czechoslovakia
   communism 223, 248–50, 256
   creation 55
   First World War 59
   German invasion 86–92

Darwin, Charles 148
Davison, Emily 22, 23
Dawes Plan (1924) 58, 105
Defence of the Realm Act (DORA) (1914) 29, 31, 33
DORA *see* Defence of the Realm Act
Dubcek, Alexander 248–9
Duma 182–3, 184, 186–7

East Germany 223, 246, 250–1, 256
Ebert, Friedrich 99
Edelweiss Pirates 119
Enabling Law (1933) 114

Fawcett, Millicent 21
Federal Emergency Relief Administration (FERA) 162
Final Solution 130–1
First World War
   Britain 25, 26–34, 37–8
   Germany 98–9

peace treaties 50–62, 82–4, 100–2
   Russia 183–5, 186, 188–9, 194
   USA 136
   women 25–7, 35
Ford, Henry 136, 138
Fourteen Points 51, 53, 54, 56
France
   appeasement 83–92
   German invasion of Poland 93–5
   League of Nations 64, 66–7, 70, 78, 80, 84
   Ruhr 70, 103
   Versailles, Treaty of 50–1, 53–4, 56, 58, 62
franchise, Britain 18–25, 35–6

Germany
   1918-45 97–131
   First World War 33–4, 37–8
   Great Depression 72
   League of Nations 66–7, 69, 70, 84
   Nazi Party 72, 107–31
   post-war division 218, 219, 220, 225–7, 250–1
   Second World War 128–31
   Versailles, Treaty of 50–8, 61–2
   Weimar Republic 57–8, 98–106, 109–13
   see also East Germany; West Germany
Goebbels, Joseph 116, 117, 131
Gorbachev, Mikhail 254–7
Graves, Robert 33
Great Britain
   1906-18 5–47
   appeasement 83–92
   First World War 25, 26–34, 37–8
   German invasion of Poland 93–5
   League of Nations 66, 70, 78, 80
   Versailles, Treaty of 50–1, 53–6, 62

Great Depression 71–4, 82, 109–10, 151, 153–9
Great Terror 202–3
Greece 68–9, 223, 224

Hacha, Emil 90
Haile Selassie, Emperor 79
health insurance 15–16
Henig, R. 54
Heydrich, Reinhard 121
Himmler, Heinrich 120, 131
Hindenburg, Paul von 110–11, 112, 115
Hitler, Adolf 82–95, 107–25
　League of Nations 66, 67
　Munich *putsch* 102–3, 108
　Soviet Union 217–18
Hitler Youth 109, 119, 121–2
Ho Chi Minh 238
Hoare-Laval Plan 78
Hobhouse, Charles 18, 23
Hoess, Rudolf 131
Hoover, Herbert 153, 155–6, 157, 159
Hungary
　communism 223, 246–8, 250, 256
　First World War 55, 60, 61
　League of Nations 68–9
　see also Austria-Hungary
hyperinflation 103–4

Industrial Revolution 8
international relations 49–95, 214–58
Italy
　Abyssinia 74–5, 77–9
　First World War 54–5, 56, 59
　League of Nations 66, 68, 70

Japan
　and Hitler 85
　League of Nations 64, 66, 70
　Manchuria 73, 75–7
　Russo-Japanese War 180
Jaruzelski, General 253–4
Jews 107, 111, 125–7, 130–1
Jim Crow laws 146
Johnson, LBJ 241–3
July Days 190

Kapp *putsch* 101–2
Kellogg-Briand Pact (1928) 105
Kennedy, J. F. 232–6, 238, 250
Kerensky, Alexander 187, 189, 192–3
Khrushchev, Nikita 231, 233–7, 246–8, 250–1
Kirov, Sergei 201
Korean War 231
Kornilov affair 191
Kreisau Circle 120
Kristallnacht (Night of Broken Glass) 126–7
Kronstadt rising (1921) 197
Ku Klux Klan 146–7

Labour Exchanges 15
Labour Party 7
Lausanne, Treaty of (1923) 60, 61, 68
League of Nations 50, 51, 53–5, 62, 64–80, 82, 84, 105
Lenin, Vladimir Ilich 180, 190–4, 196, 198, 199–200
Liberal Party 6–17
Liebknecht, Karl 99
Lloyd George, David 8, 9, 16, 35, 37–8, 50–1, 53, 56
Locarno Treaties (1925) 70, 105
Long, Huey 167
Lubbe, Marinus van der 112, 113
Luxemburg, Rosa 99

McCarthyism 231
Manchuria 64, 73, 75–7, 80
Marshall Plan 224–5
Moltke, Helmuth von 120
motor cars 138–9
Munich Conference (1938) 87–90
Munich *putsch* 102–3, 104, 108
music 144
Mussolini, Benito 55, 68, 74, 77–8, 85, 86
My Lai 240, 242

Nagy, Imre 247
National Insurance Act (1911) 9, 15–17
National Recovery Administration (NRA) 162, 168

National Socialist German Workers' Party (Nazi Party) 72, 107–31
National Union of Women's Suffrage Societies (NUWSS) 21
NATO *see* North Atlantic Treaty Organisation
Navajos Gang 119
Nazi Party *see* National Socialist German Workers' Party
Nazi-Soviet Pact (1939) 92–4
NEP *see* New Economic Policy
Neuilly, Treaty of (1919) 59
New Deal 160–71
New Economic Policy (NEP) 198
Nicholas II, Tsar 176–7, 180–7, 196
Night of Broken Glass 126–7
Night of the Long Knives 114–15
Nixon, Richard 243
North Atlantic Treaty Organisation (NATO) 227
NRA *see* National Recovery Administration
nuclear weapons 233–7
Nuremberg Laws 126
Nuremberg Trials 131
NUWSS *see* National Union of Women's Suffrage Societies

October Manifesto 182, 183
old age pensions 13–14, 164, 166

Palach, Jan 250
Pankhurst, Emmeline 21, 25
Paris Peace Conference (1919) 37–8, 50–6
People's Budget (1909) 9
Poland
　communism 218–19, 223, 246, 256
　German invasion 89, 92–5
　League of Nations 68, 69
　Solidarity 252–4
Poor Law (1834) 9–12
Potsdam Conference (1945) 219–20
prohibition 142, 149–51, 163
Public Works Administration (PWA) 162

Index   263

radio 144
Rasputin, Grigori 185
Reichstag 110, 112, 113, 114
reparations 53–5, 57–61, 101, 103, 105, 221
Representation of the People Act (1918) 35–6
Rhineland 52, 55, 70, 84, 90, 92
Röhm, Ernst 114–15
Romania 223, 256
Rome-Berlin Axis (1936) 74, 85
Roosevelt, Franklin D. 158–71, 218–19
Rowntree, Seebohm 12
Ruhr 58, 70, 102, 103
Russia
   1905-41 174–211
   civil war 195–7
   First World War 55, 62, 183–6, 188–9, 194
   League of Nations 66, 68
   Provisional Government 187–93
   see also Soviet Union
Russo-Japanese War (1904-5) 180

SA *see* Sturm Abteilung
Saar 52, 84
Sacco, Nicola 145
St Germain, Treaty of (1919) 59
Sawoniuk, Anthony 131
Scheidemann, Philipp 99, 101
Scholl, Hans and Sophie 119
Schutzstaffel (SS) 109, 114, 120
Scopes, Johnny 148
Second World War 82–95, 128–31, 216–21
self-determination 51, 55
Sèvres, Treaty of (1920) 60
sharecropping 140
Solidarity 252–4
Soviet Union 199–211
   Cold War 216–44
   eastern Europe 246–57
   Second World War 91, 93–4, 128
   see also Russia
Spanish Civil War 85
Spartacus League 99
SS *see* Schutzstaffel
Stalin, Joseph 94, 199–211, 217–20, 221, 225–7, 231, 246

Stolypin, Peter 182, 183
Stormtroopers *see* Sturm Abteilung
Stresemann, Gustav 58, 82, 105, 106, 109
Sturm Abteilung (Stormtroopers or SA) 108, 111, 114–15, 126
Sudetenland 86–8
suffrage, women 18–25, 35–6

Tennessee Valley Authority (TVA) 163
Tet Offensive (1968) 242
Townsend, Dr Francis 166
Trade Boards Act (1909) 15
Trianon, Treaty of (1920) 60
Trotsky, Leon 191, 195–7, 199–201, 203
Truman, Harry 219–21, 224, 231
Truman Doctrine 224
Turkey 59, 60, 61, 68, 224, 236
TVA *see* Tennessee Valley Authority

United Nations Organisation 218, 231
United States of America
   1919-41 134–71
   Cold War 216–44, 247–8, 250
   First World War 136
   League of Nations 64, 70
   Versailles, Treaty of 50–1, 53–5, 56
   Wall Street Crash 70, 71, 72

Vanzetti, Bartolomeo 145
Versailles, Treaty of (1919) 50–8, 61–2, 82–4, 90, 100–2
Vietnam 238–44

Walesa, Lech 252–4
Wall Street Crash (1929) 70, 71, 109, 124, 153–7, 161
War Communism 196, 199
war guilt 54, 57, 101
Warsaw Pact 227, 246, 247, 249–50
Washington Naval Agreement (1922) 70, 73
Weimar Republic 57–8, 98–106, 109–13
West Germany 225–7, 250–1

White Rose movement 119
Wilhelm II, Kaiser 98–9
Wilson, Woodrow 50–1, 53, 55, 56
women
   Britain 18–25, 35–6
   First World War 25–7, 35
   Nazi Germany 111, 123
   Soviet Union 210
   USA 152
Women's Social and Political Union (WSPU) 21
workhouses 9–12
Works Progress Administration (WPA) 164
WSPU *see* Women's Social and Political Union

Yalta Conference (1945) 218–19
Young Plan (1929) 105
Yugoslavia 55, 59, 223, 246